SIGURD HOEL'S
FICTION

Contributions to the Study of World Literature
Series Adviser: Leif Sjöberg

Benny Andersen: A Critical Study
Leonie Marx

Aksel Sandemose: Exile in Search of a Home
Randi Birn

Edith Södergran: Modernist Poet in Finland
George C. Schoolfield

SIGURD HOEL'S FICTION

Cultural Criticism and
Tragic Vision

SVERRE LYNGSTAD

Contributions to the Study of World Literature, Number 6

 Greenwood Press
Westport, Connecticut ● London, England

Copyright Acknowledgment

We gratefully acknowledge permisson granted by Gyldendal Norsk Forlag, Oslo, for permission to quote from Sigurd Hoel's *Samlede romaner og fortellinger* (1950-58) and from other works.

Library of Congress Cataloging in Publication Data

Lyngstad, Sverre.
   Sigurd Hoel's fiction.

   (Contributions to the study of world literature,
ISSN 0738-9345 ; no. 6)
   Bibliography: p.
   Includes index.
   1. Hoel, Sigurd, 1890-1960—Criticism and interpretation.
I. Title. II. Series.
PT8950.H58Z82   1984   839.8'2374   83-26470
  ISBN 0-313-24343-3 (lib. bdg.)

52,785

Library of Congress Catalog Card Number: 83-26470
ISBN: 0-313-24343-3
ISSN: 0738-9345

First published in 1984

Greenwood Press
A division of Congressional Information Service, Inc.
88 Post Road West
Westport, Connecticut 06881

Printed in the United States of America

10 9 8 7 6 5 4 3 2 1

To Bjarne,
who helps keep the past alive

Contents

Preface

As a long-time editor, Sigurd Hoel was well attuned to the biography of books, whose fates are often determined by factors other than literary merit. He was particularly irked by the constraints of writing in a "minor" language and felt frustrated by foreign publishers' seeming indifference to Scandinavian literature. Whatever recognition he received abroad was deeply gratifying to him, but the general ignorance of his work outside the North was not always easy to accept.

His disenchantment shows through poignantly in the letters he wrote during his four-month tour of the United States in 1952-53, when he had hoped to meet and exchange ideas with those American novelists who dominated the series of contemporary literature he had edited at Gyldendal Publishers (Oslo) for over two decades, the Yellow Series (Den gule serie).[1] He clearly wished these writers—Wilder, Marquand, Faulkner, and others—to think of him not as their Norwegian agent or translator but as a fellow writer. Twenty years earlier he had instructed his New York publisher to forward copies of his second translated novel, *One Day in October* (1932; *En dag i oktober*, 1931) to a group of hand-picked American authors, including Hemingway, Wilder, Faulkner, and Dos Passos.[2] Yet, after the appearance in England of *Meeting at the Milestone* (*Møte ved milepelen*, 1947) in 1951 he ·assumes—unhappily—that, whereas he had published all of Hemingway's novels and four of Graham Greene's, as well as works by Faulkner and Koestler, these authors had never read a single word written by him. And, he concludes the letter to his English publisher, now "I should like to force my novel down their throat" [sic].[3] His eagerness to become known abroad is touchingly evidenced by Hoel's willingness, during the American visit, to lend his last copy of the English version of *One Day in October* to an admirer who apparently had pleaded for the publication of *Meeting* at Putnam's, New York. Only one other book, she writes, probed for answers to the "basic problems of ethics and human behavior" with the same "troubled seeking," namely, *The Brothers Karamazov*.[4]

Altogether, of Hoel's thirteen novels—not counting his collections of stories—only these two and *Sinners in Summertime* (1930; *Syndere i sommersol*, 1927) reached the English-speaking public. Not surprisingly, criticism in English has been correspondingly sparse. It is worth noting, however, that as early as 1939 Hoel had acquired an enthusiastic American follower, Martin Joos, who lectured on his novels at the University of Toronto and contributed a highly appreciative article (in English) to the festschrift honoring Hoel's sixtieth birthday. Joos, who exchanged letters with Hoel, found the latter's work to be imbued with a profound humanity in that it shows the "importance and sacredness of the particular person's tragedy." In an age when happiness and misery are thought of as mass phenomena, Hoel, in Joos's words, "insists that the part is greater than the whole and that a human life is a sacred thing."[5] Now, almost a quarter century after his death, the time has come for Hoel to be granted the opportunity to speak, however indirectly, to that wider audience he always sought.

On his home grounds, as a central figure not only in Norwegian but in Scandinavian literature, Hoel has received a great deal of critical attention. Though after World War II he and the interwar generation were attacked and largely dismissed by the young Odd Eidem (b. 1913), in a journal article significantly entitled "Generation Change?" (1946) as well as in a newspaper debate triggered by Eidem,[6] Hoel experienced a great comeback with *Meeting at the Milestone* in 1947. While Hoel's novels of the 1950s did little to enhance his reputation, *The Troll Circle* (*Trollringen*, 1958) his last completed work, turned out to be a masterpiece for which a Danish critic nominated him for the Nobel Prize in literature.[7] Since Hoel's death in 1960 many critical studies have been written about his fiction, including numerous theses. Noteworthy among the latter is *The Blameless One* (*Den plettfrie*, 1968), subsequently published as a monograph, by the Norwegian-based Japanese scholar Masahiko Inadomi. Two more ambitious critical studies are *Sigurd Hoel: Bewitched Author* (*Sigurd Hoel—dikteren i fugleham*, 1972; lit. "author in bird-skin") by the Danish scholar Johan de Mylius and *The Giant's Heart: A Study of Sigurd Hoel's Literary Work* (*Risens hjerte—en studie i Sigurd Hoels forfatterskap*, 1975) by Audun Tvinnereim. But neither critic deals with Hoel's entire oeuvre, as the present study sets out to do.

The poet André Bjerke said at Hoel's death: "If he had written in English, he would have had a world reputation" (*Dagbladet*, 10/14/1960). In my estimation Sigurd Hoel deserves to be known to an international public. Heir to the literary depth psychology of Henrik Ibsen and Knut Hamsun, he sharpened their probings into the human psyche through psychoanalytic study. For while dismissing its conceptual apparatus and its often forbidding terminology, which might lead to "petrifaction," Hoel says that psychoanalysis "sharpens the power of observation."[8] Through the rigor and the semiprofessional quality of his psychological portrayals, he mediates insights marked by an exceptional degree of veracity, with far-reaching sociocritical repercussions. It is the psychological depth and the cultural relevance of Hoel's oeuvre, together with its highly accomplished and varied artistry, that constitutes the main justification for the present study.

While his gallery of characters is not overwhelmingly large, Hoel's range is nevertheless wide—from traditional to modernist fiction, from autobiographical novel to period satire, from breezy comedy to classical tragedy. Moreover, he was a formidable practical critic, whose incisive, stylistically immaculate reviews shaped literary opinion during a period of transition in Norwegian literature. His accomplishment as a translator and as an editor to Gyldendal's during nearly four decades cannot be overestimated. Through his editorial activities he not only decided what Norwegians would read but also indirectly influenced their ideas and attitudes by selecting works that were politically advanced, intellectually challenging, and—in relation to Norwegian developments—novel in technique. Finally, Hoel gave unstintingly of his time to help defend intellectual and artistic freedoms that he felt were endangered in Norway by an excessively moralistic conception of the nature and function of

xii   Sigurd Hoel's Fiction

literature.

Despite the wide spectrum of Hoel's activities, they were held together by an unrelenting intellectual passion which sustained, and consumed, his life. Though my main purpose will be to examine and evaluate Hoel's fiction, I shall attempt to give a sense of that life. This will be difficult, since space will not permit a discussion of Hoel's achievement as a critic and editor, two of his most impressive contributions to Norwegian literature.[9] Similarly, his plays and his numerous essays in cultural criticism will be discussed only to the extent that they help to elucidate the nature of his fiction.

I have taken certain liberties in the order of presentation of Hoel's work: in five of the seven chapters devoted to his fiction, novels are paired according to literary criteria rather than chronology. Besides simplifying the book's organization, this topical approach will better bring out the changing profile of Hoel as a creative writer.

I wish to thank the Director of the Department of Manuscripts at the University of Oslo, Sverre Flugsrud, for his interest in my work and for the materials he allowed me to use during the sabbatical leave that I spent in Oslo in 1979. His staff, like all the librarians at the University Library on whose help I depended, were models of kind, prompt, courteous service. In addition to the sabbatical, New Jersey Institute of Technology generously granted me released time over several semesters to complete the book. My brother, Ingvar, kindly took me and my daughter to see Hoel's birthplace, including the site of the notorious execution for murder from which the plot of *The Troll Circle* germinated. I wish to express special thanks to Eléonore Zimmermann for her careful reading of the entire manuscript. Finally, Leif Sjöberg has earned my gratitude for his unfailing encouragement as well as for his continuing promotion of Scandinavian scholarship in the United States.

Chronology

1890   December 14, Sigurd Hoel born at Sand, Nord-Odal, 100 kilometers north of Oslo (then Christiania).

1894   Stay at Rikshospitalet (State Hospital, Oslo) after arm fracture.

1906-1909 Attends secondary school in Oslo; graduates summa cum laude.

1909-1910 Back home; teaches elementary school while preparing for his university examination in philosophy.

1910   Works for six months for an insurance company in Oslo.

1910-1917 Studies mathematics and natural science at the University of Oslo, without taking a degree.

1911-1918 Teaches at various secondary schools in the capital.

1916   Member of the Board of Directors of the Norwegian Student Association.

1916-1917 Coeditor of the student magazine *Minerva;* first critical articles published.

1917   Considers the study of law but soon abandons the idea.

1918   Wins a Nordic short-story contest with "The Idiot," written April 30, on the eve of the deadline for submission.

1918-1919 Assistant editor to the satiric weekly *Exlex.*

1918-1931 Literary critic to *Social-Demokraten/Arbeiderbladet,* an Oslo daily, with a two-year interruption 1920-22.

1919   Coauthors a farce with Finn Bøe, *One Man's Death* . . . , performed at the Central Theater.

1919-1925 Secretary to the Norwegian Academy of Science.

1920   *Knut Hamsun,* a brief critical study, published.

1921-1924 Editor of *Mot Dag* (Toward Daybreak), a radical journal; contributes stories, articles, and most of the satiric column "Bourgeois Cultural Life."

1922   *The Road We Walk*, a collection of stories, published.

1922-1960 Editor *(konsulent)* to Gyldendal Publishers; chief editor and reader from 1931.

1923   Receives Conrad Mohr's fellowship for the study of socialism.

1924   Travels in central Europe; *The Seven-Pointed Star*, written in Achensee, Tirol, published.

1926   Visits Paris, where he meets a group of young Freudians, chiefly medical students.

1927   Marries one of these students, Caroline Schweigaard Nicolaysen, known professionally as Nic Waal. *Sinners in Summertime* published.

1928   Second visit to Paris. First prize for "Christmas Eve" ("Snow" in *Nothing*) in American short-story contest.

1929   *Nothing*, written at a summer dairy in Nord-Odal, published. Writes *Against the Wall*, a play. Begins as editor of Gyldendal's Yellow Series (1929-59).

1930   *Against the Wall* performed at the National Theater; *Don Juan*, coauthored with Helge Krog, performed at the New Theater. Award of a grant from the H.A. Benneche Endowment to Hoel and Krog causes controversy.

1931   Second prize for *One Day in October* in Nordic novel contest. Newspaper campaign waged against this and other "frank" or psychoanalytically oriented novels (the "dirty stream" controversy).

1931-1932 Stay in Berlin for several months.

1932-1933 Heated debate on the showing of Marc Connelly's *Green Pastures* at the National Theater; play closed down by the Storting (Parliament).

1932-1936 Reviewer to *Dagbladet*, an independent Oslo daily.

1933   *The Road to the End of the World* published. *Sinners in Summertime* filmed.

1934-1936 Undergoes psychoanalysis with Wilhelm Reich (two and a half years).

1935   *A Fortnight Before the Nights of Frost* published.

1936   Divorced, after unofficial separation since 1932; marries Ada Ivan. Debate about the Peace Prize awarded to Carl von Ossietzky. The Trotsky case.

1937-1938 Edits Reich's journal *Zeitschrift für politische Psychologie und Sexualökonomie* for a year.

1938   Six-month newspaper showdown on psychoanalysis and Wilhelm Reich. *Open Sesame* published. Son Erik born.

1939   *The Princess on the Glass Mountain* (stories) and *Fifty Yellow [Books]*, prefaces to novels in the Yellow Series, 1929-39, published. Trip to Mediterranean with his wife; stay in France and Italy. Son Erik dies.

1940-1943 Resides in Nord-Odal during German Occupation of Norway, with frequent visits to Oslo.

1941   *The Family Dagger* published.

1943-1945 Forced exile in Stockholm; acts as Norway's cultural ambassador to Sweden.

1945   *Thoughts in a Dark Time*, essay collection about Nazism, published.

1947   *Meeting at the Milestone* published.

1948   *Thoughts from Many Ages*, mainly travel letters and other journalistic articles, published. Government author's pension granted (for life).

1949   In Stockholm, as associate of *Dagens Nyheter*.

1950   First *Collected Novels and Stories* published.

1951   *I'm in Love with Someone Else* published.

1952   *Between the Bark and the Wood*, chiefly essays on threats to freedom from right and left, published.

1952-1953 A four-month stay in America, on grant from the U.S. State Department.

1954   *Rendezvous with Forgotten Years* published.

1955   *One Day in October* filmed; *Thoughts about Norwegian Literature* published.

1956   *At the Foot of the Tower of Babel* published.

1957   *Rendezvous with Forgotten Years* filmed. Obscenity case against Agnar Mykle takes up much of Hoel's time.

1958   *The Troll Circle* published.

1959   *The Last 51 Yellow [Books]* published.

1960   October 14, Sigurd Hoel dies of a stroke; buried in the "Grove of Honor" at the Cemetery of Our Savior, Oslo.

SIGURD HOEL'S
FICTION

1
Sigurd Hoel: Cultural Mediator and Fellow Human

Sigurd Hoel's work as author and critic is closely related to his biographical background. Growing up in an isolated rural district of East Norway that was still untouched by modern life, he became deeply imbued with the regional folkways and the skeptical cast of thought of his native Nord-Odal.[1] As a son of the local schoolmaster, however, he felt somewhat apart from the farm boys with whom he associated. This experience of being in between—neither of the earthbound peasantry nor of the cultivated professional class—may have marked Hoel's entire sociocultural perspective. During most of his life since the age of fifteen, when he first came to Oslo (then Christiania) to go to middle school, he was a resident of the city; but his early rural experience enabled him to stand aside from the life he saw, just as the wider intellectual horizons of the capital made him take a critical view of his rural past. Hoel's exposure to a succession of milieus and subcultures turned him into a lifelong mediator, between history and modernity, between rural folk literature and the latest urban literary fashion, between nationalism and cosmopolitanism.

In the heated debates of the 1930s, when Hoel was seen as one of a triumvirate of cultural radicals—the others were the poet Arnulf Øverland (1889-1968) and the dramatist and critic Helge Krog (1889-1962)—who clashed with the Establishment on a broad front of social, moral, and political issues, Hoel's rural provenance tended to be forgotten. Today it is generally agreed that his best work derives from the tension between that provenance and the radical thought that Hoel absorbed as an urban intellectual. For even books that seem entirely centered on country life, such as *The Road to the End of the World* (*Veien til verdens ende*, 1933) and *The Troll Circle*—possibly his best novels—are shot through with polarities of traditional genre and modern alienation, evocation of childhood and depth psychology, regional history and contemporary cultural conflict, ancient tragedy and social criticism. In other novels, especially *A Fortnight Before the Nights of Frost* (*Fjorten dager før frostnettene*, 1935) and *Meeting at the Milestone*, country and city are juxtaposed as the middle-aged hero explores his predicament in the light of his early experience. These are all strong novels. Where, on the other hand, Hoel deals strictly with the ambience of the city or of academia, as in *Open Sesame* (*Sesam sesam*, 1938), the emotional pressure is lower and the intellectual substance more tenuous.

Being a mediator means being a man of ideas: Hoel was an exemplary intellectual. Trained at the university in mathematics and the natural sciences, he also briefly studied law. More importantly, he read Freud and other depth psychologists and acquired firsthand knowledge of Marxism through his participation in the radical group Mot Dag (Toward Daybreak), led by the formidable dialectician Erling Falk (1887-1940). From an early age Hoel was a voracious reader of imaginative literature. Already knowledgeable in several fields of learning, through his long career as critic and editor Hoel became one of the most widely read persons in Scandinavia.

No wonder that, with such intellectual ballast, Hoel should yearn for a richer, more vigorous existence, that of a nonacademic alter ego leading a colorful, variegated life which afforded "stronger impulses, greater personal experiences, more movement."[2] His choices for the Yellow Series show a decided preference for writers with such backgrounds: Hemingway, Sherwood Anderson, Erskine Caldwell, Liam O'Flaherty, Panaït Istrati, Malraux, Koestler, Ilya Ehrenburg, and many others. Apart from discerning in these wanderers, seekers of adventure, self-exiles, and emigrés a heightened intensity of life, he may also have perceived in their unsettled, nomadic existence a characteristic of the century. In an amusing potshot at Knut Hamsun, who had insisted on the importance of roots, Hoel teasingly asks, Why this preference for vegetative analogies? Why not use an image from zoology occasionally? He also recalls Hamsun's own days of wandering and praises the author of the book under review, Nordahl Grieg, who was an incessant wanderer and world traveler (*Arbeiderbladet*, 12/1/1927).

Another wishful self-image was that of *homme engagé*. Just as Hoel the academic intellectual was drawn to the more intense life of the passions and of physical action, so he was attracted by the person totally committed to a cause. Two such persons entered his life: Erling Falk in the 1920s, Wilhelm Reich (1897-1957) in the 1930s. The latter was never replaced, but Hoel's admiration for Arthur Koestler, a man who combined adventurous experience with political activism, seems due to the same impulse. Falk and Reich were intellectuals too, but it was their leadership abilities that made them great. While Hoel responded strongly to both men—who must have fulfilled a deep psychological need—he refused to succumb to their authority.[3] Thus, during the three years he was editor of *Mot Dag*, the radical group's journal (1921-1924), he had the courage officially to disagree with Falk's populist, party-line view of literature. Several years later, in his play *Against the Wall* (*Mot muren*, 1930), Hoel dramatized the relationship between two friends, a leader and an intellectual, against the background of the Russian revolution. The play is a disguised attempt at settling accounts with Falk, years before similar literary soul-searching by other leftist intellectuals.

Hoel's bumpy relationship with Wilhelm Reich, Marxist ideologue as well as psychoanalyst, also ended in a rupture of sorts when, contrary to Reich's express advice, Hoel discontinued his analysis. Reich had characterized Hoel as a typically vacillating bourgeois intellectual incapable of committing himself to a cause; if cured, he would supposedly be able to overcome his incapacity.[4] However, the analyst could not assure his patient that the latter's talent would survive the cure, and Reich's candor in this respect may have contributed to Hoel's decision not to continue the analysis.[5] The critic Audun Tvinnereim has indicated that Hoel subsequently dissociated himself from Reich, as evidenced by deletion of references to Reich's work in essays re-

published after World War II, while Reich's ideas were retained.[6]
It is obviously significant that these men, charismatic leaders
each in his field, played such an extraordinary role in Sigurd
Hoel's emotional economy. The reason may be that they represented the two most influential twentieth-century religions:
Marxism and psychoanalysis. It is in the light of Hoel's one-time
bond to Falk and Reich that a central theme in *At the Foot of the
Tower of Babel* (*Ved foten av Babels tårn*, 1956), Hoel's next to
last novel, must be understood: "The gods are dead . . . and
people run around confused, like stray dogs."[7] In his manuscript
notes the gods are specifically designated as Christianity,
Marxism, and psychoanalysis.[8] Subconsciously, Hoel may have
been a seeker after faith throughout most of his life. In 1956 he
speaks of having undergone three, if not four, "crises of belief":
the loss of his childhood faith; the awakening from the "dream of
the millennium" after his affiliation with *Mot Dag;* the waning
of "psychoanalytic fervor" in the late 1930s; and the failure of
paradise to arrive after May, 1945, the end of World War II.[9]
Already in 1940 Hoel was out of sympathy with the kind of
"cheap radicalism" that declared religious feeling per se to be
"worthless" (Ms. Fol. 2365:8; in manuscript collection at the
University Library, Oslo). At Hoel's death his radical friend
Helge Krog wrote that he was not only "religious" but a "romantic."[10] Yet other, more rational, needs were paramount.

The inability of Hoel wholeheartedly to espouse an ideology
was a natural consequence of his early experience and his inter-
mediate social station. A fracture of his elbow joint at the age of
three, with subsequent hospitalization and repeated excruciating
dislocations by a less than competent physician, not only produced a psychological trauma but excluded him from many
physical activities, already made difficult by his extreme near-
sightedness. To disguise his permanently stiff elbow, Hoel would
even on sunny days be seen with a light raincoat on his left arm as
he sauntered down Oslo's main street. In the long run, no doubt,
the consequence of this accident was to reinforce whatever incli-
nation toward detached observation the highly gifted child—
always the first in school—may have had. Hoel's omnivorous
reading as a young man most likely confirmed this tendency;
early favorites were writers such as Anatole France and the Swede

Hjalmar Söderberg, both of whom cultivated a dispassionate, ironic authorial attitude.

In his fiction as well as in his criticism Hoel drew both upon his wide knowledge and his distancing ironic posture to carry out his work of mediation. Briefly, they were the instruments whereby he endeavored to transform unreflective, instinctively held, authoritarian attitudes and values into the elements of a genuine intellectual culture. With his habitual irony and his ubiquitous intellect he would dissolve engrained orthodoxies and newfangled ideologies alike; expose the base, primitive mechanisms underlying conventional morality, social prejudice, and collective hysteria; and penetrate to the irrational bases of individual behavior. His literary strategies themselves, often dialectic in nature, reflect Hoel's mediatory role. According to one critic, the life of Hoel's style springs from an "incessant stream of internal contradictions, an alternating current of thoughts and fancies which serve the same central idea."[11]

In Hoel's view, Norwegian culture was still "unfinished."[12] In particular he thought it was hampered by moral, religious, and esthetic puritanism, which Hamsun had fought before him. One of his chief points of praise for Hamsun at the latter's death was that, for two generations, he had been one of the most "vigorously active forces against pietism, puritanism, and obscurantism here in the North."[13] It was in large part in order to combat the stultifying, miasmatic spirit of puritanism that Hoel utilized psychoanalytic insights both in his critiques of Norwegian culture and in his fiction. The predominance of young American authors in the Yellow Series stems in part from the same motive. For along with its social radicalism, twentieth-century American literature has been vehemently antipuritan. In a wider arena, American writers were fighting a similar battle to that of Hoel and his radical Norwegian colleagues.

And yet, with all his moral-intellectual passion for enlightenment—for bringing his fellow countrymen's obscure, repressed, slandered capacities for joy and creativity into the light of day and thus helping them shape a harmoniously humanistic culture—Hoel more than once intimated that the essence of literature was lyricism.[14] This explains why the early Hamsun, with his profound nature mysticism, was so dear to him. Hoel's own novels contain remarkable spots of lyrical feeling and visionary insight, and in his criticism he frequently points to the deficiency of logic and analysis in producing and understanding great art. Though he sees no contradiction between "understanding and feeling, . . . between logic and empathy," the method of art, he notes, is "in a way the contrary of that of science: insight by way of feeling."[15] And he ridicules the scholar who endeavors to catch the "inner truth" of a great writer in the net of his elaborate analytical procedures: the "dreamed but real experience" escapes, leaving him merely with the "body" of the distortion.[16]

This emphasis on the unique nature of the imagination and its products is of a piece with Hoel's yearning for a religious perception of life, it, too, incapable of being "explained" by rational categories. Characteristically, in the essay "Religious Feeling Without God" (1955), Hoel connects religion with poetry: "Among lyric poets like Pär Lagerkvist and Arnulf Øverland I find a far richer religious feeling than what priest or bishop is capable of expressing.[17] He describes this feeling, which can be kindled by music, nature, or by being in love, as one of "rapture" and of "happiness 'beyond all understanding.' " But more essential, in his view, is the "sense of oneness . . . with all and everything," alive or inanimate. Though you are "smaller than the smallest mite," your spirit expands and opens out, making you somehow "feel infinite." The feeling partakes of "reverence and humility" but also of a "sense of triumph, of victory."[18] In Hoel's work these religiously tinged lyrical moments are usually induced through eros and form part of a utopian yearning for wholeness and perfect joy.[19]

But this aspiration remains a dream. Consequently, whatever wholeness and coherence Hoel's novels have is not that of a unified Weltanschauung. These qualities are the result, rather, of the author's esthetic "desire for harmony and beauty"; driven by that desire, he seeks to give to what is "scattered, accidental, blind and meaningless, coherence, rhythm and meaning."[20] However, the esthetic or formal coherence that Hoel achieves often coexists with thematic discontinuities.

Despite his inability to espouse an ideology, Sigurd Hoel found no dearth of causes to fight for during his life. He was always ready to man the barricades where intellectual, artistic, or other freedoms were at stake. The numerous folders in the Department of Manuscripts of the University Library in Oslo bear witness to his unflagging energy in behalf of such causes: the Ossietzky Peace Prize case, the Wilhelm Reich case, the obscenity charge against Agnar Mykle, and many more. Together with his public debates, cultural journalism, and progressive editing, these activities mark Sigurd Hoel as a sort of culture hero, no less committed in his way than nineteenth-century forerunners like Henrik Wergeland (1808-45) and Bjørnstjerne Bjørnson (1832-1910). More precisely, he was a counterculture force before the term existed, prepared to defend any individual whose rights were threatened—by religious bigotry or proto-Nazi persecution, by ecclesiastical obscurantism or narrowly interpreted obscenity and blasphemy laws.

All these activities demanded a great deal of time, and for someone who styled himself a lazy man Hoel managed to keep incredibly busy.[21] Here is an example of what he could accomplish in one week (4/22 to 4/29/1950), during which he spent one day in bed and was ill for two or three additional days: "Ca. 65 pages of notes, ca. 30 letters. One preface. . . . Read three manuscripts. Read ca. 3-4 volumes in preparation for *The World's Storytellers*. Read 6-7-8-9 journal issues. Read proofs of *A Fortnight* [part]. Made two drawings" (Ms. Fol. 2325:1). The writer in a small country like Norway is rarely able to support himself by his creative work alone, and Hoel had to take other employment to earn a living. Like most Norwegian authors he engaged in literary journalism and translation; thus he translated five or six novels by Joseph Conrad alone, besides books by Faulkner, Caldwell, and many others. Together with his crypto-political commitments and his steady editorial job, which entailed reading a minimum of one hundred manuscripts a year,[22] these varied activities left only about one fourth of all available time for his profession proper, that of a writer of fiction.[23] No wonder that his last novel, *The Troll Circle* (1958), left him totally exhausted, especially considering he had been plagued with illness during the 1950s,[24] and that numerous projects for creative work were never realized.

Nevertheless Sigurd Hoel found the time to help promising young would-be writers,[25] to lead an active social life, and to

sustain numerous friendships as well as a couple of marriages.
Contrary to the impression left by his frequently acerb manner in
debate, Hoel, as his friends have testified, was an extremely kind,
cheerful, warm, generous person. The cold, detached, intellectual
attitude that many critics deplored in his books was obviously a
carefully controlled esthetic device.[26] Interestingly, the last notes
for the novel he was working on shortly before he died contain
the following statement: "The right condition for writing is a
peculiar state of coolness, and *distance*."[27] Øistein Parmann has
dismissed the myth of Hoel as a cynic and skeptic: he calls him a
"good person, actively interested, compassionate," and so "soft"
that he must "hide behind a shell" (*Morgenbladet*, 11/17/1951).
Similarly, Ole Sæverud exposes the falseness of the popular
image of Hoel as merely an ironic observer of the follies of mankind. Sæverud points out his "tenderness toward people, his
compassion," and his "solidarity with mankind." To read Hoel,
he says, is to encounter a "fellow human."[28] Sæverud's article,
Hoel writes, caused him to cry "like a little boy." Contrary to the
widespread opinion that he is so conscious and intellectual, Hoel
writes, he says, because of an inner urge.[29]

The same attitude of spontaneous humanity, half hidden in
the author, is clearly present in the man. Its basis may be the
peculiar blend of disparate qualities that has been found in
Hoel's makeup. Arnulf Øverland mentions his almost "childlike
need for tenderness," calling this the "source of warmth" in
him.[30] To Philip Houm, the combination of "wisdom and child-
likeness" constituted an important part of Sigurd Hoel's charm
(*Dagbladet*, 10/14/1960). The union of intellectual strength with
spontaneous feeling is stressed by several friends: Ernst Sørensen
says Hoel was capable of "weighing his thoughts with his feelings" (*følelsesmessig*), an implicit attribution of unified sensibility. These and other qualities, especially his capacity for
empathy and his completely "effortless naturalness," made everybody feel like a "fellow human being" in his company.[31] No
wonder he was avidly sought out by people, not only professionally but as an adviser on purely personal matters. A fellow student compares Hoel's crowded room in his youthful days to a
railroad station.[32] With so many commitments and such charm,
he had to do his creative work in intense spurts of concentration;

often he fled to his favorite cottage when he wanted to write.
Sigurd Hoel's fiction, in Arnulf Øverland's words, has all the
"high qualities": a "penetrating knowledge of people, dearly
bought wisdom, rich humor, flaming pathos, a captivating lyrical fantasy," and—especially in *The Troll Circle*—
"overwhelming dramatic power" (*Aftenposten*, 10/24/1960).
Hoel was also a remarkable person, with a deep humanity and a
spiritual culture that make him one of the most attractive and
inspiring figures in twentieth-century Scandinavian literature.

2
Early Traditional Form: From Story to Novel

Hoel's first collection of stories, *The Road We Walk* (*Veien vi går*), was praised for its mature artistry when it appeared in 1922, though the appraisals of the individual stories varied. Seemingly amused at the critics' subjective preferences, the author reviewed his own book anonymously in a student magazine.[1] He vents his irony upon the exceptions taken by some reviewers to the "coolness" of his narrative attitude, actually an unqualified strength. In fact, weaknesses occur chiefly where objectivity falters due to an obtrusive "message" or a turgid, overheated style. The quality of the individual stories largely depends on the degree of authorial self-effacement. In the best, surface and meaning are perfectly attuned, the "message" being implicit in the self-contained picture of life presented.

In my view, four of the eight stories (originally there were a few more) are nearly perfect: "The Blind Man," "The Idiot," "Spleen," and "The Star." Of the others, "Man and the Earth," an adaptation of the deluge myth, seems a mere experiment in form, while "The Unavoidable," a contemplation of the horror of death, overaccentuates the theme and fails to generate narrative interest. In the two remaining stories, "Spring Evening" and "In the Land of Shadows," Hoel's treatment of youthful seduction and amorous grief tempered with sex seems trite and high-strung, respectively. The successful stories, while permeated with skepticism, all project a quasi-philosophical theme centered on the meaning of life.

Two stories, "The Blind Man" and "The Idiot," have one additional feature in common: both convey experience as filtered through reduced sensibilities or mental aptitudes. In the first, a young married factory worker, blinded by an accident, readjusts to his condition—after a suicidal depression—only to be deprived once more of his mental-emotional stability. Like so much of Hoel's work, the entire story is presented in free indirect discourse, whereby, while told in the third person, everything is passed through the consciousness of the main character. Because he is blind, the world of the story emerges from tactile and auditory impressions, causing other characters, for example, to be portrayed through metonymic abbreviation: as a "hand" grasping his own, or—in his wife's case—footsteps, "uneven breathing," and her "warm, trembling voice" (I, 3-4, 12). Though the disappearance of color causes the blind man's memories to lose their "fragrance" (10), through his sharpened sense of hearing he acquires a "rich world" of minute sensations as he lives withdrawn on his little farm, occupied with basket weaving. This world—of grasshoppers in the clover, chirping nestlings under the eaves, the "quick, whizzing" sound of the swallows as they round the corner, and so forth—has become "dear and familiar to him" (11). His resignation is conveyed in biblical allusions suggestive of the story of Job—"Who was he to complain? By what right did he demand that misfortune should pass him by?"—and, more harshly, that of Uriah in II Samuel: "for the sword devoureth one as well as another" (6). When peace comes after his fits of despair, he even sees something like Providence in his life. And, he learns, people are so "kind"; soon, for example, a former fellow worker helps his wife work the farm. "He had reconciled himself to life once again" (9).

Hoel prepares the startling dénouement by a conversation between the blind man and a visiting parson. Hard of hearing and thus marked by another sensory deficiency, the parson does not hesitate to articulate the "meaning" of the misfortune. He tells him: "You see more deeply in many things since you lost your eyesight. Who knows whether your true happiness isn't greater now. A thinker has said: A man experiences the deepest joy the day he discovers that what he considered his greatest weakness in reality is his strength." While the parson is still holding forth, the blind man is inexplicably caught up in a recollection with "violent force." He recalls sitting in the lilac bower one spring evening together with his fiancée: the sun was setting, there was a fragrance of lilac in the air, and the bumblebees were buzzing around them. "She sat holding his hand while speaking to him. No one had had such a warm voice as she." Suddenly, some "muted words reached his ears. And then he knew what had awakened the bittersweet recollection. The voices came from the lilac bower far down in the garden. Had he, unknown to himself, heard her voice first? Now he heard the friend—cautious and lowspoken. . . . And then came, subdued and tender, her warm, trembling voice"(12).

This moment acquires added impact by the way it is prepared. For after Hoel has raised his story to the level of theodicy by his biblical allusions, he makes the parson articulate a point of conventional wisdom: loss of eyesight is compensated by a deeper spiritual insight and by moral harmony. The story as a whole, however, moves toward an explosion of this pattern, and, ironically, the vehicle of the explosion is precisely the compensation of lost eyesight through the blind man's sharpened sense of hearing: contrary to the parson's pious thought, his greatest strength turns out to be his weakness.

Hoel himself judged "The Idiot," the story that launched him on his literary career when it fetched a Nordic prize in 1918,[2] as "the only original story in the entire book," despite the stylistic influence from Knut Hamsun. Here, he writes, "I succeeded, at any rate to a certain degree, in telling about a human fate (the story's I) without telling about it" (I, ix). While the story is indubitably one of the best, it does reveal some signs of the apprentice—a few too heavy emphases to make sure the point comes across. But Hoel's second comment is highly interesting. The story proper comes into being in the interstice between the title figure and the narrator, a young man with the usual problems of his age. To the latter, with his inordinate need for meaning, the idiot becomes a reminder of the meaninglessness of all things.

The story consists of the young man's observations of the "idiot" over a period of years. He, the idiot, habitually stands before a gate—"not much more than a hole"—in a board fence in front of a store. To the narrator his "empty gray eyes," the idiot's most notable feature, have the "staring expression" of a dead dog he once saw. They contained a "world of emptiness, they were like two holes into nothingness." These superimposed images of nothingness no doubt furnish the key to the sense of "absurdity" (*meningsløshet*) that the sight of the idiot portends. The latter's movements are minimal: apart from his rocking motion back and forth on his spindly legs, they are limited to the few steps needed to get a view of the grocery store window and an occasional motorbike ride offered by some kindly soul—then once more back to his hole in the fence. His emotions are equally rudimentary: the gray emptiness of his eyes alternates with "blind, elemental rage" when he is mocked by grownups or harassed by boys (I, 20-21, 25).

While the narrator at first receives only a glimpse of the idiot, he becomes increasingly obsessed with him; eventually he develops a curious sense of identification, as though the idiot were his double. The very thought of him fills the young man with a "kind of terror tinged with pity"—tragic sentiments, we know. The pity, shown in action as he chases away the idiot's tormentors, betrays his sense of affinity, also revealed by the reflection: "Rather die tomorrow . . . than be like him" (I, 24). Yet, in the end the young man is one step closer to the idiot: back in the same furnished room where he used to live several years ago, he has described a circle—only a little wider than the idiot's. The form of the story as a whole is the same as that of its first paragraph, which begins and ends with the same word: "today" (18); one is in a world reminiscent of Samuel Beckett. At the end the narrator reflects that "one place is just as good as another." And though he realizes that the idiot's monotonous life, consisting "year after year" of the "gray street, some tufts of dusty leaves of grass, a few trees far away, a wagtail, a sparrow, . . . the changing seasons, rain, snow," is "strange, without direction," he asks himself: "Is it that contemptible? Is it that much poorer than those of others? More monotonous, quieter, more tranquil, and happier? Nearer the goal, nearer to the great nothingness, the great happiness" (26).

Whereas "The Blind Man," written against the background of a providential concept of man's life, ends with an explosion of this pattern, "The Idiot" works by repetition of cycles of various magnitude, until the contingency of the idiot's "directionless," absurd existence encompasses the young narrator's life as well. Furthermore, Hoel seems to intend a broader reference, as shown by his description of the idiot on the motorbike: "His legs dangled hither and thither, he swayed helplessly back and forth— a kind of ironic image of all humankind as it rushes blindly and aimlessly onward, finally to end up where it started" (I, 22-23). One can understand why a young man, writing in the spring of 1918, might feel tempted to express such desperate views.[3] But this passage of excessive symbolism mars an otherwise flawless story.

"Spleen" is a psychoanalytically organized version of the same experience of absurdity. Around 1920, Hoel read a great deal of Freud and other psychoanalysts; yet, despite the freshness of the exposure, there is not the slightest sense of contrivance or ideological intrusion.

The story initially postulates a meaningful pattern of life, though only in the form of an emerging dream image. The main character dreams he is running toward a goal; but, having forgotten what it is, he has to run faster. Though he hears the footsteps of others in the "brown fog," he runs alone, with no one to ask what the goal was. Suddenly he is no longer chasing after something but fleeing: "What he had chased after now chased him." Like the circular road, this image of the hunter-hunted will turn up as a leading motif in later works by Hoel. At the sound of the church bell, he knows he is on his way to a funeral—his own—and he must not be late. Beside him a "brown devil's face" appears, a face he knows but cannot identify. The devil utters these words of Christ on the cross: "Today you shall be with me in Paradise." The dreamer screams and wakes up to hear the church bell (I, 48-49).

His depressed Sunday morning mood, only peripherally due to a hangover after the previous night's party, is evoked by grotesque images of transience—the nose drip of a female churchgoer turns into "a water clock, an hourglass, an image of time's passage"—and by allusions to Ecclesiastes concerning the recurrence of all things. But he recognizes that his depression stems from something he has repressed; specifically, he senses that the

"devil's face," whose appearance formed the climax to his nightmarish dream, is linked somewhere in his "brain" with an "evil
memory." It "lay there hidden and forgotten, poisoning mind
and senses, until he recalled it once more" (I, 50-51).
The release of the repressed begins, in true Freudian fashion,
with the young man's recall of the previous day. The thought of
the frivolous behavior of a couple of married women he had
kissed at the party "troubled him a little" (I, 51). His reflections
are interrupted by the visit of his friend, another flirtatious
woman who is collecting admirers. The first clue to his depression is offered when, soon thereafter, he takes a walk and meets a
male friend from the party the day before, married to an actress
who is unfaithful to him. In the course of conversation, the friend
happens to mention having overheard the dinner invitation extended to the dreamer by someone at the party: "His wife is
pretty, you know her. Don't fall in love. Goodbye." This is what
the dreamer, who is in love and contemplates marriage himself,
has forgotten with "such care" (55)—the dinner invitation for the
same day from a married childhood friend.

His hosts have just been blessed with a baby, seen by the jubi-
lant father as the key to happiness. However, just as the father
ends his eulogy of marriage and parenthood, the visitor, who has
been taken to the bedroom, "discovered something that liberated
him from the last residue of the day's uneasiness. In the headboard of one of the beds there was a knot in the mahogany, and it
had the form of a devil's face. A devil's face that sent him a
smile."[4]

The virtue of this story is not primarily that it handles the
Freudian pattern so well—the anxiety dream, the mood of depression, the maneuvers of evasion, and the emergence of the repressed content of the memory. It is rather the intimate
interweaving of psychoanalytic mechanisms with the search for
meaning that is the key to its artistic success.

On the surface there is an acceptance of meaninglessness,
which here becomes overtly thematized. The friend he meets on
his walk asks him: "Dear friend, who are you to demand a
meaning from life? Reason, meaning, coherence
[sammenheng]—these are all things that exist only in our
minds. . . . The meaning of life is not accessible to us. But the

meaninglessness of life is a good working hypothesis. The day
you recognize this you will feel like a reborn person, and you will
realize that everything is well and absolutely indifferent" (I, 54).
Ancient patterns of meaning have either disappeared or become
inverted. Thus, Sunday, the day intended for "rest and reflection," makes sense only in the country, where life is "simple and
has a meaning," not in the city, where life "rushes ceaselessly
onward," causing the one who stops to look back to become a
"pillar of salt" (53-54). The biblical allusion is characteristic;
except for echoes of Ecclesiastes, all these function in reverse, and
the rebirth into meaninglessness, already mentioned, is their spiritual substance. The "mocking devil's face," a leitmotif that occurs first in the dream and later in the dreamer's reflections,
finally to be observed on the headboard of his friend's bed (49, 50,
52, 55, 58), perfectly expresses the inversion of values: a devil
speaking like Christ, inviting the dreamer to a sensualist's paradise. The devil turns into a double, expressing the adulterer's real
values by contrast to his conventional desire for chastity in the
girl he loves.

This time, too, Hoel sets up a pattern of meaning later to be
exploded, namely, by the perception of the devil's face in the
knot. But the pattern consists merely of the ecstatic husband's
fondly reiterated clichés of the bliss of marriage and children—of
home life, "a gift from above." The baby is "the meaning, you
understand," he tells the "doubter," who in the next moment
realizes his own possible connection with the genesis of that
"meaning," which is treated very ironically. The husband's marital euphoria seems of a piece with his postprandial bliss: never,
he tells his guest, does he feel "the innermost pattern and
meaning in everything" as he does after a good dinner (I, 57-58).

The mocking irony of the ending recalls "The Blind Man."
But in this story neither the assumed "pattern and meaning" nor
their denial through the devil's face (infidelity) has the amplitude
and power of the blind man's Job-like predicament. The
"pattern" is that of a smug bourgeois existence, not a hard-won,
religiously tinged acceptance of one's fate, and the denial is a
seducer's leer, not the deprivation of a lifetime's peace and harmony. By compensation, the story excels "The Blind Man" both
in intellectual and psychological subtlety. It is in the intimate

fusion of psychological and religious-ethical themes that the novelty and chief merit of "Spleen" consist. "The Star" is in a different genre, a marvelously realistic retelling of the story of the Magi. Here the structure is the reverse of what we have just seen: the seeming fortuitousness of chance is converted to a cosmic design. The story, which is reminiscent of T.S. Eliot's poem "Journey of the Magi," short of Eliot's theological intrusions, deals with a religious quest. This quest takes place in a dark world, beset with the usual secular ills of rising prices, racial prejudice, poverty, and congestion. The Greek innkeeper, who complains about those "dirty Jews" everywhere, hesitates about promising lodging; but realizing the men are wealthy, he eventually proposes an arrangement: he will kick out the family sleeping in the stable, an "old scarecrow" of an artisan and his lovely wife, who has just given birth. They have failed to pay up anyway. Thus, the Holy Family is mentioned only at the end, shamefully and peripherally. Even more than in the Bible, the divine birth takes place in a corner. But as the three men walk out after lying there sleepless, facing an endless "darkness and loneliness," there is a hint of morning in the East: "Over the stable stood the star" (17).

The story juxtaposes the utter realism of everyday life with the uncommented marvel of fairy tale. The strangers are outsiders to the innkeeper's greedy materialism—world-weary seekers for a new dispensation who are viewed by others as madmen. But even their own minds are not at one about the search; what if the entire undertaking were just an "illusion, a dream, an aberration," one of them asks, when the star has failed to appear for several days. They fear being disappointed once again: "The same over and over again. When were they to learn? Once more they had dared to sustain a small hope, and once more they had called out into the vacant air. Cold and dark and silence" (I, 15-17). Whether the miraculous ending was motivated by the story's publication in a Christmas magazine is impossible to know. The influence of Anatole France, at this time an important stimulus to Hoel, stopped short at the marvelous, the fairy-tale ending. Here the "road we walk," the image contained in the collection's title and a cardinal motif in all of Hoel's production, acquires a meaningful pattern, contrary to the hither-and-thithering and circular movements in the preceding stories.

Of the remaining pieces, "Man and the Earth" and "The Unavoidable" deal with the vanity of human wishes in view of man's mortality. The former is an ironic fable of greed, in which Abal acquires a coveted vineyard only to confront death. It is a fine example of simple, objective narrative but no more. The latter presents a similar theme by portraying a group of the old and infirm who sit around in a tiny park opposite a churchyard when the weather is good. However, the potential feeling of horror implicit in the metaphysical conceit of the "island of rest" (the park) as a waiting room where they bide their turn to be admitted to the graveyard (I, 30, 35) is not brought out. This would require a different kind of art, less realistic, more concentrated. Essentially the story falls apart into a series of genre scenes, and the uncanny is not reconcilable with genre.

"Spring Evening" and "In the Land of Shadows" deal with the emotional ambiguities of youthful love. The first relates an almost too typical seduction scene in which the lovers are trapped by their subconscious desires. The subject is trite and the treatment lacking in originality. The second, more ambitious, is an attempt to evoke the intensities of erotic conflict. Years after the experience, a young man recalls how one summer day, while mourning his recently deceased love in the cemetery, he resumes a relationship with another woman. The ambivalences and conflicts are plain to see, as are the fugitive moments of release, but the story's action, largely psychological, lacks definition and, consequently, interest. What one remembers are a few images of emotional upheaval, images that will recur in later works. Thus, the persona likens his state of mind that "long, evil summer" to a "vibrating clockwork, a churning system of wheels . . . that whirled around and around in the same place without stop or rest" (I, 78), and sexual passion turns the mind into a "seething maelstrom" (82). These examples of Hoel's dark lyricism show that he was struggling to find an objective correlative for experiences that do not easily lend themselves to treatment in prose narrative. And as narrative, in my opinion, the story is largely a failure.

INGENTING: A CYCLE OF STORIES AS NOVEL

The moods and themes—and to a certain extent the form—of

The Road We Walk are continued in *Nothing* (*Ingenting*, 1929), published seven years later. The intervening works, *The Seven-Pointed Star* (*Syvstjernen*, 1924) and *Sinners in Summertime* (1927), are fundamentally different, each exploring a distinct aspect of European and Norwegian postwar reality. *Nothing*, on which Hoel was already working when the idea of *Sinners* came to him (I, x-xi), treats more universal themes. The alternation between classic and period themes will be apparent throughout Hoel's subsequent development; in some works he tries, not always successfully, to unite the two concerns.

Nothing is Hoel's first treatment of a characteristic nineteenth-century theme, the young provincial's confrontation with the big city. But neither Balzac nor Dickens, with their "lost illusions" and "great expectations," comes to mind in reading the book, which is properly called a novel of disillusionment. Rather, its sensuous lyricism and ironic detachment evoke Knut Hamsun and Hjalmar Söderberg, both deeply admired by the young Hoel.[5] The book is related to Hamsun's *Hunger* (1889) by its theme of a young outsider's ceaseless wandering in the big city, driven by a different kind of hunger; to Söderberg's *Martin Birck's Youth* (1901) by its disenchanted treatment of love.[6] Yet *Nothing* has an unmistakably original tone.

In a letter to Martin Joos, Hoel speaks about the autobiographical basis of *Nothing* and *The Road to the End of the World*. Both are based on his own life, on "personal experiences, but more on mood and atmosphere than on particular concrete experience." What is related in the story-chapters of the book, he says, has "never actually 'happened,' " though "related things," of course, did (letter of 9/29/1939). Some of the stories in *The Road We Walk* seem to have the same genesis, and in one story of 1923 not included in the collection, "Summer," the motif of wandering around the city appears.[7] Other resemblances will become evident from the following summary of *Nothing*.

The book consists of six "stories," each having the same young man, Erik, as a central figure. A youth of nineteen with a job in the city in "Nothing," the first story, Erik is next seen at home in the country later the same summer. He picks up his acquaintance with a farmer's daughter, Turi, but his tender feelings for the girl are repressed due to his intention shortly to return to the city.

With the following story, "Snow," which is related as a recollection, we are again in the city, witnessing how the young man is "betrayed" in love on Christmas Eve.[8] "The Return" describes Erik's visit home at twenty-three, to discover that Turi has just died of tuberculosis. The last two parts, "The Dream" and "Nothing," take place at twenty-seven and thirty, respectively. The first expresses a mood of existential anxiety, the second erotic disenchantment. Characteristically, the first and last story have the same title, "Nothing": the shape of the book is circular.

As in *The Road We Walk*, Hoel in *Nothing* projects his vision of experience against a background of traditional values and attitudes. In part, this background is biblical, in part secular. Often it appears in the form of leitmotifs, whose changes as the book progresses subtly reflect the young man's increasing disenchantment. Thus, in the first story a familiar road on a hill looks as though it "led directly into the heavens." The passage continues: "And sometimes a little white cloud would hang there, directly above the road, as though it belonged just there" (I, 238). In this context, charged with Scripture, the cloud recalls I Kings 18:44, portending God's answer to Elijah's prayer. In "Snow," after the young man's "betrayal," the same road image verges on "blank space, . . . emptiness, the dark night sky." And he imagines that the goal of his wandering is to retrace "his own footsteps upward toward emptiness, toward nothingness . . ." (304). In the last story, social replaces metaphysical disenchantment. This time, ten to eleven years later, the same road that had "strangely disappeared into the heavens" has a row of huge tenement houses for a horizon (334): Jacob's ladder is no more.

Other images, religious and secular, reinforce the sense of a vanishing universe of values, one that Erik can experience only in nostalgic glimpses. When, in "Snow," he listens to the reverberations of the church bells as he looks forward to spending a happy Christmas Eve with his beloved, Erik feels as though "the earth itself sang a song toward the sky in the twilight hour." After being informed by his girlfriend's landlady that she has just gone out with a "real" man (II, 298), the church bells appear more "subdued," as though "the sound were padded with wool." The last "faintly vibrating" peal of bells passes "outward into dark space" (299). In "The Return," having learned from her mother how Turi died, Erik solemnly recalls a day in church: his momentary release from self is once more evoked through auditory religious images, namely, the "peal" of the church organ heard as a boy. His thoughts as he is struck a bit later by the beauty of the hamlet—how "strong and calm [it was], how complete, self-contained, full of meaning and coherence"—are preceded by the actual sounds of the countryside, including a bell, as the working day ends. But while Erik is capable of such experiences, he is already alienated from them, and his alienation makes him feel guilty, as though "before judgment" (318, 320-21).

The theme of secular coherence and meaning, mingled with religious echoes, is best presented in the second story, "You Will Leave Me and Go Far, Far Away . . ." (II, 269-86), which is constructed around a well-known folktale, "The Princess and the Twelve Wild Ducks." Describing Erik's visit to Turi at her summer dairy (seter), it has the flavor of folk literature both in theme and style, characterized as it is by metamorphosis, nature lyricism, bits of folk song, and refrainlike motifs. The fairy tale, relating how a princess releases her twelve brothers from bewitchment, suggests that Erik, with his new job in the city, is under a spell, though at first he tries to see her as the bewitched one. Turi, though an adult, lives in a closed, coherent world transfigured by fairy tale. Sometimes, she tells Erik, she almost believes that "this moor goes all the way to the ends of the earth." If she were a crane, she says, flying day after day, she would never see anything except "moor upon moor and tarn after tarn—and the sky with a few clouds and birds—and in a way it would be beautiful, I think, almost as in an old fairy tale." Her glance conveys a sense of "peace, sincerity, simplicity," causing everything "difficult and complicated" to disappear (277-78).

Yet, despite his attempt to return to Turi after their hurried goodbye—with biblical conjurations not to look back but "flee to the hills" (II, 281; cf. Genesis, 19:18)—in the end he renounces the salvation that Turi could offer; he recalls a verse from the Bible: "I was with you, and you did not know me" (285). The epiphanic moment, with its "faint, almost imperceptible ripple [that] passed across the meadow," together with a "light rustle in the grass and the branches"—suggesting the "low murmuring

sound" signifying God's presence to Elijah (I Kings 19:13)—
clears away the "veil" and the "fog" from Erik's mind only to
confront him with a merciless truth about himself: "He did not
want to bind her. For he did not want to become bound" (284).[9]
"The Return" alludes to the question asked of Jesus by his disciples: "Are you the one who is to come, or are we to expect some
other?" (Matthew 11:2-3). The narrator comments: "But we always expect some other, and never did we know the one who
came" (318).

Thus we seem fated to an endless search, until age puts an end
to it. "Call it an evil spell [trollham] then," Erik thinks. "But he
had to roam and wander. And he didn't want anybody to sit
waiting for him" (II, 284). This reverse allusion to Peer Gynt,
where Peer asks Solveig to wait for him (Act III), is repeated in
the story's last sentence: "Nobody waited for him" (286).[10] The
theme of aimless wandering is repeated through verbal motifs
associated with the enchanted princes who had to "fly and flutter,
flutter and fly, chasing after adventure that was not adventure,"
as well as through symbolic images, such as butterflies that,
"fluttering hither and thither, approached a flower but didn't
settle, fluttered onward, onward" (II, 284, 283). The word
"onward" is a mocking allusion to the Faust theme, which re-
echoes throughout the novel in various guises: from an illusory
chase after symbols of happiness like rainbow, will-o'-the-wisp,
and "the moonbridge in the lake" (284) to a downward stumble
and, finally, a weary trudge as, Peer Gynt fashion, Erik skirts
"around" Turi's home on his way back (284-86). The "road we
walk" in life is thus aptly described by the leitmotif of the opening story, "Nothing": "And the road is long, deserted, and glim-
mering with dust" (237, passim).

These images, and the implicit existential malaise, culminate
in a realm of shadow, fog, and eternal repetition that suggests
limbo or hell.[11] This condition, one of utter loneliness, is like
being placed in "empty space" (II, 289); human feeling loses
itself, one's identity falls apart, and consciousness becomes split.
In "The Return" Erik asks himself whether hell—"the under-
world, the world of shadow"—is not the condition of the perpetually delayed commitment, causing us to "scout ourselves blind,
listen ourselves deaf, wake ourselves to sleep, go chasing around

in a circle." Curiously, as the theme is developed, these brutal paradoxes of a debased Faustian quest come to express a latter-day Hamletism, whereby "the act is dissolved before it is performed, the resolution before it is made." In religious terms, it is a "hell full of eternally trembling, eternally fluttering anxiety, of vaguely outlined, groping figures whispering: Who am I? Shadows chasing shadows." Expressed through elemental imagery, it is a condition in which "the cloud becomes fog instead of rain" (318-19). In "Snow" Hoel uses the notorious November fog of Oslo and environs to evoke this condition of evil paralysis. Every morning, he writes, there was the same "autumn fog, . . . strangely paralyzing, oppressive, depressing, as though all despondency, all hopelessness, all weakness and laxness and impurity in the world had risen out of the ground, had descended from the sky, had reeked out of the walls of the houses and filled the air, had *become* the air during this long, dark autumn" (291). This is the counter-image to resonant air, so charged with joy and religious meaning in the book.

Hoel uses dream techniques to present an intensified form of these images.[12] In "The Dream," where Erik at twenty-seven has passed his university examinations with such distinction that the future offers unlimited possibilities, the thought of death before going to sleep generates a set of dream scenes that undercut his euphoria. Curiously, the initial bliss itself is inseparable from anxiety and a sense of nemesis (II, 324-25). The dream begins with buoyant images of soaring flight, then shifts to the ground, where Erik and his beloved, clearly Turi, sit with their backs to a crowd of people stampeding by. "There was something that all of them chased toward and something they fled from. But what they chased toward and what they fled from was one and the same thing."[13] The two lovers can protect their happiness from the hurtling crowd only by remaining completely immobile. In the next part of the dream, this grotesque version of the Faustian "ever onward" theme gives way to a sinister application of the fog image. The dreamer is in a room, observed by someone in the corner whom he recognizes as the rushing multitudes reduced to one. The figure is made uncanny by the fact that his face is only an "erased, vague, diffuse surface, a *smudge of fog*, like a face seen through a dim windowpane" (329; my italics). The smudge of fog "stares at him, scrutinizes him," causing "unspeakable fear." One is tempted to conclude that, unbeknownst to the dreamer, both the rushing crowd and the "smudge of fog" are negative self-images, functioning—much like the unconscious in Jung's concept of the psyche—as a counterpoise to the initial conscious state of euphoria.

In the last part of the dream, the dreamer is sitting, together with his love, on a bench in the open air; old and seemingly prepared to live indefinitely, he resembles the figure of the Wandering Jew, also glimpsed in "The Return" (II, 309). He is like God and understands all, but is "cold and hard like stone. It occurs to him that he is dead," a thought that fills him with "ice-cold anxiety." Interpreting the experience, he sums it up through the image of a "gray, fearful abyss that he looked down into for a fraction of a second" (330). This image appears also in "Snow," where Erik would dream that he "stood before an abyss calling out something or other, not a name, but a caress, a tender word. But nobody answered."[14]

The theme of banal repetition, associated with double consciousness and with a spectral shadowy existence, is particularly well presented in the last story, "Nothing," where Erik meets a girl he was too timid to approach when he was in love with her ten or eleven years ago. Their intimate encounter has an air of unreality about it. Thus, it occurs to him that "it was not *he* who now walked here, but someone else, an old, strange man who had walked these stairs infinitely many times" (II, 339), a feeling expressed in a more rudimentary form already in the story "In the Land of Shadows" (I, 73). Throughout, the "strange, unreal sensation . . . that he had experienced all this before" made it all "spectral [*gjengangeraktig*]—as though he appeared as a living character in his own memoirs. Doubly spectral, because simultaneously he recalled other times when he had also had this double consciousness. An unpleasant sensation—to be one's own ghost [*gjenganger*]—to see oneself multiplied as a shadow of a shadow behind a shadow" (II, 340).

After sleeping with her, he knows he is a double betrayer, having "betrayed the dream [of the young girl] with the reality, and the reality with the dream" (II, 341). He fails to realize that "union of half-forgotten memory and new experience which makes one believe, for a single mournfully blissful instant, that one understands what life *is*" (334). Instead, when his unlived youth is offered to him, his desire once more to live "genuinely [*oprindelig*] and *for the first time*" is frustrated by the very fact that he "*recognizes* the experience" (Ms. Fol. 2365:3). One is reminded of the situation of Michel in Gide's *The Immoralist*, another quester for freedom, except that Michel soon gives up the attempt to recapture the past. When Erik's thoughts turn to what the encounter has meant to *her*, she seems to be his double. The possibility of being sincere and thereby beginning something "new, strong and pure" is swept aside by the Faustian motto: "Onward, onward, onward. Be free and cold" (342).

Despite the seeming pessimism of *Nothing*, the novel does embody a couple of affirmative themes. Apart from the notion of love setting us free—a thought that barely rises above a pious Christian platitude—the book has something to say concerning memory, the esthetic attitude, and the imagination. Far from being merely a medium of banal repetition, memory is a transfiguring power in *Nothing*. "Snow," told in retrospect, notes how moments of "grief and disappointment and pain" may return "richer" and "stronger" from time to time, "like a gift from the past" (II, 287). At the end of the story the idea recurs in a concrete form, as the happy "remembrance" of a painful experience causes age to vanish and happily restores a moment of youth: he "perceived the wonderfully fresh, raw smell of falling snow, he saw before him the quiet, empty street, the gleam of the snow flakes, the ascent toward a dark, cloudy winter sky" (304). All these images, so fraught with loneliness and misery at the time of the immediate experience, are now transfigured by temporal distance into an esthetically tinged joy.

Both in "Snow" and "The Return" one can actually observe the genesis of the esthetic attitude. In the former, after being told by her landlady that his girlfriend has just gone out with someone else, Erik meticulously observes the room and the landlady's gestures while taking in the story of betrayal. His minute recording of detail shields him from the pain of the emotional shock, at the same time as what he observes—in particular the landlady's vaguely obscene circular gesture of rubbing her stomach—is an objective correlative to his growing sense of life's banal repetition (II, 296-97). After he leaves, his attitude persists, generating some extremely sensitive impressions of the December evening. "His mind was calm. He noticed it himself and was a bit surprised. All thoughts, all impressions were so strangely cool, so wintrily clear" (301). The enriching moment of recall, previously discussed, is prepared by the inchoately esthetic response to his painful experience at the time it occurred.

At the end of "The Return" a similar transformation takes place through a change in attitude. Meditating on Turi's pathetic fate, Erik manages for a moment to forget his own ego and be only *"the eyes that saw.* Everything he saw was so lovely, so incredibly lovely, . . . dark and mournful" (II, 320).[15] Strangely, it looks as though the impersonal esthetic attitude confirms Erik's experience of being: his momentary sense of unity with life around him ends in his rendering "thanks for the first of all gifts, that he was allowed to perceive the world and, through happiness and pain, feel that he existed" (II, 320). This moment also illustrates the working of the imagination. For without imagination, we would be more "lonely than the animals, walking around by ourselves in a deathly still vacuum, without connection with anyone or anything, indeed, without connection with ourselves from moment to moment" ("Snow," II, 289-90). Without imagination there is no love, no self or identity, no humanity. "The imagination is the air, it is life, for the human mind. We live and breathe within it; it connects us with the people around us; it makes it possible for us to have things in common with others and for two persons sometimes to feel as one" (289). Hoel's advocacy of this basically Coleridgean view of the imagination may be a response to the contemporary philosophy of analytical empiricism, with its atomistic concept of experience.

Nothing is a sensitive rendering of a young man's initiation. Though less than tragic, the novel is very moving. While the artistic quality of the individual stories varies—the first story being the weakest, on account of its more realistic style of describing Oslo, a much vaguer city in other parts—the overall quality is very high. The lyrical passages have none of the irritating features of poetic prose, and the descriptive details form the basis of pervasive motifs that provide thematic unity to the entire novel.

3
The Postwar World: Satiric Exposé and Comic Romance

The Seven-Pointed Star (1924; lit., the Pleiades) and *Sinners in Summertime* (1927) had diametrically opposed fates as books: the former, though received quite favorably by the critics, fell dead from the press; the latter was Hoel's literary breakthrough. But the two works have many similarities. Both deal with the consequences of the war, one in the tone of macabre irony, the other in one of farcical comedy; both have satiric bite, sharp in *The Seven-Pointed Star*, more gentle in *Sinners;* their settings are abstract and hermetic respectively—in the former an unidentified city inferentially situated in Belgium or northern France, in the latter an islet southwest of Oslo. The characters are types; in *The Seven-Pointed Star* they often approach the grotesque, in *Sinners* sometimes the stereotypic. Moreover, the attempt to create a new rational order leads, in the first case, to the apotheosis of unreason, in the second to primitivistic regression. Thematically, determinism and freedom, chance and fate are important concerns, more justifiably so in *The Seven-Pointed Star* than in *Sinners.* After more than half a century, the wide discrepancy in the novels' reception seems puzzling. Though the opinion of Hoel's friend, the caricaturist Blix, that *The Seven-Pointed Star* was "one of the gems of world literature" (letter of 12/6/1938) may seem excessively generous, the relative merit of the two novels is an open question.

THE SEVEN-POINTED STAR

The plot of *The Seven-Pointed Star* hinges on the Versailles

Treaty, specifically the reparations clause. For several years the unnamed little city in the plain has regularly received cargoes of bricks from enemy country upstream. Due to the unwanted import, the town's own brickworks must soon close, causing much unemployment and driving the owner insane. Only when Director Jason, the city's chief industrial and commercial magnate—who, along with a group of compatriots, owns the enemy brickworks supplying the goods—conceives the idea of building a star-shaped super crematorium with the bricks, does the city recover from its economic doldrums. The plot, powered by Jason's mad compulsion, climaxes with a religio-politico-patriotic orgy on Victory Day, which is also Election Day. After the crematorium's inauguration the ruling political party throws a feast for the city's invalids to soothe popular discontent and garner votes.

Thus baldly summarized, the plot may appear somewhat thin. Several years after the book's publication, Hoel said in a letter to Helge Krog that, because of financial straits, he forced its completion and it came out "unfinished" (7/28/1928). Elsewhere he censures the novel for being schematic, as "precise and stiff as a correctly solved problem in geometry." Having read Kafka, he states, he became his first pupil, but a "poor" one. For while Kafka's books take place in a no-man's-land, we discover "our own dream world" between the lines. But in *The Seven-Pointed Star*, Hoel says, there is nothing to read "between the lines"— revenge for "seven years of teaching mathematics." The "vision" on which the book is based, its idea, is allegedly spoiled by being executed with "pedagogic zeal and mathematical logic" (I, x). To the present reader the book's faults lie elsewhere.

According to Hoel's manuscript notes, the basic idea was that "everything, society, is sick and crumbling." Both in the individual and in society, the "sick, disintegrating, lethal forces are those that prevail." He admits that these forces were already present before the war, but the war has afforded "a much wider scope" to evil and to the desire for destruction; it has "let loose forces that cannot for the moment be stopped" (Ms. Fol. 2313:1). This vision, seemingly conceived in the early months of 1923, took on sharper outlines on a grant-supported European tour starting in March, 1924, during which Hoel visited such cities as

Berlin, Prague, Budapest, and Vienna. This trip provided him
not only with the European milieu he needed but with "symbolic
illustrations" of his idea, including a hysterical pre-Nazi rally in
Dresden's circus and a demonstration march of Austrian war
invalids protesting the government's plan to reduce the invalid
pensions.[1] Once Hoel had gathered these live materials, it took
him only a few months—during a stay in Achensee, Tirol, from
late June on—to write the novel. It is no surprise that, after such
experiences, he offers in the book a terrifying lesson in the sociopolitical consequences of paranoia and mass psychology. One
such lesson is the rise of demagogic leaders like Jason, whose
insane dream of exterminating humankind foreshadows Nazi notions of genocide. To Hoel in *The Seven-Pointed Star*, postwar
humanity seems afflicted with physical and psychological invalidism, and the arrangements of the Versailles Treaty, a kind of
ordered chaos, are presented as being life-denying, indeed
suicidal.

These themes are largely conveyed through an inversion of
traditional moral and religious values. Thus the ruined belfry,
with its centuries-old bell, has never been restored: religion has
suffered irreparable damage. And though the bell itself was re-
paired, its sound seems "dry and cracked" (I, 96-98). The town's
religious dynamics are centered in a cult of debauchery, sexual
perversion, and sterility. At "The Merry Men's Party" (171-86),
held in the restaurant-cum-brothel of Lotus, a former painter
who lost both arms during the war, the civic leaders, the "Pleiades" group—an assembly of grotesque masks expressive of their
crippled bodies and neurotic minds—end their sadomasochistic
orgy of drinking, homosexual flirtation, and bizarre byplay by
dancing around Lotus, the "devil incarnate," and his
"barren . . . burnt-out whore" (183-85). The party, celebrating
anti-life, assumes the character of a black mass. The sinister at-
tractions of diabolism are conveyed through Dr. Conrad, the
novel's center of consciousness. In the course of the story, Dr.
Conrad, whose artificial leg is a perpetual reminder of the hor-
rors of war, undergoes a change attended by "intense pleasure":
"it was good to become another person, . . . to float before the
wind without being burdened with responsibility and will"
(177). Meanwhile the party increasingly suggests a stage perform-

ance, "outside time and place and continuity [*sammenheng*],
. . . released from the inexorable chain of cause and effect"
and "void of meaning" (178-79). Here the "bond" of true religion, like the "coherence" felt in the background of earlier works
by Hoel, is dissolved through the negative religion of diabolism.
This theme of evil liberation acquires greater amplitude
through Jason, the book's psychopathic prime mover, whose
carefully nurtured paranoia is a means of release from the burden
of existence. After his mind starts failing, he comes to see his
"contemptible weakness" as a "wonderful illness" which—since
the words and actions of the ill are "uniquely determined by
certain short circuits in the brain"—makes him "free and irre-
sponsible" (I, 243). Instead of hanging "on the cross" of his guilt,
he is now sailing "with the breeze," being "free as a bird" (244).
One recognizes the same imagery used to describe Dr. Conrad's
sensations at the "black mass."

Jason sees himself as a cog in a machine. Ironically, this is
precisely what he had refused to be as a young man, when he was
in love with a woman below him in the social scale: he would not
be another "link" in the chain of his upper-class ancestors (I,
234-35). But his idealistic euphoria—he felt like "God before the
creation," with the "ability to fly"—came abruptly to an end
with the tragic suicide of the woman he had nevertheless abandoned. He ended up on the treadmill. Once there, he tells Dr.
Conrad, there is no way "out of the machinery" (239)—except
through insanity. So ingrained with mechanical thinking is
Jason that he even speaks of the human body as a machine, an
"imperfect machine . . . [without] safety valves," and of his suicide attempt by slashing his wrists as an attempt to reduce the
steam pressure (152). Ultimately, to him, the machine image symbolizes an absolute determinism operating "all the way back to
the time before the foundations of the world were laid" (232):
indeed, the major theme dramatized through Jason is the moral
dead end represented by determinism. Jason's wish to leave society and people behind and settle in a mountain hut is a disguised expression of his desire to be "delivered from the whole
[*sammenhengen*], no longer [be] a link in a chain, but free." He
will be "like God . . . after the creation, a completely super-
fluous being" (246).

The supreme expression of Jason's illness, as of his dream of liberation, is his Christ-identification. In his extended monologues to Dr. Conrad, whose medical connivance he needs to stay out of the insane asylum, Jason keeps repeating Christ's words: Leave all things and follow me! Needless to say, this identification functions in reverse. While he presents himself as bearing the world's burden of sin on his shoulders, as being "nailed fast" by reality (I, 240, 236), and offering to "all the sick and the injured . . . a serpent to look at" by raising the star-shaped crematorium as an "emblem of unity for them all" (246), Jason speaks in apocalyptic terms of "everybody being ready for the ax" because the stupidity he sees everywhere is "evil" (156). The essence of his Messianism is a cult of death rather than life: Jason dreams of a Promised Land from which people have been eliminated (157-58). The crematorium is a fitting expression of this dream as well as an eloquent comment on the society Hoel depicts. Thus, before its inauguration, the "wedding" (300), the incidence of death is speeded up by a sort of bandwagon effect. Jason's shocking intrusion at the banquet for the invalids that follows the inauguration—he forces his way to the rostrum and shouts, "You shall die! . . . You shall die, all of you!" (333)—is only the final statement of this macabre theme.

A Satiric Fantasy

The effectiveness of satire largely depends on the skill with which the central idea is made to permeate the entire work—the handling of the action, character portrayal, imagery, and style. In this respect Hoel in *The Seven-Pointed Star* is exemplary. As one commentator says, it is executed with "bold imagination."[2] This is evident particularly in the way the entire society—the politicians, the press, the commoners—is caught up in the absurd, lethal game of erecting the monument. The articles that appear in the Establishment papers laud the planned structure as an architectural expression of the spirit of "our technological age" (I, 254), in that it combines the latest in technical expertise with a religious function. Having become a matter of technical efficiency and of profit and loss, as in the future German concentration camps, death loses its sting by the thought that one died for one's city's "prosperity and progress" (258). This example of the "big lie"—in Jason's words "everything succeeds if only it is incredible . . . enough" (233)—typifies the attitude of the city's politicians, who, in order to retain power, are prepared to appeal to the public's most "sacred" and most primitive sentiments— patriotism, self-sacrifice, memories of the war, vanity, and the need for collective identification (212).

The business of all-engrossing, all-encompassing death is brilliantly orchestrated. This is nowhere more evident than at the inauguration itself, where the most modern technology is utilized in the service of "religion." Thus, because the machinery demands that all of the seven caskets be lowered simultaneously, the seven clergymen must deliver their eulogies with perfect synchrony. One minute before the end of the allotted time, each clergyman receives a slight electric shock, communicated by a hoop fastened to his leg (I, 323-24). The computer-like precision of the ceremony makes one think of contemporary anti-utopias, satiric masterpieces like Eugene Zamiatin's *We* (Eng. tr. 1924) and Aldous Huxley's *Brave New World* (1932).

It is, in fact, the critical standards accepted for such works, rather than for the conventional realistic novel, that will determine the literary merit of Hoel's *The Seven-Pointed Star*. Effective satire does not necessarily require "round" characterization or a realistic psychology. Though the characters should not be merely "personified faults and bodily defects"—a charge leveled against Hoel's portrayals in the book[3]—figures thus conceived are not automatically ruled out, since they may evoke a spiritual essence. In *The Seven-Pointed Star*, most of the characters acquire a masklike quality; they seem like demonic grotesques whose reality is rooted in a dark, compulsive irrationality.

The irrational also manifests itself in the book's language. Its favorite figure is paradox, which not only colors the dialogue but often defines the evolution of scene. Here are a few examples: "How lofty to cast oneself once more into the abyss" after centuries of civilization (I, 134); "the earth's most inaccessible places are already teeming with people who have sought solitude" (157); the speaker brought the "crowd to such an enthusiasm for peace that it . . . [began] to kill" (155). In the last instance, the paradox shapes the entire scene. In a broader perspective, paradox informs the action of the novel as a whole: war reparations turn into an economic curse, the peace demonstration ends in a street shambles, and the victory celebration takes the form of a mass funeral. The image of the vortex expresses some of the evil intensity that powers the book's actions. Thus, the two pages describing the peace rally are dominated by the vortex (114-15), suggested also by the word "sucked" used to describe the irresistible pull of the crematorium in the book's last chapter (322).

Critical Evaluation

With all its brilliance and intensity, *The Seven-Pointed Star* does have some weaknesses. First, Hoel may be faulted for not providing a positive alternative to evil, or at least a moral standard whereby to judge his passionately evil characters. The possibilities are there, especially in the women. Olga Martel and Helene Jason embody an idea of simple happiness associated with the garden image (I, 144-46), but neither becomes a significant part of the action. Though Helene's declaration of love for Dr. Conrad is a charming piece of spontaneous behavior (288-89), it merely reveals the physician's emotional impotence. For Dr. Conrad is a divided man. The only non-grotesque figure among the central characters, he makes an effort to fight evil but to no avail. In the crucial instance of trying to save a little boy— allegedly the fruit of rape by the "enemy"—from being beaten to death by his stepfather, he is foiled by Tundra, secretary to the city council, who, along with the other politicians, plays Jason's game.

In the end, however, Dr. Conrad—who also is fascinated with Jason—asserts his independence of the demonic Messiah, whose fury vents itself through the single word "Judas." But by his betrayal of Jason, the doctor keeps faith with man, and the final mood balances his acute awareness of the transience of all things with a sense of commitment to his city (I, 333-35). Though the end approaches neither the pathos of John the Savage's suicide in *Brave New World* nor the tragedy of I-330 in Zamiatin's *We*, the note of affirmation is unmistakable.

The main criticisms of *The Seven-Pointed Star* are of a different order. Far from having the symmetry and the precision of a "correctly solved problem in geometry," as Hoel himself says, the work seems to be somewhat disproportioned. Chiefly, in showing the consequences of the Versailles Treaty, Hoel felt called upon to marshal all his knowledge of party politics, using well-known Norwegian academics as models for some of his major characters (Ms. Fol. 2313:1). This material is overlong and, in part, boring. Another excessively developed part is the story of Jason, whose passionate confessions, in the words of one critic, threaten to burst the "book's framework."[4] This can be said without denying that Jason's autobiography is by far the deepest and most subtle part of the novel. The skewed emphasis could have been avoided by relating the story more dramatically—incrementally rather than through a rather heavy-handed monologic confession for the benefit of Dr. Conrad.

But the crucial problem with *The Seven-Pointed Star* is a failure to sustain a consistent style: it oscillates between realism and expressionism. The "Norwegian" elements contribute to the former; the dreamlike mood in certain parts, enhanced by the non-Norwegian setting, aids the latter. One of the novel's best scenes, "The Merry Men's Party," is a masterpiece of expressionist evocation. On the other hand, both Jason and the politicians are portrayed according to a realistic psychology. It is a pity that, discouraged by the book's lack of success with the public, Hoel abandoned expressionism for good in favor of the more obviously palatable realistic style.

SINNERS IN SUMMERTIME

Hoel's next novel, *Sinners in Summertime*, seen by him in retrospect as his "most independent piece of work," was conceived and started while he was staying in Umhausen, Tirol, on a travel grant in July, 1927, trying to write *Nothing*. At 2:55 on the afternoon of July 12, as he felt he could no longer bear his "despondency," it was as though "the wall broke, light streamed in—and I had a new idea, for a new book." As Hoel describes it, the experience was like viewing a stage, where "figures appeared, grouped and regrouped, and changed their positions." They "began a folk dance so to speak, made bows and curtsies, passed one another and changed partners, as the custom is in the good old folk dances." With the plot taking shape, "the chapters evolved quick as a flash one after another, or—as it became more crowded—side by side on the stage. Pictures of situations appeared, with dialogue and portions of conversations. The novel was there." When he looked at the watch once more, it was 3:00. He sat down to write and went on until around 10:00 in the evening. The book was "shamefully easy" to write, perhaps "a little too easy," he admits: it was finished in slightly over two months, in between other pressing work. Hoel ascribes the ease of writing the book to the period, a "happy break" between the wars. The previous year he had met a group of young radical academics, and in *Sinners*, he says, he portrayed "their imagined cousins." He knew that such groups existed in "all countries" and thought that, if they gradually became influential in society, things would work out well (I, x-xiii).

The plot of *Sinners* deals with a group of graduate students in their mid-twenties who decide to spend the summer together on a working vacation. These eight to nine enlightened men and women want to eradicate the self-deceiving mentality of preceding generations and make a fresh start, "create order from chaos" (II, 97). Under their patina of postwar disillusionment, they are filled with a "fierce and reckless faith," radical faith (39). In particular, they believe that sexual relations can be more rationally arranged than hitherto; they acknowledge none of the evils "inextricably associated with love" in the past, such as "jealousy, mendacity, dishonesty, duplicity": "no dramas, . . . no fisticuffs, no murders or suicides" (19). The result is easy to predict: at the end Fredrik, the narrator, admits they were all a bunch of self-deceivers, having committed all the "old stupidities" one after the other (212).

When Evelyn, a sexually liberated mathematician, joins the group, the island paradise begins to show disturbing signs of change; they become "more nervous and irritable," possibly because, as Fredrik suggests, she was so "open and free and without fear, . . . absolutely whole, uncorrupted, . . . and authentic." She is also "intense, capricious and perversely sincere," particularly about sex, and introduces a "more vehement, more dangerous tone." As Eve, or the serpent, she "bewitched" the members of the group, causing them to hate and love in a more impassioned way (II, 56-57). In short, reality has entered the garden, with all the predictable consequences. By taking Erik, the group's Don Juan, for herself, Evelyn upsets the entire sexual balance; a catalyst of emotional change, she triggers erotic displacement and new attachments, with frustration, jealousy, and tears as a result.

These effects are subsequently compounded by the visit of the fiancé of one of the women, Astri, and his friend, Fearnley Jensen, who, with their upper-class status, represent the intrusion of "society." At the dinner party arranged for the occasion, the emotions that have been simmering under the surface, now strengthened by resentment produced by a sense of inferiority, are projected upon the outsiders as Johan, the budding psychoanalyst, coarsely insults them. Though this first outbreak is smoothed over by Erik, during the night Erna—a rather histrionic woman smarting under the seeming coldness of her idealistic common-law husband, Alf, the group's oldest member and already a doctor—takes Fearnley Jensen to her room. In the morning, the visitors embark and Astri along with them, but are forced to return because of a storm—a romantic backdrop to the subsequent action. Alf refuses to fight Fearnley Jensen, but Johan, stung by the latter's "self-satisfied, triumphant smile" as Erna lightly strokes his hair in passing, first slaps and then fights him, with all the formalities of a duel.

The action is rounded off with two encounters, linked together through Fredrik, who participates in both. Sigrid's suicide attempt by drowning—she has been spurned by Erik for Evelyn, who, abandoned in turn, seeks out Fredrik—causes Sigrid and Fredrik, who have previously been in love, to get together again, at which point Hoel introduces the only overt sexual act in his purportedly sinful book. However, this resolution, which is followed by readjustments for the better in other relationships, is overshadowed by the concluding savage fight between Erik and Fredrik, best friends and rivals. Afterward Fredrik, the narrator, feels "infinitely well"; the blood courses through his veins, his muscles are alive, and his brain is "sharp" (II, 212). Then, sitting in his boat after saying goodbye to Erik, he "looked at the sea and sky and laughed" (212)—presumably a laugh of liberation.

After the book was completed, Hoel felt uncertain about it. He dismissed his uneasiness, however, as being due to puritanism—the thought that a "book which had been such fun to write had to be a trifle." And the fact that it was condemned from the pulpits of the land—it is said that one Sunday no fewer than seven sermons were preached against it[5]—convinced him that there had to be something to it. Without knowing how, he says, he "happened to strike a new tone this one time" (I, xii-xiii).

Generational Comedy

Hoel's doubts about the book's merit are interesting. Some reviewers found it to be journalistic, immature, and pretentious, with banal themes, weak character portrayal, and contrived situations. Those who praised the novel stressed its satiric or comedic properties, along with Hoel's psychological deftness and verbal brilliance.[6] One unsympathetic reviewer, C.J. Hambro, discerned the influence of Anita Loos's *Gentlemen Prefer Blondes* (1925), which had been translated by Hoel—an extremely dubious contention. On the other hand, Floyd Dell, who reviewed the English translation favorably, says that Hoel had given, "in his Scandinavian setting, a truer account of the young men and women of these United States than any as yet given by their literary compatriots."[7]

Hoel's intention becomes fairly clear from a letter to his Dutch publisher, where he ascribes the confused reactions to the book to its indeterminate genre. He says it is not a "realistic novel" in the usual sense, because there are too many "palpable exaggerations." Though he admits that the latter, along with his intention to portray "*types* who say and do typical things," might point to satire, it is satire with a difference, written by someone (Fredrik) who is a member of the group he satirizes. The book, therefore, also becomes a "satire" of the narrator himself. Though Hoel makes no further attempt to define the book's genre, his description of the work confirms the view of those critics who have stressed its comedic aspects. Thus, he refers in the letter to the "many comic . . . traits" of the young generation portrayed (Ms. Fol. 2314:5). Like so much of Hoel's work, the book took shape under the impact of foreign authors—

Shakespeare, Oscar Wilde, Bernard Shaw, and Aldous Huxley, whose *Antic Hay* he reviewed for the Yellow Series in 1927. The Shakespeare connection has been ably argued by Arne Røed.[8] Though he admits that Hoel may not have been consciously aware of *A Midsummer Night's Dream* when writing the book, Røed shows convincing intrinsic similarities betwen *Sinners* and Shakespeare's romantic comedy. Apart from their common emotional mode, with fall from Eden followed by a happy ending, both treat love, or "being in love," similarly: in their groping toward the right partner, the characters constantly change their attitudes. In doing so, they are simply acting like puppets—in Shakespeare, of Oberon's "herb," in Hoel of affective obsessions, however rationalized: "Love deprives us of reason, reduces us to automatons, like fools; whatever it does to us is delicious." But the clown image, as in the case of Johan, is compensated by the book's air of innocence. Røed correctly notes that its title is misleading, the proclaimed "sin" being mostly "bluff." Even the outbreaks of violence serve the comedic intent. In conclusion, Røed calls *Sinners* a fairy tale—indeed, a poem about youth and romance. A similar perception may explain why another critic speaks of *Sinners* as a "magic grove, a pagan sacred isle."[9]

The comic range of *Sinners* reaches from high to situation comedy, at times approaching farce. On the one hand, Hoel has the knack of producing a glittering surface of verbal play, perfected, one surmises, by the study of such masters of wit as Wilde and Shaw;[10] on the other hand, he has an innate sense of comic burlesque. These two sources of comic form and feeling coexist in *Sinners*. As in *The Seven-Pointed Star*, paradox, for example, not only informs the movement of thought but shapes situational development as well. The typical situation in *Sinners* invariably turns into its opposite. The first chapter is a good illustration of this pattern. It begins with Johan addressing a crab he has just caught, "You are a self-deceiver and as such belong to the previous generation" (II, 7). As Johan goes on lecturing his two friends, Erik and Fredrik, on this subject, the crab escapes into the water, whereupon the friends throw Johan after it, thus turning Johan's point of self-deception against himself. The chapter as a whole forms an ironic loop, shaped by the merging opposites of paradox.

The burlesque goes deeper. As the young men are wandering around the islet, they suddenly stand "face to face" with a sheep, its expression one in which "thousands of years of stupidity had become petrified in character" (II, 12). The sheep accompanies the action throughout. For example, after the men have dampened and brushed their best clothes for the dinner party, they smell of "wet wool" and even toast each other as "old ram" (89, 91); the air feels like "gray wool" (136), the clouds are "woolen gray" (144). And when the company arrives at the dueling site, the sheep is there ahead of them; at the climax it clinches Johan's victory by intervening in the scuffle. The burlesque millennial regression suggested by the sheep is sustained by allusions to primordial times (18), to Valhalla, and to the Viking custom of "holm-going"—fighting duels to the death on a small island. While paradox and aphorism provide brilliant intellectual and formal means of access to the underlying irrational forces—those that move the action and the characters—the low burlesque bodies forth the same forces through crude, pungent sensations and primitive allusions.

Psychoanalysis and Character

Different as these devices may be, their combined effect is to relativize the ideas and attitudes of all the characters, including the narrator, Fredrik. Indeed, with the possible exception of Evelyn, everyone seems to embody Johan's concept of personality as a "system of weak points," the "invalidism" that life imposes on everything alive (II, 8). The crab in the first episode, with its hard shell and soft insides, comes to symbolize this insidious concept of personality, which adumbrates Hoel's later Reichian ideas. Only when, in rare moments, the shell is broken, do people grow whole, happy, and at peace with their surroundings. This feeling is illustrated by Fredrik when he discovers that, unconsciously, he has been victimized by a sense of inferiority to Erik. Only after his personality—"hard shells of pride and vanity"—is broken down is he again a "living human being" who feels open to reality, both good and bad (124).

The psychoanalytic themes of *Sinners* are obvious in one sense, obscure in others. Hoel says that, from 1924 to 1927, Freud had superseded Marx as "the man of the day"; in fact, in those years Freud was the most important subject of discussion in several Oslo intellectual circles.[11] Though Hoel himself was clearly somewhat of a Freudian, during the debate occasioned by the book at least one psychoanalyst claimed that the book was a "mockery of psychoanalysis."[12] Another, Hoel's friend Trygve Braatøy, discovered a pattern that Hoel himself seems to have been vaguely aware of when, in a manuscript note, he raises the possibility of a "hidden homosexuality" in the friendship-rivalry between Erik and Fredrik (Ms. Fol. 2365:3; 7/13/1927). In Braatøy's view, Fredrik's itch to fight Erik after the duel between Johan and Fearnley Jensen was an expression of a sexual bond: rage is directed to what subconsciously attracts. The same explanation accounts for the fact that Erik constantly troubles Fredrik's thoughts and "disturbs him in his love-making." To Braatøy, therefore, the savage fight between Erik and Fredrik at the end is intercourse in disguise: "killing is often close to sex murder, and the fight close to intercourse."[13]

This interpretation has been elaborated in a thesis by Arne Lauritz Holden, who stresses the emotional predicament of Fredrik: Erik intervenes in and disturbs Fredrik's erotic moments with Sigrid; on the other hand, Fredrik desires a "two-sided sexual experience," namely, "to be together with Sigrid and Erik at the same time"—which, of course, he cannot admit. Erik's relationship with Sigrid is similarly explained: he loses interest in her when he learns she has not been enjoyed sexually by Fredrik. Fredrik's feelings during his first intercourse with Sigrid at the end are "pale" by comparison with his feelings of happiness after the fight.[14] Despite the fact that, in his manuscript notes, Hoel says the interest ought to "concentrate" on the women (Ms. Fol. 2314:1), the relationship between the two friends constitutes the book's deepest plot motif.

Criticism

With all its surface brilliance, its evocation of the period, and its obvious entertainment value, *Sinners in Summertime* is an emotionally ambiguous and intellectually self-indulgent book. Thus, while the women pursue "masculine" studies like mathematics, engineering, law, and biology, the novel seems permeated with antifeminine bias. The intellectual self-indulgence is particularly apparent in Fredrik's drawn-out reflections after Sigrid's not-so-serious suicide attempt. His internal debate concerning "blind chance" and "fated" happenings exceeds the occasion, revealing an intrusive authorial obsession. When Fredrik tries to soothe his fear of commitment to marriage, of exchanging dream for reality, by posing philosophical questions, such as, "Was it chance which had brought us together again?" "How broad a place in the chain of cause and effect was occupied by her own feeling—that is, her feeling for me!" and so on (II, 187-88), he seems either neurotic or absurd, and that can hardly have been the author's intention. The dread of meaninglessness, of the consequences of the closed deterministic system that are an underlying concern also in this book, has failed to find an adequate objective correlative.

Like *The Seven-Pointed Star, Sinners in Summertime* is a work of uneven artistic quality. Although with his next novel, *Nothing*, Hoel wrote a nearly perfect piece of fiction, its form is that of a cycle of interrelated stories. Only with *One Day in October* (1931) does Hoel reach full artistic maturity as a novelist.

4
Two Oslo Novels: Formal Experiment and Roman à Clef

One Day in October (1931) and *Open Sesame* (1938), however disparate in literary value, both have Oslo as their setting and represent distinctive milieus within the Norwegian capital. They each introduce a considerable number of representative characters, whose portraits are laced with satire. While the mode differs, *October* leaning toward dark comedy and tragedy, *Sesame* toward parody and situation comedy, they end alike in the characters' acceptance of a somewhat shabby status quo. The author's irony alone enables the reader to transcend the futile vicious circles that determine the shape of these novels.

ONE DAY IN OCTOBER

The most striking difference between Hoel's earlier work and *One Day in October* is the immense gain in objectivity, partly due to its nontraditional structure. A cross-section, collective, or contrapuntal novel—the terminology varies—*October* represents the first significant impact of modern English and American fiction in Norway. Though thirty years earlier Hoel's countryman, Jonas Lie, had published an excellent contrapuntal novel, *When the Iron Curtain Falls* (1901), a technical stimulus from abroad seems to have been necessary to shake the hegemony of traditional narrative. Curiously, this stimulus may have been provided by an American play, Elmer Rice's *Street Scene* (1928), shown in Oslo in 1929 as *The House and the Street* (*Huset og gaten*). The action of *October*, which spans fifteen to sixteen hours, occurs in an Oslo apartment house and the adjacent streets. The story is carefully clocked: besides four general time zones—afternoon, evening, night, and morning, used as titles of the main sections—individual chapter titles designate more specific ones: 7:30 p.m., 10 p.m., midnight.

Secondarily, the increase in objectivity is due to Hoel's perfected mastery of free indirect discourse or *erlebte Rede*. Formally third-person, past-tense narration, such discourse converts in the act of reading to a first-person, present-tense mode—a kind of interior monologue of the character being portrayed—without eliminating the reader's awareness of a narrative consciousness. The greatest merit of this method is its aptness for combining authorial distance with presentational immediacy. Hoel had already used the method skillfully in depicting characters close to his own sensibility; but in *October* he portrays with psychological penetration an assortment of characters of varying ages, occupations, and temperaments, reproducing the very rhythm of their perceptions, thoughts, and feelings by the use of this method. Owing to the author's critical distance, the portrayals at the same time become self-exposures of the dramatis personae. Generally the method is handled discreetly, with only occasional lapses into direct satiric commentary. The satire, of which there is a good deal, is usually implicit in the characters' exchanges and the inner monologues.

The plot of *October*, a novel completed in forty-one "writing days,"[1] turns upon the repercussions of an exceptional woman's tragic predicament in the apartment house where she occupies a furnished room. Tordis Ravn, having left her husband, a research chemist, and put behind her a three-year-old strife-torn marriage, suffers an emotional breakdown after a few months of solitary struggle against a hostile environment. It is her repeated cries, "Take me home again! I want to go home!" that trigger the action of the novel's main section, "The Afternoon" (III, 7-165): except for the drunken janitor and a deaf and blind couple, the tenants experience a moral-psychological crisis from listening to her pleading words. Mrs. Ravn remains the matrix of the action throughout, until—and even subsequent to—her violent death due to a fall from a second-story balcony. (It is uncertain whether the fall was accidental or intentional; she is frightened by a jealous neighbor watching over her late at night while her landlady is out.) In his manuscript notes Hoel envisages the plot by way of a biological analogue: Tordis Ravn—whose presence has already evoked much ill feeling, envy, and jealousy among the women, and desire and dreams of erotic conquest in the men—is a "foreign body" in a "good bourgeois house." Her rejection in less than twenty-four hours assumes the form of "violent convulsive movements (spasms)." It is in the course of these spasms of expulsion that the principle of the book's central underlying action is realized, namely, to "unmask" the marriages of the agitated tenants (Ms. Fol. 2318:1).

The usual rhythm of the individual chapters, most of which deal with marital or other family relations, moves from an initial state of equilibrium to a highly emotional, seemingly critical scene in which the characters break through their "psychic defenses" and recognize the truth about themselves, followed by a covering-up of the glimpsed "abysses" (Ms. Fol. 2318:1). Hoel has been true to his plan as delineated: for though virtually all the characters confront the "abyss" at some point, mostly they turn their eyes away from the terrifying possibilities it conjures up. In the end their problems are either resolved by the course of events, or their situation reverts to the beginning with the onset of the new day, which makes the "events of the night" appear "unreal" (III, 273). There is one difference: the weather, at the outset unseasonably warm, has turned appreciably colder (7, 272).

This basically comic rhythm—comic in the sense that it ends in a slightly ignoble return to normalcy—is counterpointed by the tragedy of the Ravns. A brief chapter about Dr. Ravn, based on a visit to his wife's room earlier in the afternoon, contains the information that Mrs. Ravn has lost her job, suffers sexual harassment, and is pregnant. But their marital history is presented in "Dr. Arvid Ravn's Report" (III, 166-232), a lengthy apologia in which the husband tries to explain his seemingly harsh, unyielding attitude to his wife. This report is fitted into the clocked time scheme through Dr. Ravn's reading of his account, recorded soon after his wife moved out, before he decides how to respond to her frantic call for help—predictably only after it is too late.

The insertion of this first-person account within a third-person cross-section novel, while stylistically bold, is justified for several reasons. It allows Hoel to treat one marital situation at length and analytically; it effectively contrasts the average philistine humanity of apartment house No. 27 with the truly exceptional Ravns; and it offers a detailed, though biased, portrait of Mrs. Ravn. For, despite the words of an American reviewer to the effect that Tordis Ravn's "beauty, vitality, charm, loneliness and weakness are abundantly evidenced in the effects of her presence on the other tenants of No. 27,"[2] her tragic dimension eludes the mosaic of her neighbors' casual impressions, which seem less revelatory of her than of her observers. Mrs. Ravn is clearly intended to dominate the novel, and that she does so is due in large part to her husband's "report."

Character Portrayal

The tenants of No. 27 are what Hoel would call representatives of the "economic, but especially the spiritual, middle class."[3] The manner of their portrayal bears traces of both Marx and Freud.[4] Seemingly, already before his knowledge of Wilhelm Reich's "character analysis," a sociopsychological synthesis of Marx and Freud that was influential among Norwegian cultural radicals, Hoel had effected such a synthesis on his own.[5] Reich's incisive analyses of the mentality of the German petite bourgeoisie are paralleled in *October;* the novel's meaning can be elucidated in terms of Reichian concepts of patriarchy, a system synonymous with women's oppression, class discrimination, and sexual repression. Needless to say, under such a system love between the sexes loses its quality of natural affection. Thus, in describing "marital love" in his manuscript notes with reference to the "business man" (Mr. Hammer), Hoel says it consists of "*habit,* gross—and injured—*egoism, the instinct for property, vanity,* direct and unadulterated *rancor* and *hatred,* perhaps also some primitive eroticism (idea of jealousy). But tenderness, really genuine tenderness and genuine pain? Hardly a trace" (Ms. Fol. 2318:1). By contrast, Mrs. Ravn's strongest point is precisely her capacity for "tenderness" (III, 82).

In letting his characters expose their innermost drives in re-

sponse to lovely Mrs. Ravn—to men, a "wishful dream" of ideal
womanhood; to women, the rival "bewitching" their men (Ms.
Fol. 2318:1)—Hoel strips them of their pretenses, their "armor"
in the Reichian sense, and reveals them as pitiful bundles of
loneliness, anxiety, and selfishness. Men and women alike are
vulnerable, the men less so only because of a firmer self-
definition through social roles. As for the women, those who are
not completely subservient to their men show definite pathological symptoms. One critic uses the term "abreaction" in reference
to Mrs. Ribe's daily sessions of reverie and tears, and he speaks of
Mrs. Hammer's "compulsion neurosis."[6] Far worse, Mrs. Gabrielsen is a termagant and intriguer who vents her bitter sexual
frustrations through vicious slander and persecution. Through
the extremity of Mrs. Ravn's situation, all these members of the
"spiritual" middle class have their eyes opened for a brief moment to the horror of their empty, meaningless existence.

While the milieu is presented in a sociopsychoanalytic perspective, Hoel's character portrayal is eclectic. Thus, the middle-aged
married men are portrayed according to received images: the ped-
ant (Mr. Ribe), the average sensual man (Mr. Hammer), the
power seeker (S.P. Eide), the academic drudge (Mr. Gabrielsen).
A certain unity of portrayal is achieved by implicit sexual characterization. Mr. Ribe, constipated, sexually sterile, and in thrall to
his ritualized routine, is an anal-compulsive type. Mr. Hammer,
the merchant, with his habitual infidelity, is a jovial embodiment
of genital sexuality, somewhat skewed by vanity and self-flattery.
The sexual nature of Eide—lawyer, real estate tycoon and the
landlord of No. 27—is defined by his primary goal of power; with
him, in fact, desire arises from power and has a predatory, sadistic, and at the same time oral quality (III, 126, 131, 132). Gabrielsen, the high school teacher, seems sexless, an impression
that helps explain the malicious oral compensations of his wife.
Similarly, most of the other figures have fairly distinct psychosexual characteristics.

By contrast with the authorial viewpoint, the above-mentioned
characters see themselves in *moral* terms, in accordance with their
bourgeois values. The reviewer for the *New York Times* praised
this part of Hoel's portrayal: "The way in which a character
rationalizes his conduct so as to appear not unbearably contempt-

ible in his own sight is wickedly well done."[7] Ribe sees himself as a champion of order who, opposed by the women, is allied with the government for which he works; Hammer reacts to the news of his wife's infidelity with conventional moral outrage; Eide, thwarted in his amorous scheme by Mrs. Ravn's sudden death, discerns a moral "point" (*meningen*) in the event: that he restrain his passions so he can continue gathering wealth (III, 259). The portrait of Eide, arguably the novel's richest, merits further discussion. While Hammer is the capitalist manqué, the social substance of Eide is that of the capitalist pure and simple. With him all values—religious, artistic, human—are reduced to the level of material properties and are treated in commercial terms. His attitudes and behavior seem to be determined by a tacit philosophy of social Darwinism, a ruthless exploitation of everything and everybody for his own profit; yet he sees himself as one of the "pillars of society" (III, 119). The consciousness of power pervades his very being, causing him to feel that he "existed" (130); one suspects that Hoel had read Alfred Adler as well as Freud.[8] Though Eide's sexual predatoriness can be seen as an expression of the same Darwinian immoralism, its recognized potential for threatening his capitalist ethos turns it into a complicating drive and humanizes the portrait of a ruthless man.

The younger men, being socially unsettled intellectuals and therefore lacking clearly defined or confirmed social roles, view their experience in a broader frame and project their self-images in philosophical terms. Once more the author's interpretation is evident through tone, imagery, and sexual characterization. All of them—Ellefsen, a former Communist who supports himself through tutoring and other odd jobs; Malling, journalist and failed writer; and Amund Moen, a peasant student—are at odds with their circumstances.

Ellefsen, who has had a brief affair with Mrs. Ravn, is a rootless person whose identification with her predicament betrays his own social alienation. His appraisals of her position lack consistency, oscillating between sociological, psychological and quasi-philosophical perspectives that seem to be alternative explanations of his own malaise. On the one hand, he explains Mrs. Ravn's destruction by her separation "from the human mass" (III, 79); on the other, he sees women's social rebellion in psychological terms: they can think only "on behalf of the sexual organ" (80). Or he adopts a fatalistic determinism, envisaging a dark apocalypse where the "past ages of suffering" are repeated in an indefinite future time (87). These ideological twists and turns are indicative of self-deception. To his credit he suspects that there is a "deeper truth" (*sammenheng*) to his wretched experience and that everything could be saved if he were able to find it (87). One wonders whether a childhood memory of being locked out from his mother's room when his sister was born—a quandary that drove him to beat his hands to "shreds" against the door—is not intended by Hoel as the key to a "deeper" explanation of Elefsen's powerlessness, his inability to help Mrs. Ravn, as well as his own social alienation. Significantly, he turned into a child, crying between her breasts, when he was with Mrs. Ravn (82, 85-86). Yet, Hoel avoids a schematic Freudian interpretation: the possibility of a mother fixation is made casually and holds no privileged position.

Mr. Ellefsen is treated with sympathy, perhaps because his situation is reminiscent of Hoel's own: that of a disenchanted Communist sympathizer. Conversely, Ove Malling, the journalist, is profoundly unlikable. Married to a slattern and thwarted in his literary ambitions, he projects his own predicament upon society—seen in paranoid fashion as conspiring against him—and upon the cosmos, which plays "blind man's buff with human destinies" (III, 89, 96). Consistently with his paranoia, his self-images are projected through pompous, inflated language: an eagle's flight, warlike conquest, bullfighting. And his passion is conveyed through images of cloudburst, hurricane, and typhoon. When, in a moment of self-recognition, he realizes his hollowness, "egoism and vanity," he falsifies the experience by blowing it up into a struggle with "the powers of darkness" comparable to Jacob's wrestling with the angel (253). This is also the way he excuses his one act of egregious bad faith, namely, helping to write the letter of complaint to Mrs. Ravn's employer: it becomes an example of his Dostoyevskian demonism (97). Malling's self-dramatizing, self-deceiving imagination culminates the moment when, having to renounce Mrs. Ravn, he thinks of her while having intercourse with his wife: in "demonic triumph" he deceived the one with the other and "took revenge

upon fate" (254). Apart from the hyperbolic self-inflation, Malling's chronic moral confusion is manifest from the helpless,
grotesque images used to characterize his thought: "flapping
wings," a "flock of crows" (94). As in the case of Eide, the implicit authorial vision seems to be based on Adler rather than
Freud: Malling's portrait is a superb study in overcompensation.

Amund Moen and Ellinor Welland, daughter of Mrs. Ravn's
landlady, are the only characters who undergo basic change, one
that enables them to take a more active hold of their existence.
Significantly, this change comes about through sexual experience. The fact that they are the two youngest characters may
hint at Hoel's hope for the future.

Amund Moen is reminiscent of Erik in *Nothing*. As with Erik,
his existence appears insubstantial, like shadows, and his loneliness is projected through images of "desolate, empty space" (III,
139); but he is fully aware that this and other figurative perceptions are engendered by himself. Occasionally these perceptions
generate a muted melancholy lyricism, as when, under the impression of being on a "hopeless errand," he sees the spiral stair-
case in Dr. Ravn's apartment house as the symbol of a fearful
cosmic recurrence: "things took their course, . . . the planet
rolled on, mighty, big, blind, unconscious. The spiral repeated
and repeated itself from the darkness infinitely deep down to the
darkness infinitely high up—over and over again" (149). An ineffectual dreamer, Moen is afraid of women, whether Ellinor or
Mrs. Ravn, and he is incapable of maintaining discipline as a
substitute teacher. In the course of the novel, however, he is per-
force brought into varied contact with people, being called upon
by Mrs. Welland to help move and watch over Mrs. Ravn and to
deliver the latter's message to her husband; by Ellinor to be her
companion for the night, apparently her first ever. Already before
he sleeps with Ellinor he has lost the fear of facing his class, and
the sexual experience completes the cure.

Amund's change is chiefly conveyed through variants of the
cosmic imagery used previously. Feeling older and calmer after
making love to Ellinor, he realizes that the weather has cleared;
he notices a twinkling star and imagines himself "sitting on a
light-beam, riding forward through space." Perceiving the "coldness" in the star's twinkle, he thinks of it as a "lighthouse in vast

ice-cold space." These humanized images of cosmic events signify an adjustment, without surrender, to the modern scientific
perspective. In practical terms, though he feels he has become
"colder, . . . less good," he is "firmer, . . . harder," too. And
though he reflects, like Erik in *Nothing*, that his love was fulfilled only after it had lost its value for him, the gain in manli-
ness, maturity, and balance is unquestionable. Thus he knew, for
example, that the ability to keep discipline had "come along with
the coldness" (III, 270). As for Ellinor, her seduction of Amund is
as deliberate and daring as her lovemaking, compared to
plunging into the "swing of sensuality, onto the dizzy abyss."
Though her action may, as Amund reflects, have given birth to a
new "female destiny," equally "difficult and lonely" as that of
Mrs. Ravn (269), she clearly does not belong to those women
who, in Fredrik's words in *Sinners*, were "doomed to tragedy" (II,
198). She, whom Amund in self-mockery had called a "star," is a
New Woman whose personality, like Amund's final mood, is
epitomized in the penultimate line of the chapter: "the star
twinkled, cold and remote" (III, 268, 271).

The Ravns: Escape from Eros

Dr. Ravn's "report" is based on the premise that science/tech-
nology is the most important factor in modern society. As the
"superman" of the new age, the scientist is at odds with the
married state, since his "erotic fund" is transferred to his work;
and if he nevertheless follows custom and marries, he perceives
woman as a "vampire, invented by the devil to bleed him white"
(III, 230). This fear of sexuality and consequent attraction to
asceticism are not unprecedented among intellectuals; one is reminded of Kierkegaard and Kafka. A related theme, the conflict
between the man who "incarnates the philosophic consciousness
of Life and the woman who incarnates its fecundity," found a
classic expression in Shaw's *Man and Superman*.[9] Closer to
home, there is Ibsen's treatment of the theme of life versus calling
in *When We Dead Awaken*.[10] Hoel, in presenting the conflict in
the guise of scientific research versus eros, hoped to treat the
theme in a *"slightly* new manner" (Ms. Fol. 2318:1), while undermining the credibility of Dr. Ravn's anti-eros position.

In the description of the course of his marriage, Dr. Ravn shows some awareness of psychoanalysis; Hoel has endowed the chemist with part of his own cast of mind and expertise. Dr. Ravn deals with processes like sublimation and repression, speaks of "libido" withdrawal from everyday existence in favor of science, and looks to his past history for explanations of his marital pattern. Yet, except for a few glimpses of insight that have nothing to do with psychoanalysis, Dr. Ravn despairs of finding the truth; he admits being a victim of uncontrollable, irrational psychic drives and behavior patterns, which can all be traced to a remote past.

It is ironic that he, who suffered grievously because of his father's humiliating treatment of his not-always-truthful mother, marries a woman with whom he repeats the very pattern he has sworn to avoid. He wonders what "accursed law," what "deadly drive" leads a person to choose a woman "who made us re-experience all our most painful experiences yet once more" (III, 195-96). This pattern corresponds, of course, to the "repetition compulsion," allegedly Freud's "first motive for his postulating a death instinct."[11] Momentarily, the situation takes on a spectral Ibsenesque quality, as he and Tordis appear to him like "pale ghosts," an example of the "eternal recurrence of things" (195). Once when he caught her in a lie—to cover up a meeting with an old friend—it struck him that they were not only "ghosts" of his father and mother but "repeated much older, far more famous scenes: the inquisitors' torture of the witches" (211). One is reminded of Jungian archetypes, with which Hoel was familiar through his reading. Similar repetitive patterns, involving increasing marital deterioration, are conveyed figuratively through "vicious circle, the wheel of evil"—perhaps the central image in all of Hoel's fiction (168, 231). While aware of these experiential repetitions, Dr. Ravn concedes that, in things human, he knows next to nothing! He finds woman enticing precisely because she is "like the sphinx, the riddle of the world," which "cannot be solved" (231); and about himself, he admits, he knows even less than he knows about women (227).

Against this background of seeming humility, it is somewhat incongruous that Dr. Ravn should put so much weight on his "poetic vision" soon after his wife's last emotional collapse before her departure. This vision is described by means of similar imagery. He thought he "saw a pattern [*sammenheng*], a long, eternal pattern, where we were only a small and fortuitous link." In this "Old Testament mood" he felt that both he and his wife were "under the finger of fate." Admitting that he has no "personal feeling" for her, he merely voices a sense of her "pathetic, . . . moving" situation: she had been caught in a "wheel of fate which rolled around and around with her, further and further, and would some day crush her" (III, 213-14). Though he trivializes the vision, he takes it seriously enough to let it absorb the potential guilt of his brief infidelity with a married woman: "I felt what I had done as a logically correct thing. Or, rather, as something unavoidable. A link in a chain which I once . . . had seen in its entirety" (221-22). His tragic vision becomes a means of absolving himself from responsibility.

This self-deception places Dr. Ravn on a level with the other characters in the novel. He is a man with most of the limitations of his class, with, in addition, a disabling professional blind spot. In his manuscript notes Hoel writes that Dr. Ravn "clings to *truth* as to a crutch." It is his refuge from the "*life* he is afraid of," the life his wife represents. This theme, "specialized science as escape from existence" in Hoel's statement (Ms. Fol. 2318:1), anticipates Max Frisch's classic portrayal of technological man in *Homo Faber* (1957). Only on the supposition that, as his wife suggests, Dr. Ravn has subconsciously sabotaged their marriage from the very beginning can his behavior toward her be fully understood. Indeed, this thought occurs to him during the composition of his report: "Have I gone around with a secret desire for escape from the very first moment?" (III, 191).

His actions toward Tordis are certainly quite damning: thus, while admitting her "real understanding" of the subject, he mocks her attempt to study chemistry so as to prepare herself to become his assistant; and he dismisses as a "fixed idea" her learning shorthand and languages in order to supplement the family finances (III, 191). At the other end of the spectrum, one wonders about the logic of keeping a maid if funds are short and the wife is burdened with free time and untapped energies. Her periodic illnesses, emotional breakdowns and extreme jealousy, which he seemingly attributes to her being a "neurotic" (184), are largely due to neglect, as shown by her speedy recovery on their excursion to the mountain. His persuading Tordis to have an abortion manifests the same attitude of marital sabotage. In any case, his admission at the end of the apologia that his wife has suffered a great injustice through her wrecked marriage, on the ground that she was the only woman he knew who "could have become what the new age must demand of woman: to be the man's comrade in thick and thin" (228), undermines any personal accusation against her and places the accent on Dr. Ravn's alienation from life. Significantly, he admits being "sad and depressed to death" at her departure, as though he had "committed a shocking outrage, killed something noble and proud" (227). The inner being of the superman avatar of science is, appropriately enough, associated with an image of coldness suggesting death: a "large frozen lake" (205).[12]

It is evident that, as in the case of the middle-aged male tenants of No. 27, Dr. Ravn's professional role is largely a means of escaping reality. Contrary to a criticism that the author had not "seen through" Dr. Ravn,[13] Hoel's entire portrayal of him is determined by the idea of self-deception. This is concretely demonstrated when, after "weighing" his hefty manuscript against his wife's seven-word missive, "Help me I am so lonely Tordis," he rushes downstairs to answer her call (III, 233-34): her simple appeal outweighed a treatise. That he arrives just after the gate is closed is partly due to his unresolved ambivalence.

The reality Dr. Ravn flees from, and which he participated in during the early part of his marriage, is conveyed through an experience on his wedding day and a number of striking images. The experience was one of "initiation, of something sacred," where all of nature partook with him in a "tacit pact." His bride's "deep dark glance" connected him at once with the "unconscious world of animals and plants and with the supersensible world of ecstatic dreams." It led one to think of the "eye of the first living thing, where all drives, all wishes, all *life* lay . . . *shamelessly* exposed . . . : as though a luxuriant, lovely tropical flower had received an eye to see with—so unconscious, so passive, so fated was the glance in those eyes." He imagines that, while most mortals experience momentary intuitions of an all-encompassing significance, this mode of "exposed" vision was hers every day (III, 181-83). At the same time her eyes could be "bright and merry" like a little boy's.[14] It is because of this immediate relationship to reality that Mrs. Ravn becomes a symbol of life itself and capable of exposing the emotional poverty in the existence of her contemporaries.

Form and Structure

Compositionally, *One Day in October* combines two seemingly contrary principles: circularity and linearity. The former is manifest in its overall form, with a return to the initial state of affairs, as well as in thematic repetitions and special devices, such as the "smell of wet potatoes" motif, the people in the street at the beginning and the end, and the newspaper woman's reappearance in the last chapter to rerun her first-chapter circuit. As Johan de Mylius has noted, beginning and ending are mirror images of one another: the action begins with a man, Dr. Ravn, leaving No. 27; it ends with a "bareheaded man," evidently Dr. Ravn, approaching (III, 8, 278).[15] The completeness suggested by such a circular structure creates the impression of a community; and indeed, the author notes, though at first it may look as if the tenants have nothing in common, "the action shows to what extent they are entangled with one another" (Ms. Fol. 2318:1).

More importantly, perhaps, the little apartment house community becomes a microcosm of the city, as Hoel intended: he notes that the book would gain if it could "give a kind of picture in miniature of Oslo now, in 1930." This symbolic expansion is aided both by thematic and other means. One of Ellefsen's visitors, a "poet," launches into an excoriating monologue about the evils of Oslo existence. He stresses in particular the city's shabby treatment of people from the provinces, whether literary men, peasant students, or talented people generally. The poet's words extend a thought in Hoel's manuscript notes concerning the social attitudes of the members of the bourgeoisie: they have "abjured the solidarity with those who are on the losing side, those who need help, 'the displaced and the oppressed' " (Ms. Fol. 2318:1). It takes very little imagination to perceive the parallel between Tordis Ravn's position in No. 27 and the situation of the outsiders, such as Amund Moen, in the city of Oslo. The

poet finds the city's spirit epitomized in the not uncommon autumn fog referred to in previous works: it is as though "something evil has been buried here from time immemorial and
slowly oozes out of the ground, out of the hills, evaporates and,
following the law of eternal recirculation, descends from the sky
again as a kind of fog—malice, envy, poverty, hatred, meanness,
slander, faultfinding" (III, 71). This theme of virtual social ostracism is of central importance in several subsequent novels of
Hoel.

The linear structure, contained within the overall circular
form, is provided by the drama of Tordis Ravn. A familiar paradox emerges from Hoel's evident desire to produce a sense of the
"fated, inevitable aspect of her case" (Ms. Fol. 2318:1), while at
the same time undermining the validity of Dr. Ravn's tragic vision. The paradox stems from a discrepancy between ethical and
esthetic categories: whereas ethics has its basis in the possibility
of voluntary decision and action to change the course of events,
esthetics demands a sense of inexorable progression to generate
the tragic emotion. *October* avoids the static quality of many
cross-section novels by a dramatic suspense that carries the plot to
a tragic climax. Though Hoel makes considerable use of coincidence, the interplay of human weakness with circumstance is so
intimate as to obviate any sense of contrivance. It is a well-
composed book.

Critical Reception

One Day in October appeared at a time of increasing polariza-
tion in Norwegian cultural life between traditional humanism,
based on Christian or national values, and cultural radicalism,
also traditional but recently powerfully reinforced by Freudian
and Marxian doctrine. The publication of *October*—which won
second prize in an all-Scandinavian literary contest[16]—and of
several other novels that combined frank treatment of sexuality
with exposés of middle-class moral sordidness, triggered a confrontation between the two groups that went on for months, even
years. Hoel himself called the immediate clash a "sort of cultural
battle" (*kulturkamp;* I, xiv), a not infrequent phenomenon on
the Norwegian literary scene. It has been popularly referred to as

the "dirty stream" controversy, because it was started by a reviewer from *Morgenbladet*, Fredrik Ramm, with an article entitled "A Dirty Stream Flows across the Land," in which he charged these books with being pornographic. Though no confiscations were made, the novels in question were removed from many booksellers' counters and display windows (I, xiv).

The stream of "lubricity" that Ramm envisaged flowing from Gyldendal Publishers was allegedly so harmful, especially to the "young girls and boys" who usually are the pretext for censorship in such cases, that the damage done to a child by a "drunken rapist" was small by comparison.[17] Subsequently, none other than the future primate of the Norwegian Church, Eivind Berggrav, entered the fray with an article called "Can Psychology Kill?," in which he coined the term *psychochondria* to express the harmful, withering effect of psychoanalytic knowledge upon literary spontaneity. Calling Hoel a "psychological laboratory worker," he asserts that he "constructs" his books on a Freudian "scheme."[18] A few years later the respected critic Eugenia Kielland wrote a long article about Hoel's work in which she made similar charges. Generally, she says, there blows a "cold draft" from Hoel's books; nothing living can in the long run grow in the "thin air of intellectualism." In *October,* which she calls an "intelligent but quite barren product of the brain," Hoel, she says, portrays a "purely animal existence" with "copulation as the central function."[19]

This is depressing reading. The only consolation is that this debate eventually led to a more enlightened view of sex, higher tolerance for sexuality in literature, and a freer, more open intellectual climate in Norway. It is also comforting to know that there were reputable critics who found *October* to be an "artistic masterpiece" and a "wise, fine, and superior book."[20]

OPEN SESAME

The confrontation over *October* and its companion novels provided part of the inspiration for *Open Sesame,* the idea of which had come to Hoel already in January, 1932 (Ms. Fol. 2365:6). But the novel's plot derives by way of parody from the controversy caused by Marc Connelly's play *Green Pastures* (1930). This play had a deplorable fate in Norway, in that it was closed down on the alleged ground of blasphemy after one limited showing to a delegation of the Storting (Parliament). The debate over the play went on from November, 1932, to the summer of 1933. In *Open Sesame* it is represented by an anonymous play, a takeoff on Ibsen's *An Enemy of the People* that is accepted by the National Theater, subsequently to be removed from the production calendar because its rumored content provoked a furor in the press— it is election year—and eventually a Storting resolution. The story of the controversial play is the substance of the second of the of the book's three main parts.

The first part deals with a literary anniversary celebration— there had recently been several centennials, Ibsen's, Bjørnson's, Jonas Lie's—the Ibsen centennial in 1928 being the principal model. The relationship between Part I and Part II is one of sardonic irony: the great master's work was the apotheosis of freedom, yet in his centennial year an Ibsenesque play—about a patent medicine discovered to be poisonous—is prohibited from being shown. The third part deals with the response of the intellectual left to this situation: they decide to start a journal.[21] But having learned that few men of wealth are willing to put up money for such a venture, they hit upon the idea of marketing a patent medicine in order to procure the needed capital for the journal—fighting the devil with Beelzebub. But soon what was meant to be a means of fighting all "magic, superstition and sorcery" becomes itself somewhat of a "magic formula" (VI, 282-83). And eventually the journal gives place to the patent medicine in their minds: means become ends. Finally, they are bought out by the entrepreneur, an astute cynic named Kramer, and the book fizzles out in the story of a young journalist named Bårdsen and his bride.

The restricted setting of *Open Sesame*, which has been called a "dazzlingly witty, indiscreet and infamous" book, enabled Hoel to catch, in the words of the same critic, the "entire spiritual life" of Oslo. The book's indiscretion and infamy in the eyes of native readers are due to the transparency of its satiric portraits, based on well-known newspapermen, politicians, and writers, who allegedly were "flattered to be butchered so elegantly."[22] The portraits are clearly intended to help characterize the intellectual and political climate of the period, during which Fascism and Nazism were triumphant in Europe and Communist Russia had just undergone years of "witch trials."[23] There are direct allusions to the magical-religious basis of these ideologies, which, along with related phenomena, are symbolized by the patent medicine, a piece of modern magic. The book's central theme is how people's irrational yearning for panaceas, for instant solutions, is exploited by the newspapers, advertising, politicians, and other leaders. Because such a yearning is religious in nature and involves a collective willingness to believe, to suspend criticism, and to be deluded, it can be conveniently manipulated by the mass media, particularly the press, in order to create a public opinion— whether in support of a product or a political candidate. Hoel had made a similar diagnosis of mass psychology in *The Seven-Pointed Star*, against a European background.

Open Sesame can be compared to the newspaper clippings of Trond Blaker, Hoel's proxy. These clippings "constituted the history of the time in miniature." The work that was to come out of them was to show "contemporary man as a slave to his own creations, in thrall to his own technology, his own machines and instruments. . . . It was to be the first step to the liberation of man" (VI, 87). And, true enough, as the story of the patent medicine is developed, it becomes a burlesque representation of most sociopolitical phenomena of the time, whether so-called democratic election campaigns, the rise of dictatorships, or the banning of a play. However, the element of liberation is missing.

Essentially what Hoel does is to show, as the banned play supposedly did, how "public opinion" is formed—speaking ironically, how a "disinterested conviction combines chemically with self-interest, vanity, cowardice, and other virtues and thereby moves on to a higher plateau and becomes sacred, becomes religion" (VI, 108). While the many animal and mechanical analogies produce an effect of low burlesque, Hoel also uses the companion device of high burlesque. Thus, a sequence of chapter titles deriving from a poem by Bjørnson about the genesis, growth, and victory of a truth, "Battle Hymn for the Freedom Lovers in the North" (1874), casts the ironic light of parody upon the entire process of shaping the book's big lie: the tradition of liberty has succumbed to technological-commercial quackery. These burlesque devices, with the consequent ironic parallels, are handled deftly and vigorously.

The satire is brilliantly malicious as long as it deals with politics and the press; and Hoel's caricatures of himself and of his closest associates, Helge Krog and Arnulf Øverland (the characters Blaker, Gram, and Valemo, respectively; VI, 69-89, passim), are good-humored and amusing. There is a point, however, at which satire of oneself and one's own party turns sour and self-pitying, and that point is reached here. Besides, Part III, which deals with the radical intellectuals' counterattack, is too drawn-out, and the success of young Bårdsen after much adversity ends the book with a digression. Anyway, this pattern ineptly copies the ending of *October,* where similarly the sexual union of two young people hints at a new beginning. Though this is an acceptable resolution to the problems of Bårdsen, who marries and leaves Oslo to become editor of a hometown paper, it does not offer a satisfactory dénouement to the predicament of the Oslo radical intelligentsia.

The lack of such a dénouement seems to be implicit in the book's very structure: like so many of Hoel's stories and novels, *Open Sesame* has a circular shape. Compositionally it forms a circle in that it begins and ends with an important anniversary: first the poet's, then the scientist's. More importantly, circles of all kinds, mostly evil—vortices, eddies, backwaters, and so forth—are used to characterize all aspects of the intellectuals' life, their daily routines, their work, their thinking. The opening description of the intellectual elite is done in terms of the "circle" their movements trace in Oslo's civic center—from the "newspapers to the publishers, from there to the theaters, on to the cafés, back to the newspapers, and the same over again." In fact, there are several "circles," and where they intersect vortices form, in which people may "whirl around" for "hours, days, even months and years" (VI, 10-11).

The basis for this imagery is the close connection between being a writer and various other occupations, such as book reviewing, drama criticism, miscellaneous journalism, translation, and editing, activities that often demand more of a writer's time than he can give to his vocation. It is wearisome to walk this circle from year to year, "ten, fifteen, twenty years" (VI, 217). The image occurs in many variations: rowing in a circle in foggy weather instead of making headway upstream (221); getting caught in a backwater or eddy, where things drift around forever in a circle unless the water level changes (386); walking around and around, like a horse or ox pulling the threshing machine, driven by the "publishers, the theater directors, the editors" to help produce "circuses" for the people (387); getting sucked in by the mill of "cultural life" (218). And, as usual, Hoel discerns everywhere the evil dynamics of the vicious circle, whereby things of necessity go from bad to worse. With such dominant images—and they are pervasive—no wonder young Bårdsen is the only one who escapes: by flight (386).

Another kind of image, probably Reichian in inspiration, is used in portraying the reason for the intellectuals' failure. They are divided men, separated from their own emotions, their wives, the common people.[24] In his manuscript notes, Hoel writes extensively about being "work-shy": how to pierce the "glass-hard armor that separates my affects, i.e. my feelings, my incentives, from this work?" In one note, work blockage is equated with sexual fear (Ms. Fol. 2321:1; 7/30 and 8/6/1935). The same point of view is implicit in the novel. Thus, Gram reflects that his compulsive "sense of order," which serves as an excuse to postpone work (VI, 80-83), was perhaps nothing but a "protective fence" around his inner chaos; among other things, it protected him from his wife's "warmth" (235). All it takes to remove the inward barriers, at least temporarily, is a sudden intuition of "meaning" (sammenheng), which they share in the moment the journal is conceived. As soon as they were fired by something that transcended their egos, it was as though "a lot of fences, cubicles [båser], and dividing walls melted and collapsed within them" (216). Subsequently, their "banal" fate is generalized to embrace everybody: "standing isolated in his cubicle, the individual longs for contact with others and for the strength that only the many can give. Divided by inward fences into many separate parts, he longs for contact with himself and for the strength that only unity and integrity can give" (221). It is this personal and collective unification that the journal was intended to effect.

In Open Sesame Hoel has a great many things to say, perhaps too many. It is not a very successful novel, even from a strictly

Norwegian perspective. (Naturally, much is lost to the foreign reader, unable to recognize the possible models for the characters and the situations.) Brilliant in part, scintillating with paradox in Hoel's most spirited manner, it is also dull, trite, garrulous. One critic has said that it would have been a great novel if distance had simplified the material: it ought to have been written in Madeira.[25] According to a reviewer, the book has two faces, as though it were written in two periods. Parts I and II show Hoel as the "gay mocker," reminiscent of young Hamsun in his "insolent disrespect," while Part III, the not-very-funny second half of the book, shows the face of a "disillusioned cynic."[26] There is a dearth of memorable characters, however amusing some of the caricatures may seem to initiates. The novel would have profited from a drop of the poison that makes *The Seven-Pointed Star* an excoriating work of satire. That would have called for a different narrative perspective, excluding Hoel's ironic treatment of himself and his radical intellectual kinsmen. But he was too honest for such a strategy, and not enough of an ideologue.

5
Childhood and the Provinces

The Road to the End of the World (*1933*) and *The Princess on the Glass Mountain* (*Prinsessen på glassberget,* 1939) both focus on the themes of childhood and community life. In their wide use of folk and fairy-tale motifs and techniques, they also draw upon the same stylistic models. The two books represent Hoel's literary artistry at its very best.

HOEL'S NOVEL OF DEVELOPMENT

The Road to the End of the World was one of two books—the other became *The Troll Circle*—that Hoel was resolved to write as soon as he became conscious of his literary vocation.[1] Its actual inception may have been due to his meeting a group of Freudians in 1926. Hoel notes that the book required "all [his] free time during seven years" (I, xv).

During its long gestation, the plan underwent great alteration from the cycle of stories originally contemplated: "stories waste most of the time on unessential things," he writes in December, 1930. The essential things among his childhood recollections, he decided, were not actual happenings but sensory and emotional experiences and the aura surrounding them: the "crusted snow in spring, the light in the sky, the taste . . . of new things, human sorrow and joy in their purity" and their commingling. Though he fears that, having reflected on his childhood as literary material, he may have dispersed its "very fragrance, the aura," these, he notes, are the "invisible, subtle things" for whose sake stories are composed (Ms. Fol. 2318:1).

Another alteration pertains to the narrative attitude. By the time he wrote the bulk of the novel, in 1932 and 1933, Hoel felt critical about some chapters dating from 1926, before he had realized "how strictly such material had to be treated." The chief problem was the "sentimental-ironic, kindly condescending tone" so often favored in stories of children, which now struck him as the "falsest of all." Among authors who showed him how such stories *"could* be done," he mentions the Swede Dan Andersson (1888-1920) and the Russian Osip Dymov (1878-1959). The latter's novel *Vlas* (Norw. tr. 1931)—allegedly Hoel's favorite book[2]—was apparently more important than a work like Joyce's *A Portrait of the Artist as a Young Man* (1916) in teaching him to take the child's experiences "seriously" and to present them with a minimum of adult distortion.[3] That he also picked up some leads from Joyce will become evident from the novel's texture.

In a letter to Martin Joos six years after his book came out (9/29/1939), Hoel explains its underlying purpose and plan: to "portray the genesis of a human being." *The Road* is described as the first volume of a major work, the subsequent volumes of which would follow his hero, Anders, from the age of "fifteen till . . . today." *Nothing* is a "chapter [of this book] that came a little ahead of time." Yet another novel belongs to this plan, a "book that will show some of the roots," Anders' story having dealt with "the stem above ground." This plan was realized as *The Family Dagger* (*Arvestålet*, 1941; lit. "Family Steel") and *The Troll Circle.*

Though his underlying idea, as stated, implicitly stresses the universal aspect of childhood, Hoel admits the novel is "autobiographical in the artistic sense of the word," partly in the "usual sense" as well. Like Anders, he grew up on a farm in the East Country and had a severe accident and operation at the age of three. Hoel broke his elbow joint in a fall, Anders his ankle. From three to four, Hoel writes, he underwent several operations, "with and without anesthesia"; at one time he nearly died.[4] Though the experience is forgotten, it "lives in my dreams," he says, a fact that has enabled him to "verify it." This does not make him unusual, he writes, for many "have undergone a some-

what similar period of illness and terror during these same decisive years." He has included as much of the episode as is
necessary for the "truth of what follows."[5] The "human being"
that he set out to portray, therefore, was neither an abstract statis-
tical average nor an exceptional person, one whose fate had been
sidetracked by an "accidental misfortune." Because of this careful
balancing between extremes of generality and specificity, Anders'
experience seems paradigmatic even to readers who have grown
up in widely different circumstances.

Structure and Form

Hoel's decision to respect the child's perspective ruled out as
inartistic certain elements of the traditional development novel,
fairly exemplified by *Sons and Lovers* (1913). Lawrence begins
with an extensive description of the setting and a concise history
of the Morells' marriage. In *The Road*, as in Joyce's *Portrait*, the
reader from the very beginning experiences the world through
the child's mind and senses. Setting, plot, character interest, and
other conventional elements of narrative are, so to speak, provided incidentally. Thus, only the final chapter presents a bit of
delayed exposition about the parents' marriage, as part of the
obligatory scene between father and son.

Plot and setting in *The Road* compose a time-space contin-
uum: the incidents that happen to Anders from year to year form
a constantly widening pattern of concentric circles. The circular
road that, like some Midgard serpent, runs around the hamlet,
and around Anders' world, connotes time as well as space, and
the circles, or loops, of time rise ever higher. Indeed, they are
spirals, because each year one "could look straight down to where
one had stood the year before" (IV, 204-5). The book's very structure reflects this developmental concept in that the first part,
called "The Garden of Eden," focuses on Anders' relations with
his family, while the second part, called "The Hamlet," represents his widening experience of community life, of servants, comrades, girls—an experience that is increasingly viewed from the
perspective of a perpetually recurrent cycle. By contrast, "The
Garden of Eden" is seen as the "old days before repetition entered
the world" (196).

The same developmental concept determines character portrayal. Initially outlined through sensory fragments glimpsed by a little boy—impressions that are often magnified to mythic proportions—the characters gradually change from being projections of a child's mind to becoming more or less independent figures. Their portrayal usually goes hand in hand with the involuntary self-characterization of Anders, by means of a superbly handled free indirect discourse. An excellent example is the first chapter of Part II, "Embret," where the author shows a new, psychologically interesting aspect of the permanent hired man— a proud person who has given up his right to the family farm in a fit of pique with his father and is irked by his inferior position. At the same time the portrayal of Anders gains in emotional depth as his ambivalent feelings toward both Embret and his own father come to the fore. Anders dreams that the lightning, associated with the God-father figure, has "struck him, paralyzed him and cleft him in three—Father, Embret and himself" (IV, 163). ¹ The book contains a variety of narrative forms, each adapted to the boy's stage of development. In general, the text shifts back and forth between emotionally charged situations and scenes, on the one hand, and developed incidents with a more or less dramatic structure, on the other. This entails a rhythmical alternation between static and dynamic representation, each assuming a different form depending on Anders' age. In Part I, the former is exemplified by evocations of fear, diurnal cycles, and brief vignettes of village life; the latter by a fairy-tale-like episode ("To God to Complain," ch. 5) and family occurrences. Among the latter are Anders' accident, hospitalization, and recovery; the birth, illness, and death of a younger brother; the story of Anders' learning to say r and of the writing desk. In the last episode, instigated by a bragging remark dropped by a "bad" older boy, Anders incurs a grievous defeat when, wishing to please his father, he cuts an ornamental pattern into the latter's desk only to encounter his father's wrath. In Part II, while these elements tend to mix, the same rhythm persists as the narrative moves back and forth between genre scenes—Christmas, the outing to the mountain dairy, Embret's death and funeral, Anders' confirmation and departure—and Anders' mostly ill-fated or unfinished adventures with his comrades and his favorite girls.

Texture: Recurrent Motifs

The texture of *The Road* can instructively be compared to that of Joyce's *Portrait*. The basic unit of the book's composition is the sensory-emotional motif. To show how the motifs are organized, one of the principal clusters will be examined, that of fear or anxiety, usually combined with aloneness. Already in chapter 1 fear is associated with darkness, with a figure—personifying the moon—trying to grab Anders, and with staring eyes.[6] The personified north wind is as real as the chimney sweep and becomes confused with the name of a seasonal hired hand; and the troll with its ugly red eye is as terrifying as a toad or a snake. An early chapter, "The Snake," consists of five scenes depicting actual and dreamlike fear, each featuring the fixed, staring eye, an image that gathers added meaning as Anders' circle of experience widens. Worth noting is the boy's impression of a writhing snake in its death spasms; nothing had ever seemed so alive to him as the dead snake, which "came crawling out of a bad dream." It "stared" at him with its unblinking, reddish eyes until he felt "completely alone" (IV, 57).

Most of the images forming the fear cluster become absorbed by the figure of a passing cattle dealer, Svartbekken, whose "red-rimmed" eyes are only one of his repulsive features: his "face red like raw meat" and his "nose like blue intestines," he "hissed and cursed and squirted spit" into his scraggly beard. His whiplash winds itself "like a snake" around the muzzle of his horse. Anders fears his father will sell him to Svartbekken, who becomes an incarnation of "death and the devil," seen by Anders as one and the same figure. The snake, which "knew everything" (IV, 58), also becomes associated with God. Thus, at the end of the chapter "The Snake," Anders envisages Svartbekken driving across the earth "with his whistling whip, under a menacing mute sky that did not strike him down—and an evil, triangular head with evil eyes without eyelids stared mutely and calmly at all the evil that happened and let it happen. He had seen it once that way—or dreamed it, he wasn't sure" (62).

In subsequent episodes the fixed, all-knowing eye acquires a more immediate relevance for Anders' self-image and moral awareness. When he is trying to pronounce the letter *r*, people's

teasing makes it seem as though "the whole world stood
. . . staring at him with an unblinking eye" (IV, 110). This
snakelike gaze, comparable to Sartre's *regard d'autrui*, paralyzed
him: his tongue "withered" in his mouth (111). And after the
vicious episode where, led by Albert—a somewhat older boy—
Anders and his friends kill a baby goat by throwing it repeatedly
into the water to see if it will walk ashore on the bottom of the
lake ("Sunday in August," 219-47), the "stiff, dimmed" eyes of
the goat are projected upon the entire islet—indeed, upon the sun
and the sky, as a "menacing" and "huge staring eye" (243). Similarly, after Anders has received a small-bore rifle from his father,
its look of cold steel reminds him of the killed viper of several
years ago: "it was as though its muzzle stared at him with a black
eye" (272). When he ends up winging a crow despite his decision
never to kill an animal, Anders notices its "black eye staring at
him." In a state of emotional upheaval he tries to finish off the
bird, only to be pursued by a flock of crows, like furies. Knowing
that his father will soon be home, he returns to pick up the rifle,
which he has dropped in his fright, but the thought "viper"
occurs to him as soon as he touches it. "And before he knew what
he did, he had flung it into the water" (279). Thus, as Anders
grows older, Hoel expands the application of the "fixed eye"
image to take in situations of trial and moral choice.[7]

A cluster of similar images of terror, one that eventually absorbs most of those already examined, is formed around the indefinite pronoun *noe*, meaning "something." If a distinction is to be
made, this cluster discloses the uncanny. Its seed seems to be
Anders' paralyzing fear of a neighbor's bull on the rampage. The
following night he has a terrible dream: he stood alone in a
"huge, white, empty and desolate yard, and *something* came toward him. Everybody had abandoned him" (IV, 53). The dream
returns in various guises, and the word *something* becomes associated with rats and toads, as well as with the snake (61).

In the chapter entitled "Something," the emotional content of
the developing cluster is augmented by its association with overheard snatches of dialogue: a disagreement between Anders' father and mother; a disturbance caused by Crazy-Fredrik, a local
lunatic; adults playing on children's fear of the dark; and so
forth. The indefinite word *something* is part of all these ex-

changes. In each case it connotes a hidden, undisclosed reality that, in the meantime, presses upon Anders' senses from all sides: from the silence; from the shadows in the corner; from the knot in the door frame resembling a coldly staring, laughing face; from spiders reaching out after him with their "long crooked arms"; from the "big, dark cross" in the window, associated with Jesus being sacrificed by his Father; and from the eyes of Crazy-Fredrik, who, after killing his son, becomes identified with the "man in the knot" (IV, 94-102). Just as Svartbekken absorbs most of the individual images in the "fixed eye" cluster, the figure of Crazy-Fredrik seems to sum up the *something* cluster: the unspeakable horror of his words to the effect that, after beating his son unconscious, he decapitated him out of a sense of pity, is emphasized by italics and repeated in four sections of the chapter.

In the end *something* acquires a shapeless shape of its own: as a troll-like creature that "looked at him and smiled without a face, with only a big hole for a face . . . that led to nothingness." It makes a tiny sound, *sssssssss!*, which causes Anders to freeze with terror (94-101).[8]

Point of View and Narrative Perspectives

While shaping the novel's texture, the deployment of these motifs mirrors the growth of a child's mind. But though Hoel was resolved to respect the child's point of view, the book contains an implied author, whose presence evoked disparate reactions from the reviewers. Eugenia Kielland found the novel too clear and coherent to reflect truthfully the kaleidoscopic confusion of scattered impressions, separate ideas, and vague thoughts in a child's mind. Only if one assumes that the author meant to render the child's mind as interpreted by an adult, she says, can it be considered successful (*Morgenposten*, 11/24/1933). Helge Krog, on the other hand, stresses the authenticity of the presentation of the child's consciousness. Hoel "feels and thinks, learns and experiences" with Anders; all, he says with some exaggeration, is seen through the child's eyes, and the child's feelings are rendered in his own language, "without sentimentalism." Hoel's ability to represent "internal experiences, moods, impressions, psychological states," Krog writes, is not a feat of memory alone, but a "quality of the imagination . . . a creative power."[9] Krog's view seems to be confirmed by Hoel's account of how he used "the method of free association" (*innfallsmetoden*) for the first third of the book, with his own memories functioning only as control (*Dagbladet*, 11/7/1933). The point is that *The Road* is a work of the imagination, and as such combines the representation of experience with implicit if not direct interpretation.

Though Hoel does not use the terms, he intended Anders' mental growth (ontogeny) to recapitulate the history of the species (phylogeny), as well as the "corresponding mental notions" as embodied in "primordial myths, fairy tales, tall tales, novels" (Ms. Fol. 2319). His adherence to this "law" of development is largely responsible for the success of his portrayal of Anders. The child's early experience consists mainly of emotionally charged perceptions; his thinking is entirely concrete. Time, for example, is at first a "tall, lean old woman" (IV, 17), later someone who revolves the "big, big wheel" of the year (125). Then, at eight years of age, time's passage is perceived through drops of rain trickling down the windowpane and through the ticking of the clock (195, 202). As these motif clusters demonstrate, Anders' thinking is not only concrete but steeped in primitive animism and in personification. It is also magical, as shown by his desire to drown Gorine and his sister in effigy (37-38), fear of losing his leg, and anxiety about being turned into a girl by a witch after his accident (64-66).

Physically, Anders' growth is indicated by the changing angle of vision from which he perceives things. At first he sees the world from below; he is intimate with what is at his level—the grass, flowers, insects, the cat. One chapter ("To God to Complain," 30-40) is based on his experiences with this lower world. As he grows, his sensory impressions not only acquire wider scope but are received at a different level. His mental perception is clearly stimulated by sensations of height—from his being lifted to the ceiling to his being on top of a hill. Height and depth perceptions play an important role in Anders' emotional life and are thoroughly value-charged from the very beginning.

The language used to convey these perceptions is also adapted to Anders' stage of development. While false naiveté is avoided, the vocabulary in the first part is fairly limited, the sentences mostly short or extended by parataxis and coordinating conjunctions, with generous use of repetitive figures like anaphora, epiphora, and epizeuxis.[10] These features are such that are also found in fairy tales and the Bible. Myth and fairy tales, it may be recalled, represent to Hoel the same kind of thinking that is characteristic of the child.[11]

Nevertheless, without the reader's awareness of an authorial consciousness that shapes and discloses the meaning of Anders' childhood experiences according to certain formal and intellectual expectations, the book would probably seem trivial. By "authorial consciousness" or implied author is not meant the occasional violations of Anders' point of view, either in the boy's precocious reflections or in intrusive authorial commentary. These are blemishes, though difficult wholly to avoid. The book's art consists largely in the achievement of a double resonance: while the reader experiences the world from the perspective of a growing child, he is simultaneously aware of patterns of form and meaning that the child could not see. This dual perspective can be exemplified by almost any chapter in the novel. In "To God to Complain," for example, the fairy-tale form may seem a perfectly transparent medium, the natural vehicle for the child's naive enterprise: Anders' walk toward the sunset, interrupted as it is by distracting sights and sounds—the grunting pig, a bunch of sorrel, a stray cat—that he cannot allow to delay his self-appointed mission, is the very substance of fairy tale. Yet, when one recognizes the model and notes how carefully its pattern has been followed—the obligatory opening phrase "once upon a time," repeated situations, the formulaic language—it becomes clear that the author, despite the sympathy with which Anders is treated, is engaging the reader in a literary game. The resulting humor is a cue to the double perspective, also evident in the *explosion* of the fairy-tale form. For after the paradigmatic opening pages, Anders gets so engrossed in his own mini-world of beetles, earthworms, and modeled clay figures that he forgets his complaint and eventually dozes off.

The chapter "R" illustrates a different kind of double resonance, one that pervades most of the novel. Briefly, Anders, who is deeply embarrassed that he cannot say *r*, discovers one morning that he has done it without trying. His triumph is completed by his father's present of an ax, which he immediately tries out in helping Embret chop wood. However, he becomes so carried away with his success and with Embret's praise that, continuing to chop alone after Embret goes in to eat, he ends up "dirtying" his pants.

Anders is already aware of certain patterns in his experience, especially the change of mood from high to low. He has a cleverness with words, immensely increased because of his need to avoid all words with r in them. The thought of how clever he is makes him feel superior. However, when he considers why he is so clever, "it was as though he sank from a high peak down into a deep black hole." His mother has told him of Jesus' temptation, of how the devil took him to the top of a tall mountain and showed him "all the kingdoms of the earth and their glory." Different from the others, whom he thinks of as stupid, Anders envisions himself standing "on a tall mountain . . . [looking] down upon them" (IV, 109). These thoughts precede the story of his success with the letter r and its humiliating aftermath. After the disaster his first thought is that God has taken "revenge" on him: "He sank and he sank . . . down from a vast height, from a tall mountain, and down down down into a deep, black hole."[12] At the same time he has perceived an inner voice telling him all the time that he was "lying and bragging," but because he wanted "praise" he failed to listen to it (117).

Though Anders seems already to have a primitive sense of nemesis, even hubris, he does not fully grasp the interrelation between his triumph and the biblical allusion, and between his father's gift and the humiliating accident. For this, one requires the benefit of a wider view, one that is beyond Anders. The biblical allusion is one of many images of height in the novel. First, God and Anders' father are seen as being "on top" in their respective domains: they are psychologically equated. But Anders' desire to be "like God and know all" (IV, 21) is morally ambiguous, and his wish to be like his own father—stated immediately before Anders disobeys his father's commandment not to see Martin, the bad boy and the indirect cause of the mutilation of the writing desk—seems mixed with deep hostility. In his manuscript notes Hoel records the phrase "man's rebellion against God" after a comment on an early chapter where the father is equated by the boy with God (Ms. Fol. 2319:1). When Anders is being questioned in the desk episode, his father, who in the same chapter is compared to "God in the Bible" (130), grows so tall that he almost reaches the ceiling; yet Anders refuses to answer him. At his mother's death, toward the end of the book, Anders feels "rejected by God, consecrated to the devil for all eternity." Then, by way of an afterthought, he reflects that he "recognized" neither of them, not since the episode with the desk (294). However, by studying the image structure one realizes the presence of the demonic dream of power and knowledge from an early age, though Anders could not have been aware of it at the time he was having difficulties with saying r. Nor would he understand the alternative explanation, "infantile omnipotence" or overcompensation, which the text equally allows for. In his notes Hoel says that in a way the chapter "R" deals with the "sense of inferiority" (Ms. Fol. 2319:1).

Though the relationship between his father's gift and the humiliating episode ("dirtying" his pants) may seem coincidental, comparison with other incidents reveals an underlying pattern. First, as he grows older, Anders generalizes the meaning of the episode: he applies it to Martin, the bad boy his father forbade him to associate with ("so often he stood making poo-poo in his pants, so to speak" [IV, 134]), as well as to Embret, with whom he identifies to some extent in the latter's futile rebellion against his father ("To see him stand there making poo-poo in his pants. Right in front of Father's eyes. That was the worst of all" [162]). In several episodes Anders' deepest desire seems to be to receive praise from his father, but he fails miserably: he dishonors the ax his father gave him by reverting to an infantile nursery pattern; having failed to please his father in the desk episode, he can only project his own sense of worthlessness and fling a "nursery" expletive at him ("stinker"; lit. "bag of shit," *drittsekk*); and when the gun his father gave him takes on the semblance of a "snake," he throws it away, thus rejecting his father, along with full genital sexuality. After one has read the entire novel, the perceived hostility toward the father acts upon one's understanding of each episode. Specifically, the seeming simplicity of the nemesis pattern in "R," of which even Anders is aware, becomes complicated not only by hints of demonic rebellion in

Anders, but by a deep-seated aggression against his own father.

Psychoanalysis and the Portrayal of Anders

The preceding has incidentally commented on the portrayal of Anders in connection with the book's image clusters and its dual narrative perspective. A fuller examination of Anders has still to be made, along with a more systematic interpretation of his experience.

Hoel clearly did not wish to portray a typical artist in the making. Yet, to some extent, this is what he has done. Several circumstances separate Anders from other people, a fact of which he is himself aware: his phonetic quandary, his accident, his creativity. The first forces him to play with words, so as to avoid those with *r* in them. Paradoxically, his linguistic defect becomes his strength: "No one could turn words like him. He played with this thought. And he felt strong and wise and happy. He could be so glad that he sang" (IV, 109). His accident, which hampered him for a longer period, made him "different" from others; a visiting old woman calls him a "fox," seeing how he exploits the difference (68, 76). Unable to skate, he feels like "king of the entire lake" as he sits watching those who do; and seeing how his sisters envy him and avoid quarreling with him, he feels as though "he ruled over them with his foot. . . . It had made a man of him" (75). Finally, his incipient creativity is shown in "To God to Complain," in which his frustration is totally forgotten as a result of his truly esthetic fascination with the clay figures he shapes and, subsequently, with the rhymes he makes up. Suddenly he realizes that he has made a song, and it was "as though he grew as he stood there." On the strength of this accomplishment he takes possession of everything around him— the field, the horse, the hill, the sun, and so forth. "It was as though the words changed each time he called them out and meant all things, and he owned it all" (40). But Hoel's portrait of the artist in the making is limited to Part I; on the whole, Anders cannot be described in such terms.

He is a lonely child, intelligent, sensitive, proud. Hoel concentrates on the relationship with his parents, which colors all his other relationships. Though he claimed in an interview that his book was not psychoanalytic, he significantly admitted that he did not consciously avoid a psychoanalytic viewpoint either.[13] Considering that Hoel had known Freud's work for a dozen years by this time and that he was married to a child psychologist who had studied with some of the most distinguished professionals in the field, it would be extremely surprising if the book failed to show traces of this exposure.

Interestingly, Hoel's manuscript notes contain elaborate self-analyses of a psychoanalytic nature. Thus, after listing the people he had been tied to by a "sense of shame," Hoel examines the family atmosphere of his childhood home and his relationship with his parents. Having identified his two basic traits as "excessive ambition" and "excessive sensitivity" and characterized them as "obviously infantile," he explains their continued presence as due to a "not abreacted childhood situation, that is, neurosis." Though he does not remember it, he has no doubt that it is one of *"Mutterbindung"* (mother fixation). Then he mentions his "tiny attempts as a child to keep up with the grownups (my father, my twelve years older brother) and defeat them with my mother," though again he has no such recollection. Nor can he detect any "castration fear," which theoretically ought to be part of the picture. In the end he expresses dissatisfaction with his formulation, feeling that it is "distorting and misleading" (Ms. Fol. 2319:1). Nevertheless, Hoel's self-analysis articulates the underlying emotional pattern of Anders' development.

The clue to an understanding of the psychological dynamics of Anders lies in the Oedipus complex. In the book, the manifestations of this complex exist on two levels, familial and cosmic: the relationship with the father is projected upon the world at large and upon the divine. However, the repressed aggression against the father, coexisting with intense idealization, appears in reverse form: the father, divine and human, sacrifices or kills his son. Thus, God the Father wanted his son to be crucified, Crazy-Fredrik axes his son to death, and Anders fears his father will sell him to the itinerant cattle dealer and butcher. The associated castration anxiety is evident in several ways: in Anders' fear of losing his leg and of being turned into a woman, and in direct threats by an evil father-substitute like Albert. The repeated references to "dirtying" one's pants, always connected with a regressive self-image in relation to the father, are on one level symbols of unmanning. Anders' latent hostility to his father becomes overtly conscious in the desk episode, where the damage is effected by means of a knife: as soon as he hears his father's thundering voice in the office, "he immediately understood what he had done" (IV, 141).

Anders' relationships with others, whether men or women, are basically determined by his parental situation. In his manuscript notes Hoel speaks of his own lifelong tendency to identify with unworthy individuals: "Throughout my entire childhood, in fact until today, it has been this way with me that, if a person close to me (I can't know him extremely well, I think) behaves in such a way that I feel ashamed on his (her?) behalf, then I risk precisely to become dependent on and bound by that person." He notes that, in such a situation, he is ready to do anything to prevent the other person from being exposed. "The peculiar thing, psychologically, is that it is the other person, he who commits the stupidities, who symbolizes *me*, and I myself am, so to speak, reduced to a third person, a being who must carry the burden to prevent me from being crushed by the shame of an intolerable exposure" (Ms. Fol. 2319:1).

All of Anders' important relationships in the book follow this pattern to some extent: those with Embret, with Martin, with Ole. All three "symbolize" himself in the role of antagonist to his father or, in Ole's case, to a substitute father-figure, Albert; every one is seen to be "unmanned" in some way or another. In the case of Ole, who provides the boat for the excursion in "Sunday in August," the self-projection seems reciprocal: after the horrible killing of the baby goat—only a literary murder, according to Hoel (*Aftenposten*, 12/12/1950)—Ole and Anders have a savage fight where each appears as a mirror image of the other. The moral-emotional dynamics of the episode's climax, which Hoel leaves for the reader to untangle from the spare, Hemingway-like narrative, is based on Anders' shame, on Ole's behalf, for his breaking down in front of Albert and only weakly crying in protest against continuing the cruel game with the goat. Though Anders seems to wish Albert dead, in conformity with the oedipal pattern, he is flattered by the equal footing on which the evil father-figure treats him. As a result Anders becomes a party to a heinous act that, in retrospect, looks like a reenactment of man's primal fall: "He had seen all, taken part in everything, knew more than he ever had believed he would know—and he knew that he could tell nothing of all this to any human being. He felt as alone as though he stood there alone at the ends of the earth" (IV, 246).

Contrary to the comments of some critics that Hoel has largely neglected the child's sexuality, the novel contains a considerable amount of it, despite the near absence of overt sexual activity. Anders' relationships with women are clearly determined by a sense of unrequited love for his mother, who, when she is not with the father, pays more attention to the younger children. More crucial is her "betrayal" of six-year-old Anders in the desk incident, where, after cajoling him to confess, she goes and tells the father. This act, whereby the wife offers up her son to the avenging God-father, is never forgotten by Anders and, seemingly, never forgiven. The juxtaposition of the mother's illness, and her futile last attempt to get through to him, with an incident of mixed nude bathing in which Anders seems paralyzed before the girl he likes (IV, 285), shows the close connection between his maternal and other love relationships. Significantly, the pattern of "betrayal" or "escape" is present in several of the episodes with girls. In his notes Hoel comments on some incidents from his own life that turn up in the book. In one case, after starting school, he told off a girl on the telephone just because his sisters laughed at him: "I knew that I betrayed her—and myself. . . . I knew—without knowing the word—that I committed an act of Judas. I suppose I walked out of that affair with an impairment—a little poorer, weaker, more despicable than before. A first pattern was formed for many future instances of cowardice and treason."[14] The escape pattern is also seen in his attitude to his father's pathetic attempts at confidence before Anders' departure to the city. By this time he feels "strong and hard, as behind an armor"; though he realizes it is an escape maneuver, at the same time he experiences a "cold joy" (320).

Like most of Hoel's characters, Anders, too, is concerned with "coherence" or "meaning," which either eludes him or seems frightening. In "The Garden of Eden" a primary unity can be inferred, if only negatively; toward the end of this part, Anders finds it "more difficult than before to see the interconnection of things [*sammenhengen*]." And when he dreams of it, it is associated with *something*, "big and terrible," and wakes him up with a scream (IV, 126-27). As he grows, he finds it increasingly hard to explain things, including his own behavior. The genesis of the desk episode turns into a "long series of many things, one thing behind the other, as far as he could see. He couldn't quite see the farthest one" (141).[15] After the rifle incident, he feels equally incapable of explaining what had happened. No wonder that at the end it seems to him "that it was the world out there that had to give a meaning to everything. Here all was so confused, nothing hung together. The connection [*sammenhengen*] was in the outside world" (316). Therefore, he is poised for flight (322). But his soaring anticipation of the future seems ironically undercut by a recalled saying of Embret's that smacks of Freud: so many strange things will happen there, and "afterward . . . you will understand that everything had happened to you before you were ten years old" (315).

Summary Evaluation

The Road to the End of the World is a remarkably rich novel. It combines a vivid representation of everyday life with profound archetypal patterns. The psychology of childhood is sensitively explored, and the concrete, lyrical style effectively conveys its changing moods. For those who wish to delve deeper, Hoel's portrayal of Anders invites psychoanalytic interpretation. Moreover, through mythical, religious, and folkloric allusions the inward experience of one developing individual acquires universal significance. A strong ingredient of inserted local stories and of genre figures, pathetic and grotesque, evokes an idiosyncratic milieu with perfect mastery. Embret, the permanent hired man, is an embodiment of an entire way of life. The wide range of excellent portraits from a vanished age, made more real through moderate use of dialectal speech, gives the book a slightly nostalgic quality. These are ample pleasures, for which one is quite willing to pay with slight irritations over an occasional infraction of point of view or a bit of authorial commentary. Hoel has written a classic novel of childhood that ought to be available in all the major languages.[16]

SCENES OF RURAL LIFE

The stories collected in *The Princess on the Glass Mountain* had all been published separately before. The original contribution of the book consists of the five stories that deal with community life. Their depiction of a closed rural milieu, of the psychological effects of poverty, and of the situation of the outsider within such a milieu, looks forward to *The Troll Circle*. In terms of narrative technique, their most interesting facet is Hoel's skillful handling of the collective point of view: the stories are mostly told by the "folk," drawing upon rumor, local tradition, and old recollections; sometimes they are relayed by Anders, who also functions as observer.

"Love One Another," the longest and most serious story, is notable for the intimate fusion of narrative method and theme. The story's main subject, namely, how a community can be made to turn against a nonconformist, is conveyed through various mechanisms such as overhearing, gossip, slander, paranoid constructions, and voyeuristic observation, all of which are part of the very forces that Hoel wishes to expose. The young married couple, Jon and Inga—he a returned local boy, she a town beauty—eventually raise a storm in the community. A watchmaker and a seamstress respectively, they cannot help offending against certain vested economic interests. Worse, their sexual mores, such as kissing in public and swimming in the nude, cause a scandal. Besides, Jon seems to lack proper respect for the authorities, whether secular or religious: it is told that he dropped the word "organize" to a group of lumberjacks and threw an inquisitorial clergyman out of his house. All these factors, economic, moral, political, release the mechanisms of the mass mind, similar to those that underlie the forming of "public opinion" in *Open Sesame,* which Hoel was working on when "Love One Another" was first printed in 1935. Suffering loss of business and open harassment, the young couple are defeated: Inga soon falls ill with tuberculosis and dies, Jon packs up and leaves.

"Love One Another" can be read in several ways. First, it is a

story of social ostracism due to being different; as such it presents
a subconsciously motivated conspiracy of growing complexity
and does so with great dramatic suspense. But with its ironic
allusion to Romans 13, it is also about the terrible consequences
of a sexually repressive morality. The young couple's acceptance
of a joyous sexuality is the chief stumbling block to being assimi-
lated to the community; it seems to challenge the very foundations of marriage and of "Christian" ethics. From a third
perspective the story is an impressive dissection of the genesis of
evil: even arson and murder are contemplated as weapons against
the offenders.

By comparison with "Love One Another," the remaining four
rural stories are minor accomplishments, though each is perfect
in its own way. They, too, deal with characters who deviate from
the average, mostly through honesty, simplicity, naiveté, or a
spontaneous joy of life. In three of them, "The Murderer,"
"From Cotters' Country," and "The Old Ones on the Hill," the
climax or turning point occurs through physical violence. In a
manuscript note for *The Road* Hoel mentions the tendency toward "acts of violence" displayed by people who lack "other
means of expression" (Ms. Fol. 2319:1). Martin, Hans, and
Amund in these stories, respectively, are not very bright, but they
are kind and allow themselves to be exploited by the sly foxes
around them or by the authorities. Martin, being thrown out of
his cotter's plot four times in succession after it has been decided
to convert the plots to forest land again, receives a prison sentence
for beating up the lumber company's representative: this experience has marked him for life and given him the cognomen
"murderer." Hans, helplessly inarticulate, is strung along by
Amalie, whose father and brother-in-law profit unconscionably
from his good nature. After the banns have been read for Amalie
and her widowed brother-in-law, Hans brutally murders her. The
murder is obviously a substitute for speech, for communication
(VI, 66); he seems to have been totally unconscious of any intention to kill (67). Amund in "The Old Ones on the Hill" leads a
life of poverty due to the consequences of a fight with his rival,
who turns Amund's simplicity and guilty conscience into a nice
source of profit and eventually takes over Amund's farm. All
these stories give compassionate and at the same time humorous

descriptions of the condition of the poor and the disenfranchised, while, as in "Love One Another," the exploiters are treated with comic irony.

In "The Hunting Accident" ("Vådeskudd"), the exposure of the avarice of a farming family has an almost tragic poignancy. The elder brother watches at the wounded man's side; he reflects how much he loves his dying younger brother. At the same time, having once saved his life from a raging bull, he feels that he has the right to his brother's money. He unlocks the chest of drawers, but in the moment when he has gotten his hands on the bills, his two sisters storm in. In the midst of the ensuing heated exchange, the wounded man sits up, protesting, has a hemorrhage, and dies. The story, with its macabre climax, is instilled with restrained moral passion.

These stories present a microcosm of an entire social, psychological, and moral universe. Their art is one of great economy, governed by the principle of understatement. Yet, the picture of life that Hoel evokes is vivid, colorful, and saturated with an unmistakably local atmosphere. Some of the characters are roughly hewn, as though cut out of wood or stone; others, especially the women, suggest grotesque miniatures in a softer medium. Most are excellent examples of comic portraiture, in which one physical trait can give the clue to an entire personality: Martin's fear of touching things with his huge, powerful hands for fear of breaking them; Hans' habitual drunken howling, a substitute for speech; Amund's helpless hemming and hawing. The economy is also evident in the method of narration, in that the stories, so to speak, tell themselves: their tale of poverty, social injustice, and moral squalor is reflected through the distorting medium of the collective psyche. At the same time there is a guiding intelligence behind it all, mediated chiefly through the observation and reflections of Anders; these help the reader correct the distortions, make moral evaluations of the stories' substance, and assemble the individual tales into an integrated vision.[17]

6
Psychoanalysis and Quest for Identity

Two novels twelve years apart, *A Fortnight Before the Nights of Frost* (1935) and *Meeting at the Milestone* (1947), display so many resemblances that they can profitably be discussed together. Both are Oslo novels and contain vivid descriptions of peasant student life in the capital; both represent a peculiar combination of confessional and quest novel; finally, they bear a strong imprint of psychoanalysis, not only in their themes and images but in their very technique, that of retrospective narration from the vantage point of crisis. They even share some weaknesses.

A FORTNIGHT BEFORE THE NIGHTS OF FROST

In 1935, when he wrote *A Fortnight,* Hoel was undergoing analysis with Wilhelm Reich. Starting in January, 1934, and lasting until June, 1936, when Hoel broke it off, it was allegedly a training analysis; and indeed, for a couple of years, Hoel was Reich's associate and had a few patients of his own.[1] His immediate aim, however, seems to have been to control the self-observations he had made in preparation for writing *The Road to the End of the World.* The analysis entailed a great deal of suffering on Hoel's part. Apparently it came to focus on the most painful incident in his childhood past, the fracture of his elbow joint and the subsequent complications. The effects of breaking through to the repressed memory, with its associated anxiety, were so shattering that, according to a friend, for months at a time in 1934 and 1935 Hoel was in a state of deep depression. When, during the summer of 1935, Reich took a vacation and interrupted the treatment, Hoel felt "betrayed" by the man on whom he had come to rely emotionally, notwithstanding the attendant suffering.[2] Yet, by August 15, 1935, he had recovered sufficiently to start *A Fortnight,* which was finished the same fall (I, xiv).

The novel covers a few weeks in the life of Knut Holmen, a successful Oslo doctor, married and father of two children, whose solitary celebration of his fortieth birthday sets off a series of incidents that take him on a kind of time travel in the past: the images of journey and of "crossroads" are pervasive. The quest theme is initiated in the moment when Holmen thinks he recognizes, in a passing woman, a girl he loved twenty years earlier. His frantic pursuit of this lost love, Helga, leads him to roam the streets of Oslo and to revisit the haunts from his lonely student days. Soon, however, his quest of the past is complicated by his meeting a young woman, Vera, put in his way, as we learn later, by an acquaintance, the engineer Ramstad, who asks Holmen to look after his apartment while he is away on vacation. His relationship with Vera, viewed at first as an interlude, assumes depth and passion at the seashore, where they spend a few rapturous days together. Back in the city, Holmen rents an apartment for Vera and himself. By this time his pursuit of Helga seems a mere delusion; it is compared to a "twenty-year-old phonograph record" (V, 159). After waiting in vain for Vera to turn up, however, he begins a second frantic pursuit, this time by train and car, to recover his most recently lost love. The novel's structure suggests a Chinese box or a spiral, a physical figure used to describe Holmen's wandering (168). After tracing one circle after another, in the end Holmen finds himself at home with his wife, though under altered circumstances: he has traveled in a "large circle," but "not only in a circle" (267).[3]

The book's climax and dénouement come about through two scenes of extreme physical violence. Soon after his return from the shore to the city Holmen is visited by Ramstad, now back from vacation. Ramstad, a demonic Nietzschean with sadistic proclivities, seems furiously jealous over Holmen's affair with Vera, despite his having thrown them together in the first place.[4]

He had wanted to "test" his values, he tells Holmen (204); judging by his long monologue, however, the object was rather to test his own power, including his sexual power. The fight between him and Holmen is provoked by Ramstad's taunting boasts about reconquering and sexually subduing Vera. Though Vera, frightened by Ramstad's manner, visits Holmen, they—she and Holmen—never get back to their former footing, even after it becomes clear she is leaving Ramstad. And one day, instead of Vera, Knut's wife, Agnete, finds her way to his little apartment. Having learned through a friend of their stay at the seashore, Agnete feels bitterly insulted and ready for a reckoning, which—ironically—occurs after the relationship with Vera is already a thing of the past. It takes place at their summer island spot before closing up for the season. Agnete, who has spent the summer there with the children, asks Holmen to drive her down to pick up their things. The scene of violence, facilitated by his ladylike wife's getting drunk and triggered by her taunts in regard to the children's paternity, is extremely brutal: Holmen nearly strangles his wife in an attempt to force the truth. The critic Hans Heiberg called it "one of the most devilishly revealing pieces of pure hell in Norwegian literature" (*Arbeiderbladet*, 12/21/1935). In revulsion against this degrading incident, Agnete rushes out into the storm. Though Holmen saves her from drowning and both resume their normal everyday lives, the marriage is seemingly held together only by Holmen's concern for the children: he refuses to put them into the hands of a wife who has become a convert to the "life-changing" upper-class revivalism of Frank Buchman (1878-1961), leader of the Oxford Group and later of Moral Rearmament.

The Man Without Identity

The foregoing resumé acquires meaning only if seen in relation to the book's underlying theme: "forgotten anxiety over forgotten transgressions lies like shadows on our lives" (V, 151). The moment that has determined the life of Knut Holmen, we discover, is linked to his affair with a young, innocent girl who gave herself to him, without calculation, when he was a poor lonely peasant student in Oslo. In the very midst of their rapturous union they were plunged into a "stinking sewer": suddenly his landlady stood in the doorway shouting expletives—"tart, whore. In *my* bed. . . . Swine!" (41, 105).The experience was so paralyzing that, though they exchanged some letters, Holmen made no efforts to renew his physical contact with Helga. When he relates this episode to Vera at the shore, it is emotionally more revealing: in a recurrent dream the night after his encounter with Helga, a dream in which the ghastly experience is reenacted, it was not the landlady but his mother who stood in the doorway. This dream, in turn, is connected with a childhood incident involving his mother. Having decided that the only way not to have more children was sexual abstinence, his puritanic mother indirectly caused his father to have an affair with the maid, whereupon his mother temporarily abandoned the family: she did not wish to stay in a house where a "hussy" had lain in her bed (150). Besides learning all the "dirty" details later in the servants' quarters, the boy felt guilty of his mother's abandonment. The pattern is subsequently extended to include Holmen's wife, who during their quarrel uses the same words about Vera as those spoken by the landlady and his mother (228).

The upshot is that Holmen's personality has been warped by a prohibitive sexual morality that was instilled in him in the nursery. Confirmed by an unfortunate experience in youth, his childhood fear and guilt became a "sneaking anxiety that hindered him from giving himself completely to anyone"; having betrayed Helga, he also betrayed himself (V, 106, 112). Instead of following his true desires, he has embraced an existence dominated by material success, social respectability, and moral, intellectual, and emotional mediocrity.[5] As a man of the world—a status seeker who is a worthy representative of his class—Holmen is proud of his sartorial elegance, his flair for good food and wine, and the admiring glances he can still elicit from pretty young women.

In the course of his impromptu vacation, Holmen becomes painfully aware of his "unlived life," his "unused possibilities" (V, 36). He becomes veritably obsessed with the "road not taken": research, writing, intimate friendship, passion. The route he has followed, with all its crossroads, is seen as a succession of fortuitous occurrences: he has not truly *chosen* a direction for his life.

While signifying his desperate quest, his erratic movements in the course of the novel—expressed in the chapter title "Hither and Thither" (181) and exemplified by pacing the floor, wandering about the streets and in the environs, traveling to the seashore and to the mountains and back—also reveal Holmen's spiritual and moral disorientation. In both respects the novel appears to be a boldly sustained series of symbolic actions. Holmen's indeterminate state of being is conveyed by his repeated sense of "floating" (*sveve*), of being suspended in between—be it places, roles, or fragmentations of the self: "*He* was always in many places and no place" (137). The most extended example of this feeling is found in the scene with his wife, which to him seems to be played on a stage, with two simultaneous sets of actions: "And he himself was in both places at the same time, but therefore not entirely in either place; he was floating somewhere in the middle, observing himself" (229). The prohibitive morality represented by his mother is also the source of Holmen's self-alienation: visiting the servants' quarters as a boy of seven or eight against his mother's wishes, he felt he "ought to have been somewhere else" (85).

One recurrent image used to convey the insubstantial, spectral quality of this state of being is "shadow."[6] "One of his shadows was running around some shadowy city blocks, another sat in an empty office, other shadows were still in other places, and one was here," he reflects at the seashore (V, 137). Moreover, the shadow is seen as a force of fate: "Where could he have broken the circle, the circle of shadows that surrounded his youth?" (119). In the wretched neighborhoods where he used to live in furnished rooms as a student, shadows were emitted by the very houses, covering them like a "gray fog" (102). As previously mentioned, the book's central theme is expressed through this image: repressed anxiety and guilt lie "like shadows on our lives" (151). Sometimes it is as though the shadows chased by Holmen were "just behind him and chased *him*" (114), a sinister reversal already used in *Nothing*.

Before Sartre made the theme of identity fashionable, Hoel in *A Fortnight*, a novel about middle-age crisis, presents a deep-probing treatment of identity on a psychoanalytic basis, with no Proustian esthetic redemptions. Holmen, as his name—meaning "islet"—suggests, is a world unto himself; as Ramstad tells him, his crisis is due to his lack of commitment to a cause larger than himself (V, 200). He is a product of contingency, having allowed chance circumstance and conventional expectations to dictate his choices. His bad faith is evident everywhere: at Geilo, on his search for Vera, the arrival of an Oslo-bound train becomes a sufficient reason for him to retrace his steps (174), and he defends his investment in war-related stocks by the thought that "*he* couldn't change the world. He couldn't stop the insane game of the great ones" (167). His moral dependency on others is shown by fear of being detected in a compromising situation by Ramstad in the latter's apartment. Generally, his sexually conditioned anxiety is inseparable from fear of being watched, stared at, and condemned. Culturally, he has chosen the first of two possibilities open to the member of a rural subculture in the capital: he has acquired all the externals, "the manners, the repartee, the style, the flirtation, the jargon—thereby risking to become nothing but an empty shell" (21).

A puppet of his milieu (V, 45), Holmen is a perfect example of inauthenticity. His dream about having become a stone can be viewed both as an instance of what Sartre calls objectification and of the Freudian death instinct (169). Holmen himself seems to understand it in the latter sense: "the freedom that consists in being dead" masquerading as the art of living (171). That such a man, when the ultimate question, Who was he? came to him (137), could find only a congeries of different shadows is not surprising.

Nature and Eros: A Failed Ideal of Integrity

At the seashore, Vera frees Dr. Holmen from the shadow world, as well as from the "tethers" and "burdens" that seemed to deprive him of freedom in the city (V, 132). Being with Vera made Holmen feel "whole and part of a wholeness. Nothing separated him from himself, nothing separated him from her" (154). This feeling, though momentary, expresses an ideal, as against the fragmentation of his everyday personality. At the shore he and Vera follow the timeless rhythms of the sea instead of the ticking of the clock; they also develop a close relationship with the rest of their environment, whether natural or man-made. Everything they touch, hear, and see acquires a meaning by becoming part of the inward plenitude of their daily existence. Within this context of unity of being, the lighthouse, which sends a "white fan of light around the horizon from twilight to dawn: three times and then a break, three times and then a break" (133), comes to seem an appropriate symbol of the divine. That Hoel wishes to remind the reader of paradise regained is evident from his serious, non-ironic allusion to Genesis: "And the evening and the morning were the first, second and third day. . . . slow swells of time that merged with eternity" (135).

The basis of their newfound integrity of being is erotic. Reich's doctrine of the orgasm, which Hoel accepted, has left clear traces both in *A Fortnight* and *Meeting at the Milestone*. The healing, liberating power of eros is shown by the "miracle" that had happened to Helga: "Nineteen years of threats and terrors and anxiety dropped from her like a bundle of old rags in the course of five minutes—until she stood there as God had created her, free, happy, enraptured" (V, 112). Here as in *Meeting* the principal image used in evoking the transcendent nature of sexual pleasure, specifically of orgasm, is a typical dream symbol, flight, and the problem of Holmen could be defined as fear of flying. In thinking of Vera after their experience at the shore, Holmen envisages her face as it appeared just before the moment of highest rapture, when he knew that "now she rose, now she soared." Then he associates certain values and personal qualities with the orgasmic experience: her face was "wild, free, untamed—and it was radiant. It radiated light." And something more, it was "brave. It radiated courage. . . . It was the courage he remembered. Some of it passed on to him, and he knew he rose to heights where he had never been, except perhaps in dreams." But then, at a "certain point of the journey, she left him and continued rising." Dizzy and afraid to fall, he "did not dare to follow her further." All that a doubter like him can hope for— and *that* she gave him—is a "glimpse of the Promised Land" (176-77). But he will not reach it, owing to the fact that, with him, once desire or happiness has reached a certain height, it generates anxiety (126). Significantly, fear of happiness is one of the great Reichian themes.

The same theme is evident in Holmen's changing relationship
to nature, from which, despite his rural background, he seems to
be alienated; he is as afraid of the "starry sky" (V, 43) as those he
mocks. The "empty, remote, lonely" sound of the dial tone, with
its suggestion of "outer space" and "endless desolate distances"
(54), expresses this alienation. The virtual self that emerges
during his stay at the shore with Vera, one that is in tune with the
natural world, seems to languish with the end of the affair. After
the crisis with his wife, his sense of confrontation with an indifferent nature is once more present. Having awaked during the
night, he steps out on the veranda: "He stood there for a while
staring, tiny and unnoticed in the midst of the mighty, austere
vastness, which stared at him in turn, without sympathy, without
giving comfort, without seeing" (244). The way he perceives his
wife's eyes, beyond love and fear, "mute, completely resigned"
(247), is not very different. In a psychological novel, this is something more than a naturalistic cliché; the alienation from nature
and from eros is coequal, each indicative of a crisis of identity.

Fiction as Figurative Psychoanalysis

In a marginal comment to Arne Stai's book about him, Hoel
says about A Fortnight: "When I wrote the book I did not realize
to what extent Reich was a model—or to what extent the problems he represented showed up in Ramstad. Nor did I realize the
degree to which the book gives a figurative representation of an
analysis. Many years passed before I saw that."[7] The very names
of the principal male characters, Holmen and Ramstad, are transparent derivatives from Hoel and Reich, whose love-hate relationship forms the background to the fictional characters' rivalry
over Vera. But the most interesting comment is what Hoel says
about the novel's psychoanalytic form. External marks of this
form are the retrospective technique, the return of the repressed as
the defense mechanisms weaken, dreams and dream symbolism.
More subtly, the book's action, a mimesis of Holmen's mental-
emotional life, is a reenactment of a primal situation expressive
of a mother fixation.[8] The consistency with which this reenactment is executed appears clearly through one detail of Holmen's
behavior pattern. After the harrowing scene with Ramstad,

which convinces him that Vera is lost to him, the quality of his mental life reverts momentarily to that of childhood: his room appears "vast," and all objects in it grow "gigantic" and "threatening," whereas *he* seems very small. And when Holmen goes out for a walk, he eventually finds himself in a thicket outside the city, just as, after rushing through the empty house when his mother had left, he was discovered in a thicket of the pasture. Only afterwards does Holmen realize that he has "repeated himself" (V, 150, 207-8). Similarly, his search for Vera at the shore includes the same image of roaming through empty rooms calling her name (178): the crisis of his relationship with Vera re-enacts a childhood trauma.

The question arises whether Holmen's successive recognitions of having "repeated himself" generate the kind of insight that, in analysis, would enable a person to modify his behavior pattern. Does the book, in short, imitate the form of a successful analysis? The answer is largely determined by one's interpretation of its total form: is there in the end a break in the vicious circle? In psychological terms, the vicious circle is expressive of neurosis: emotional failure in the past, though regretted, leads to renewed failure in the present, which, while similarly regretted, is followed by a return to the point of departure. Holmen's persistence in his old patterns of behavior is particularly clear from his failure to act on Vera's unmistakable hints after the marital blowup that she would be willing to resume their relationship. The dynamics of his neurotic state is fearfully conveyed through a dream in which Holmen is repeatedly struck by a bolting stallion that he tries to tame. Being symbolically stallion, tamer, victim, and observer, he sees enacted before his eyes the Reichian dialectic of rebel and slave, without any break in the vicious circle (V, 242-43).[9]

While the description seems to indicate a negative answer to the question posed, some comments by Hoel suggest a somewhat less pessimistic view. Writing to Martin Joos, Hoel defines the book's problem as follows: "To what extent, after reaching a certain age, can we at all, 'by our own effort,' straighten out our existence?" (9/29/1939). In this connection, the view that Holmen is unable to assume responsibility for his life, and thus to develop emotionally, because of his creator's "determinist view of guilt"—one that makes guilt into something "irrational and negative"[10]—is based on a crucial oversight of one of the book's central themes, namely, that liberation from past conditioning, including sexual guilt, will increase one's capacity for self-responsibility. Speaking of Holmen's "journey" in his notes, Hoel stresses the liberating power of new perception per se: "if on the way he acquired a little more self-knowledge, his circle became not a closed circle but a spiral, which—possibly—led him to a higher perspective. It may be that this is the utmost a person can demand." He also makes a statement that, however indirectly, bears on the power to change one's life: "Man cannot determine his own destiny, but to the extent that one accepts the existing state of things, adapts to it and profits from it, to that extent he is responsible for all the evil that occurs in the world at large" (Ms. Fol. 2343, A 29). It is important in this context that Holmen finally sells his war-economy stocks, thereby shedding his glittering role of man-about-town and ending his complicity with one kind of social evil (V, 263). Emotionally, this means a step toward personal wholeness, one aim of psychoanalysis; morally and existentially, it signifies a victory over "bad faith" and a gain in authenticity.

The last manuscript note quoted shows that, in writing *A Fortnight,* Hoel planned to apply psychoanalysis not only to the fictional representation of the individual but to that of bourgeois society and the world at large, though only by metonymic extension. Hoel discerned a connection between the personal crisis of Dr. Holmen and the international situation. "The crisis of Dr. Holmen is one of fear, confusion and hunger for life, in a manner similar to the world crisis. He rushes around in a circle, just as the world rushed around in *its* circle" (Ms. Fol. 2343, A 29; also V, 193). Throughout the book there are repeated references to the world situation, by means of Holmen's stocks and bonds and otherwise. The servants' quarters on his father's farm come to seem a microcosm of the world, where evil is tolerated on the ground that nothing can be done about it and where feelings of inferiority and fear are masked by overcompensation (86). A series of oxymorons in Ramstad's monologue, including an entire social philosophy that will not be further examined, illustrates some of the ways in which the rebel-slave complex is implicit in the contradictions of bourgeois society: "sincere hypocrites," "constructive destroyers," "gangsters in uniform," and virtuous "sex murderers" (192-93). Though Ramstad's point is that this situation will lead to an explosion, viewed in relation to the book's plot and imagery it seems to represent a nearly irremediable situation of evil social stasis.

Esthetic Evaluation

Hoel thought that the time pressure in finishing *A Fortnight* caused its second half to be less than successful. "Seduced by the ecstacy of work, I believed it contained a clear depiction of a number of things that now, afterward, I can see it merely suggests, sometimes barely that" (letter to Joos, 9/29/1939). The revision that he would have liked to undertake was never realized. Perhaps the book's greatest weaknesses are Ramstad's long monologue (V, 188-201) and the perfunctoriness of the concluding section. The former was seemingly a result of Hoel's feeling that the book's intellectual substance was not fully embodied in its action, character development, and imagery; the same recourse to essayistic amplification will be seen in *Meeting at the Milestone*. Even if one accepts the essayistic digression—a not uncommon device in the modern novel—as a valid element of fiction, the mishmash of Nietzschean, Reichian, and Freudian ideas that Ramstad spews out in his jealous fury with Holmen carries conviction only to the extent they have already been embodied in the book's narrative, and such embodiment is on a limited scale. Ramstad himself, while interesting in ordinary dialogue, becomes a pompous bore as an amateur philosopher. The book's conclusion is weak for two reasons: first, it is asserted instead of being fleshed out in scenes; second, Holmen's justifying his continued marriage, and the renunciation of Vera, by the duty to protect his children from fear, the kind of fear that the book has so thoroughly documented in his own case, is a pious deception, a last instance of bad faith.[11]

But the novel's shortcomings, though not minor ones, are more than compensated for by the book's brilliance and depth. Hoel's mastery of free indirect discourse, here the chief form of narrative, is superb; its nimbleness, varied pace, and capricious turns and twists render the rhythms of modern life as well as the movements of consciousness. At the same time, by its impressionism of perception and memory, often influenced by the momentary state of the body and by idiosyncratic associations, it yields an in-depth portrayal of the central character. One is reminded of Leopold Bloom's volatile reveries as he wanders around the streets of Dublin. The first chapter (V, 7-72) is particularly brilliant, achieving a marvelous immediacy of portrayal. In the witty, whimsical mind of Knut Holmen, self-styled epicurean and master of the art of living, all things are reduced to a mundane level: women, cigars, and cars are interchangeable. Things become animated and people are objectified; we move in a chaotic universe, one without moral order. As the internal pressure mounts, Holmen's light, carefree mood vanishes, and he becomes increasingly bitter, defensive, and self-assertive. But by this time he has captivated us, and we are willing to perceive the world and people through his eyes.

Throughout the book all sorts of perceptions, thoughts, superimposed memories, allusions, and fancies pass through Holmen's mind; but however multifarious, they are all held together by his moods and obsessions, a fact that sometimes lends an expressionistic quality to the style. Thus, the details of the external world become images of Holmen's changing states of mind and feeling. While he and Vera make love, the thundering noise of a passing racing car is transformed, first to the sound of a river, then to the roar of a waterfall, until they are overcome by the "vortex" of passion (V, 91). Aside from landscapes, insects in particular—beetles, bumblebees and mosquitoes—serve as effective objective correlatives of Holmen's moods (143-44, 178, 263). The beetle image, after being associated with vicious circles and emotional stasis, is applied in figurative fashion, with sinister, near-surrealistic effect, to technological civilization. Looking from his window in Oslo after returning from the shore, Holmen perceives the cars as "giant beetles which dashed off into the fabulous world of a dark future" (156). The combination of realism and expressionism, which did not work in *The Seven-Pointed Star*, is one of the novel's great merits; it contributes toward achieving, through style, a unity of literary perception and representation that somewhat mitigates the impression of the central character's tragic division.

MEETING AT THE MILESTONE

Meeting at the Milestone is, in some ways, a more impressive performance than *A Fortnight;* its thematic range, moral urgency, and probing analysis of evil are unprecedented in Hoel's previous work. The book's impact is partly due to Hoel's impassioned fight against Nazism, particularly during the Occupation, when his wide knowledge of the Nazi ideology was given focus by the direct impact upon mind, heart, and nerves of living under a brutal, oppressive tyranny. In an interview Hoel asserted that "the strongest impressions life has given me I received during the Occupation."[12] His contribution to the Resistance Movement included over fifty articles in the illegal, underground press. Before his escape to Sweden by "organizational decision" in the fall of 1943, he was, by his own account, in danger of arrest at eleven different periods. Nazi journalists, he reports, saw him as the "evil spirit" of Norwegian intellectual life. In the winter of 1942, he was abused on the German radio, both from Hamburg and Berlin.[13] In view of this personal history, partly reflected in disguised form in the novel, it is no wonder that *Meeting at the Milestone* has become a classic of the Occupation. Adverse criticism on a neo-Marxist basis to the effect that it approaches the problem of Nazism in an individualistic, liberal-humanistic spirit has done nothing to diminish its popularity.[14]

Convinced that the idea was the best he had ever had for a novel, Hoel had hoped to publish the book in the fall of 1945, at a time when the public was book-hungry after five years of Nazi censorship.[15] But the publication was repeatedly postponed due to other commitments. Started in the summer of 1942, work was continued briefly in Stockholm in 1944, but the book was largely written "at terrible speed in less than two months" in 1947.[16] This delay may have caused minor alterations in his plan, though there is no evidence, contrary to Audun Tvinnereim's suggestion, that originally it was intended to be a reworking of *A Fortnight,* with its theme of self-renewal.[17] Hoel's intention to focus on the question of Nazism appears clearly from his earliest manuscript notes (Ms. Fol. 2324:3; 8/8/1942). Just before he re-

sumed work on the book in Sweden in 1944, Hoel read the manuscript of Aksel Sandemose's *The Past Is a Dream* (*Det gångna är
en dröm*, 1944)—the Norwegian original came out after the
war—and this book, with its complex narrative structure, may
have influenced Hoel's adoption of what one critic called Conrad's "documentary technique."[18] The following summary will
show the resemblance to Conrad's time-shift technique as well as
to his use of multiple narrators.

Story and Structure

The novel's intent was an ambitious one, namely, to show "the
roots of Nazism" (Ms. Fol. 2324:3),[19] a subject about which Hoel
published an essay, "On the Essence of Nazism" (1945), originally conceived as part of the book. At the same time the novel
has many of the earmarks of confessional fiction, and in some
ways it embodies Hoel's own wartime experiences, including that
of writing the book.

Meeting consists of three parts and an epilogue, all presented
as dated documents by the principal narrator, a lawyer-banker
who is also the central character. The compositional rhythm
reflects the novel's genesis, as previously explained: the three
main parts are dated 1947, 1943, and 1944, the epilogue 1947, thus
forming a narrative loop. Hoel's intent to include the book's
compositional history is evident not only from the sequence of
dates and geographical locations, but from the fact that in subsequent references he mistakenly stated the novel was begun in
1943, the date of the "I's" first notes in the published work.[20] Yet
he indicated that the book's "I" was "at most" only partly "related to" himself, that "he is me and he is not me."[21]

Worthy of note is the clear family resemblance to Holmen in *A
Fortnight*, despite the "I's" more ambitious project. The gradual
change of focus from the collective problem of Nazi treason to the
moral and psychosexual problems of an individual, or a group of
individuals, makes it necessary that he, like Holmen, review his
past. Hoel has chosen to do what he does best: to deal intensively
with a limited number of characters and their youthful erotic
experiences. But far more systematically than in *A Fortnight* he
also desires, by symbolic amplification, to put the searchlight on

a grave social, moral, indeed national problem. The patently idealistic premise of this dual purpose is stated in the epilogue, where the "I" argues that if we followed the pattern of one person's life with sufficient clarity and empathy back to its origins, eventually we would become omniscient concerning this person and capable of predicting his future. More than that, we would understand "all human life, that of families, groups, societies, *everything*" (VIII, 375). Though the narrator admits he failed to find the "pattern" in his life (376), this idea remains the philosophical premise of Hoel's novel.

Since the story is inseparable from the manner of its telling, it will be summarized from the point of view of the narrating "I," nicknamed the Blameless One on account of his spotless record as a Norwegian patriot. A self-righteous man in his forties, he seems to judge a person purely by his contribution to the "cause": human weakness, even fairness and a sense of justice, is put down by him as being *stripete* (lit. streaked), that is, as leaning toward the Nazis. His attitude at the outset could be called Pharisaic; in a Danish radio interview with Philip Houm in 1951 Hoel said the book was "intended as a struggle against the Pharisees."[22]

Part I (VIII, 11-68), recorded in 1947 but dealing with what happened in August, 1943—with cutbacks to some twenty years earlier and a few observations from the vantage point of 1947—introduces an underground agent, Indregård, who is cracking up. In his conversations with Indregård, the Blameless One, whose house is used as a cover for endangered members of the Home Front—usually before they are dispatched across the border to neutral Sweden—assumes a condescendingly ironic attitude. While traveling around the country as an insurance man secretly working for the Front, Indregård has discovered that there are good and bad Nazis, good patriots and bad ones. Worse, he has come to realize that he is directly responsible for another person's, indeed an entire family's, having "gone to hell"—that is, become members of the Nazi Party (45). As a one-time substitute teacher at an Oslo junior college (*gymnasium*) he interfered—out of unconscious jealousy and repressed sexuality, it turns out—in the seemingly innocent relationship between his young colleague, Hans Berg, and a gifted female pupil. Berg was not only summarily dismissed but was informed that he could save himself the trouble of applying for another teaching post in Oslo. Now, having met him more than twenty years after in the small town where Berg buried himself without completing his degree, Indregård feels he is partly to blame not only for Berg's wretched marriage but for his joining the Nazi Party as well.

Throughout Indregård's confessions and his vignettes of provincial life during the Occupation, the "I" maintains the same ironic attitude, indicative of profound contempt and ultimate dismissal. He acts as though he has taken Andreas, his superior in the Home Front, as his model, despite being fully aware that the latter is "through and through hard and ruthless, strictly speaking a completely insufferable fellow" (VIII, 19-20). The recurring phrase "through with him," used to characterize his attitude to former friends who have turned Nazi, also applies to his feelings about Indregård (47, 64). Nevertheless, Indregård's predicament strikes home, since it is he who "in all his confusion" sets the narrator thinking, first, about his own acquaintance with Hans Berg, then with others who have turned out badly (64). Moreover, the fact that in his last words to Indregård he mimics the latter's "magic formula," "Excuse me!"—which epitomizes the agent's guilt-ridden mind (26, 45, 57)—sets up a suspicion of underlying moral kinship between the two men. This suspicion is strengthened when, much later, one discovers the nature of the narrator's marriage, a tragic failure ending with his wife's suicide and his son's death. The Blameless One eventually attributes this misfortune to his hiding behind a great love in the past as a "protection against a new love," a pretext for "escape from life" itself (345). His attitude is not so different from Indregård's confirmed bachelorhood, clearly due, despite his denial, to his love for the high school student some twenty years ago.

Part II, the narrator's notes from 1943, begins with the story of Hans Berg and continues with thumbnail sketches of other fellow students who became Nazis. But mostly it presents his own erotic autobiography (VIII, 137-239). The account of Hans Berg (71-101) alternates between scenic presentation and general narrative and moves from boyhood to youth, with interspersed questions and reflections from the standpoint of 1943. Most memorable is the ghastly account of how Hans's puritanic father spent most of a Sunday nearly flogging his eleven-year-old son to

death because he refused to apologize for some innocently
dropped curse words. This piece of ritualistic sadism turns Hans
into a self-destructive Satanist. While inwardly a slave to his
father's sin- and guilt-ridden conscience, he must always be in
opposition, a rebel. The narrator adds an allusion to a similar
incident in an American novel, evidently the insensate beating of
Joe Christmas in *Light in August,* a book Hoel had translated;
this allusion is intended to universalize the experience. The
"Gallery of the Damned"—except for Carl Heidenreich, who will
play an important role in the "I's" own life—is a collection of
peasant student grotesques that illustrates many of the seven
deadly sins but gives few clues to what the "I" seeks: the "roots"
of Nazism.[23] Most suggestive is his final comment pertaining to
the difficulty of acculturation: "there is a long road from a poor
little fjord in the West Country or a remote hamlet in the East
Country to college, university, and modern life in Oslo. A person
can go astray many times on that road" (136).

The "I's" research into his own life, resulting chiefly in his
erotic autobiography, follows from his frustration at failing to
find what he was looking for, the roots of Nazism. If, he argues,
exploring the past helps to understand the present, you should
examine the person "you *ought* to know best at any rate—
yourself." He overcomes his reluctance to disturb the "web of
remote experiences, of remembrance, longing and dream," a
"cobweb" he has himself spun over the years, though he understands that it springs from a deep fear of what he may discover
(VIII, 137-38). Most of the events related occur from spring to fall
in 1921, when he was in his early twenties; but here too is a
cutback to an earlier period, chiefly a scene with his father six
years before (169, 173-78), as well as a brief encounter in 1943 with
the first girl he had an affair with in 1921 and her husband
(179-83). The underlying idea is accentuated by the vast gap between the opening "Prayer for Love'" and the declaration by
Kari, his girlfriend, at section's end that she is pregnant. In between these extremes of longing and despair, the episodes run the
gamut from casual sex and infatuation to passion. The ecstatic
experience with Kari is a glorified version of Holmen's brief
affair with Helga, except that, instead of an outraged landlady, it
is pregnancy that separates them.

At this point the notes abruptly stop: as in *A Fortnight* the psychological quest is interrupted by life itself. The aftermath to the pregnancy, related piecemeal in Part III, dated 1944, includes the narrator's futile efforts to find a surgeon to perform an abortion and some vague thoughts about that ultimate trap for young men, marriage. His last attempt to find a doctor causes him, unwittingly, to complete tying the knot of his fate and of the book's plot. Not knowing that Kari has had a relationship (arranged by her possessive stepfather) with Heidenreich, a medical student of his acquaintance, the narrator turns to him for help in finding an abortionist—just two hours after Kari, his love, has in desperation asked Heidenreich to marry her. When Heidenreich—who probably guessed the identity of the girl involved—refuses to help him, the narrator curses him, wishing him "to get children where you do not want to and none where you do!" (VIII, 300-01). Next day Kari tells him there is no longer any danger. This information is offered incrementally in Part III, interspersed with the political events that constitute its main substance.

In Part III, dated Sweden 1944 (VIII, 243-353), the "I" reports how his search is prolonged by real-life happenings; as he says, he was "overtaken" by what "slowly and uncertainly approached" as he was writing (247). Because of continued leakage of information in the small town where Indregård had been unsuccessfully operating before his breakdown and where he had met Hans Berg, the "I" is sent down, under cover of bank business, to meet with the Resistance group in an attempt to discover the source of the trouble. In an atmosphere charged with mutual suspicion and fear, he does his detective work with creditable skill, but the solution to the problem comes about by chance, and a startling discovery it is. Looking from his hotel window at a Nazi rally, he sees Inga, the lovely maid to one of the group's members, drop a slip of paper into a flowerpot outside the hotel entrance, whereupon a young Nazi storm trooper (*hirdmann*) picks it up. (It appears later that Inga was in love with the storm trooper, Heidenreich's son, who had asked her to play at lovers with the youngest member of the Resistance group for spying purposes.) A few moments later, having a chance to look more closely at the young Nazi as he addresses the rally, to his horror the Blameless One recognizes his own youthful image: "It was myself. I saw myself from my youthful years" (288).[24] He has already learned that Heidenreich lives in town and is married to Kari (Maria), facts that he may have known for a long time but repressed.

The remainder of Part III includes the narrator's meeting with Heidenreich, his subjection to a gruesome beating in Heidenreich's basement—used by the Gestapo—and his rescue through Maria, who takes him to a contact. The rescue, the nocturnal escape to Oslo, and the posthaste departure from his home for Sweden in the very nick of time before the arrival of the pursuers, led by his son, the storm trooper—this is all consciously narrated in the manner of the crime thriller, a favorite of Hoel's used here with symbolic purpose.

The movement of the book's plot can be compared to an infernal vortex. The novel begins with a collective theme that touches the Blameless One only peripherally, since he feels immune to the idea of treason. But after he begins his self-examination, the circles grow smaller and the speed of events faster until he is overwhelmed by the final revelation of having fathered a Nazi. Imagery supports this analogy. Thus, the walk in torrential rain from his hotel and back to report his findings to the group is described in infernal terms: heaven and earth seem reduced to primal chaos, and he feels "on the edge of hell" (VIII, 301). When he enters his hotel room, Heidenreich sits there waiting. The following chapter, "Deep under the Earth," maintains the infernal image, adumbrated already in an early description of the sounds emerging from a German precinct adjacent to the narrator's house in Oslo (18), and continued in the story of Hans Berg and "The Gallery of the Damned"; it is even ominously alluded to in the account of his passionate affair with Kari (232).

The inferno occasionally blends with another image of the central action provided by a modified version of the story of Bluebeard: the "locked room," which acquires an increasingly sinister connotation. It is introduced in connection with Kari's reluctance to be completely candid with him; this is the "serpent in [their] paradise" (VIII, 237-38). Before continuing his notes in Sweden, after learning what Kari's "locked room" in a different sense had contained more than twenty years ago—a Nazi storm trooper—he says that what awaits him is "like opening a door to a dark room, knowing that an adder lies waiting in there, a large one. It says hsss! and strikes you in the throat" (249). The Blameless One applies this image both to the encounter with himself, in revolting distortion, as "traitor, spy, pimp" (291) and to the struggle against Nazism. He feels that he has discovered a vital truth, which takes the form of a tied knot; but he fears that, if he tries to untie it, it will turn out to be "no ordinary rope but a snake which . . . strikes the moment I have untied the knot" (250). The plot is based on a fearful paradox: truth inexorably means tragedy and death. The situation is reminiscent of that of King Oedipus, another searcher for truth whose revelations spell doom.

There exists a dialectic tension between the fearful, often violent energies implicit in these images, energies that impel the plot movement, and the involuted narrative with its many time shifts. One reviewer, the novelist Johan Borgen, suggested a possible danger of the chosen technique, namely, the absence of a coherent action, plot or fiction serving to "fasten reality to the canvas of the imagination." Others saw no problem with Hoel's technique. Thus, the *Times Literary Supplement* reviewer of the English translation noted that the "digressions and self-questionings of the narrator do not retard a dramatic, well-told . . . novel."[25]

Fortunately, one does not have to choose between such extreme views. Clearly, the narrator's reflections and shifting perspective as he moves back and forth in time, until narrative and narrated time merge in the end, slow down the book's pace by in-depth probings into the meaning of what happens. But, conversely, the staggered, dated entries and attendant circumstances, besides contributing to credibility by lending the novel a semi-documentary quality, turn the novel's very telling into suspenseful action. Moreover, some of the great scenes are so overwhelming, in their physical violence, danger, passion, or grief, that the more meditative sections provide a needed esthetic balance to their fierce drama. After the slow reportorial and introspective movement of Part I and Part II respectively, Part III builds up to a furious pace, which is maintained until the epilogue, a coda of calm observation and urgent exhortation. Some individual chapters contain several strata, each with its own distinctive character; consequently, paradoxical conjunctions of pace and rhythm appear, as in the chapter "Shadows from the Past" in Part III, where, during the narrator's rescue by Maria, involving constant risk of detection and death and therefore producing suspense, the former lovers simultaneously enact their obligatory scene after some twenty years of separation. The novel is masterfully constructed, with internal as well as external suspense—so well, in fact, that one forgets that much of the story is based on coincidence.

A Thematic Replay

The following analysis will amplify the previous discussion of familiar Hoel themes like patriarchal tyranny, erotic primitivism, and bad faith. These themes are articulated in *Meeting* with unusual power.

Hoel's view of Nazism was psychologically conditioned. The "roots of Nazism," he writes in a note, are the "human structure that is engendered by sexual repression (and other suppression related to it)" (Ms. Fol. 2324:3), while those who are "in tune (with life, woman, work) are protected against the great mass suggestions."[26] The chief agents of suppression are the fathers, and *Meeting* is Hoel's fiercest attack on the patriarchy. The last part of the epilogue—where the "I," having given up on the all-encompassing synthesis he had hoped for, casts up some fragments for the reader to forge into a pattern—consists largely of imprecations against rule by the old: "It was youth and the life of youth I saw—in a world led and governed and driven into the abyss by old men" (VIII, 379). Preaching a repressive morality predicated on the total depravity of man, the patriarchy eliminates the freedom of natural man and puts up "fences and walls . . . outside you and within you," enmeshing social man, internationally as well as nationally, in a prohibitive network of restrictions whose purpose is "dignity. It [dignity] is the highest form of freedom, and it consists in your no longer being able to move." Instead of love, joy, zest for life, adventure, and rebellion, the patriarchy inculcates career, duty, patience, school, and obedience, with the result that love—and in turn everything else—is betrayed. Prevented from expressing themselves through love, youth's energies become warped in "hatred, rancor, envy and suspicion" (380-81). These feelings are a good soil for Nazism.

This Reichian view of the patriarchy clearly underlies central portions of the novel's action. It accounts for the moral perversion of Hans Berg, whose engrained Christian guilt, despite Satanic revolt, unconsciously pushes him toward self-denigration and self-destruction. In the final analysis, his becoming a Nazi is also a consequence of his repressive upbringing. Similarly, the patriarchy accounts for the "I's" fear of happiness, probably the deepest reason for his abandoning Kari. Both during the love-making with Kari and at the pregnancy crisis, his father is morally present (VIII, 213, 297). But if the failure of the Blameless One to stand by Kari is due to the life-denying morality of the patriarchy, then so is his unwitting implication in Nazism through his illegitimate son, an involvement that is no less real for being practically disavowed. In another concluding fragment, he writes: "I saw Nazism as our illegitimate child. Begotten blindly and cowardly, betrayed in his mother's womb and abandoned, left to fend for himself. And I saw us, the blameless and self-righteous ones, stand there and look at this creature, our child of flesh and blood, and say: 'We do not know you!'" (381).

In *Meeting* erotic primitivism is celebrated even more fervently than in *A Fortnight*. The nature of eros is sacral; the "I's" feelings for Kari are distinctly religious. Because of its transcendent nature, sexual experience poses similar difficulties of description as mystical union, but instead of choosing the path of negative predication often used by mystics, Hoel tries to render the "magic rhythm of joy" through a series of lyrical and apocalyptic images: the overflowing cup, an unfolding rose, flight, the opening of the heavens (VIII, 199-200). Like Vera in *A Fortnight*, Kari is "freer" and "more courageous" than her partner (211); she has within her some of the primordial power that breaks through "walls and fences and reaches the innermost part of us" (212).[27] Through his love of her, the narrator says, he felt he was able to "follow the vibrations of her mind all the way back to her birth, even further, back to the prehistory of mankind. Through her I could behold a remote past when people were happy, sincere, innocent, with a joy as pure as that of the child, like the joy of Adam and Eve on the first day" (236). As in *A Fortnight,* the Reichian concept of matriarchy merges with a biblical Golden Age archetype. By means of his love, the "I" underwent a psychic transformation: all problems were solved once the "meaning of life" had been found: "to love, be loved, be loved, love" (237). He adds a general reflection—a possible reminiscence from Lawrence's *Sons and Lovers*—to the effect that someone who has loved and been loved cannot go entirely wrong in life: he will always have a "domain to fall back on, a fixed point that maintains his equilibrium" (238).

Bad faith and *regard d'autrui* are intimately related to Hoel's conception of Nazism. Hoel says in his notes for the radio interview with Philip Houm in 1951: "We are responsible not only for our own immediate actions. We are also indirectly responsible for all the crooked things we let happen without protesting; we are responsible for all the injustice that others do to others—if we know about it and fail to protest" (Ms. Fol. 2324:6). This view is analogous to Ignazio Silone's idea that the only way to remain free under a dictatorship is to fight it.[28] In this respect the "I" is impeccable: instead of acting like a majority of his countrymen, he is actively fighting tyranny; indeed, he is staking his life in the fight. Nevertheless, this model patriot, the Blameless One, has been guilty of serious bad faith in his relationship with people, particularly women: instead of making a deliberate moral choice, he allowed parental conditioning, conventional notions of the married state, and Kari's silence about the possibility of marriage to determine his actions. Later, in his own marriage, the romantic memory of Kari acted as an alibi for never committing himself to his own wife. This condition of existential inauthenticity is best shown by a trait that haunts many of Hoel's heroes, psychic fragmentation. Thus, arrested on his spying mission, the "I" at one point feels divided into four persons: himself, an observer, young Heidenreich, and Carl Heidenreich (312).

Hoel presents a couple of striking variants on the inauthentic: one concerning Hans Berg, who became a Nazi, the other concerning the founder of Nazism, Adolf Hitler. The intense conflict in Hans Berg between rebel and slave leads to a moral impasse, leaving his actions to be determined by a spiteful, self-destructive obeisance to the *regard d'autrui*: "He who knows he is a pig [from being judged a pig by the standards of morality as mediated by his puritanic father] may think it is good to be allowed to behave like a pig" (VIII, 90). Thus he marries to "expiate a sin," but at the same time "to take revenge on fate, God, the world, himself" (100). Hans Berg fails to exercise authentic moral judgment; he acts, though reversely, as a puppet of parental and social conditioning. The dynamics of Nazism, as the "I" understands it in his "vision" after the torturous beating, operates in the contrary direction, having started with a failed corporal's glorified mirror image of himself—as "lieutenant, captain, major, colonel, general, field marshall, . . . lord and master of the world, trampling with jackboots on all the kneeling peoples of the planet." He watches his mirror image—that is, himself as object—until he is hypnotized; then he hypnotizes others until they see him "as he saw himself" (322). These extreme instances, of the Nazi follower and the Nazi leader, show how Hoel intuitively was able to frame and utilize existentialist concepts to explain crucial sociopsychological phenomena of his time.

The Blameless One: Mask and Reality

The Blameless One, patriot and covert traitor, moral idealist and perpetrator of evil, champion of humanity but deficient in his love of individuals—this man is in some ways a paradoxical figure. The situation is complicated by Hoel's device of "mirroring," whereby a crisscrossing network of psychic identifications is set up between different figures: between Heidenreich and Kari's stepfather, who feels he possesses Kari if his young relative does (VIII, 336); between the narrator, on the one hand, and Heidenreich and Hans Berg; finally, between young Heidenreich and the narrator. These mirrorings, which may suggest unanimism, esthetically resemble the device of the double. Significantly, all characters with whom the Blameless One has an affinity seem to be lower in the moral scale than he. Because of his intimate involvement with some of them, such as Heidenreich and his son, he feels an encroachment upon his moral integrity.

The narrator's moral position is clearly ambiguous. While finally admitting his co-respondibility for Nazism and urging others to wake up and recognize their own covert complicity with evil, Hoel's main character in *Meeting* seems incapable of changing his attitude in concrete situations of choice. This predicament could be viewed as Ibsenesque tragedy. For in the course of the "I's" review of his past, ghosts appear to haunt him, as they haunt Mrs. Alving and John Gabriel Borkman. He has committed an egregious moral crime that overtakes him: like Mrs. Alving he learns that he is by no means "blameless"; like Borkman he has sacrificed a woman's love and thus killed her soul—Kari says her existence is a kind of death-in-life (VIII, 334). But unlike Borkman he did so merely from petty fear and cowardly indecision.

It is certainly possible to understand the "I's" experience in the light of naturalistic tragedy, a form that knows no catharsis. There are signs, however, that Hoel did not intend the tragic wholly to usurp the ethical interest. The decisive argument in this respect is that, after the story proper is ended, the "I" adds an epilogue with a distinctly didactic purpose. But any attentive reader of the conclusion of *Meeting* will perceive a harsh incongruity between the idealistic, quasi-religious sentiments in the epilogue and the total moral impotence of the Blameless One in his last meeting with Kari as well as in his continued refusal to accept his son. Thus, like a modern Christ he embraces the evil-doers, all except the scientific torturers (VIII, 370), but his Nazi son inspires him with the utmost ambivalence (364). One is tempted to conclude that the passionate intensity of his moral zeal and humanitarian rhetoric increases in inverse proportion to his ability to change his own life and to help those for whose predicaments he has acknowledged responsibility.

It seems that Hoel has set up the "I" as a mask, a persona that is, in part, treated ironically. In any case, as the previous discussion shows, there are obvious contradictions between words and deeds, as well as within his system of dominant ideas. Thus, his cognitive orientation is scientific, but the values he assigns to it are religious: he truly believes, judging by the epilogue, that by pushing genetic or causal analysis to the beginnings of individual existence, he can achieve a sort of *unio mystica* with the primordial "roots of things," as they were before we had "specialized" and "isolated" ourselves. If this individual's life could be written down, the reader would also understand his or her own life, with an effect of "deliverance" (*forløsning;* VIII, 375). Once more, ideas of matriarchal prehistory merge with religious redemptionism. The narrator admits, however, that the grandiose, all-encompassing "vision" he supposedly had during his torture, a vision in which the meaning of human history itself was revealed to him, cannot be reproduced. Ironically, the "solution" and the deliverance do not come from his vision but from a fellow human being, Maria (Kari), whose unexpected appearance in the torture chamber, "like a glimpse from an everyday reality," strikes him as "almost disturbing" (324). He is "delivered" by a woman in a practical and ethical way, not by his visionary knowledge of himself and the all. The juxtaposition of mystical rapture and moral praxis cannot be coincidental: Hoel's tacit judgment of his character is felt behind the events.

In any case, the "I's" subsequent behavior shows that he has not really changed as a result of his painful experiences; nor has he been delivered by knowledge. A clue to the reason why this is so may be had from his feelings during the beating, in which Heidenreich is a passionate participant. These feelings are ones of satisfaction at being punished, which he mockingly ascribes to a "Christian view of life" (VIII, 317). His thoughts during the torture circle around "guilt and debt"; at a certain point, however, it occurs to him, "Now we are quits!" (318).[29] Equally significant is his recall, at this time, of how Hans Berg was flogged by his father. *Mutatis mutandis,* the same phrase—"something inside him had got jammed" (*var gatt i baklås*)—appears in both passages (77, 318). Despite its deep satisfaction and its visionary aftermath, the "I's" experience of being beaten seems to have been largely a discharge of guilt accumulated by a residual Christian conscience—a discharge so complete that afterward, with all his protestations of a zealous concern for an erring mankind, he is empty, cold, and indifferent. Notably, after being bandaged by the doctor he feels "armor-plated" (349), and he is as closed off from people at the end as at the outset.[30] Thus, the openings Maria gives him are not picked up; he seems humanly and morally impotent. Moreover, the parallel with Hans Berg makes one wonder whether the narrator, too, is not unconsciously self-destructive.

His attitude is that of the cold, ironic observer, an attitude that finds hyperbolic but meaningful expression through a terrifying dream inspired by the report of Nazi medical experiments he has just heard of. His dream about the anthill connects with an experience that happened, as he notes, in the "eternal and famous year 1921," the year he had his passionate affair with Kari (Maria). After a discarded match set fire to an anthill, he and his friends deliberately fed the flames while studying the behavior of the ants with scientific impassivity. The incident, with its Easter setting, is reminiscent of Raskolnikov's dream in the epilogue to *Crime and Punishment* and, differently, of a recalled incident in Hemingway's *A Farewell to Arms*. But, contrary to the cathartic effect of the dream in Dostoyevsky's novel and the image of life as a trap in Hemingway, here the effect is morally sickening. The dream is particularly ironic because it is preceded by the narrator's passionate condemnation of those who, under the mantle of respectability, use science for evil ends (VIII, 370). While the dream may symbolize something as uncharacteristic of Hoel's view of man as original sin, suggesting that all of us have evil proclivities, the very fact that the narrator has the dream in the first place bespeaks a mind attuned to cold, scientific observation rather than human compassion.

A further point supports this view, while enabling the reader to see the development of the narrator in perspective. In his youth he saw love as an absolute, as a religious experience that justified everything. One of the images used to convey its ecstasy is the ascent of a tall mountain, with an allusion to the temptation of Christ but without any taint of sin in the ability to "see all the kingdoms of the earth and their glory" (VIII, 200). The vast distance traveled by the narrator—who feels totally alienated from his youthful self (183)—is suggested by the use of this same image in a political context, D-Day: "I sat on the bench [in Stockholm] as on a cloud and looked out over all the kingdoms of the earth and their glory" (246). The absolute at this point is the fight for his country's freedom: eros has been sublimated to a political passion. And in this domain he has been anything but a failure. The words in the epilogue, "If you betray love, you betray everything" (380), do not apply to him; they are an instance of guilt-laden rhetoric. However, his active sublimation of the erotic experience, through pursuit of knowledge and politics, has warped the "I's" personality.

Eros united him with another human being and with the all; once it was gone, he could only seek the wholeness he then experienced by intellectual means. This may account for the excessive value he places on knowledge generally. But instead of enabling him to recover and, however imperfectly, participate in the primal harmony he longs for, the research into his own past unveils a horror that he is unable to cope with: knowledge, unlike eros, is not redemptive. The inefficacy of his self-search is shown by the fact that, once it is over, he returns to his previous harsh political attitude. Even after the war is over, this attitude takes the form of an absolute. Consequently, just as at the beginning his reaction to Indregård excludes humanity and compassion, so at the end (1947) he writes about his just-sentenced son, the Nazi storm trooper, and his mother: "All this does not concern me, I know. It is the lives of strangers" (VIII, 7)—a variant on the formula "through with him" applied to former Nazi friends at an early stage of his writing. His passionate concern for mankind, coupled with inability to love individuals, is reminiscent of the predicament of Ivan Karamazov. No wonder Hoel said in a letter that he does not, "without reservations, stand behind the 'morality' which the main character derives from his experiences."[31]

What has been stressed here, to be sure, is not his morality per se but his moral contradictions. Still, Hoel's refusal to be equated with the Blameless One is a sound basis for approaching the novel. One may also note what Hoel says in an editorial comment about Kjølv Egeland's originally rather harsh judgment of the Blameless One in *Guilt and Destiny* (*Skyld og skjebne*, 1960). While disagreeing with Egeland's view, he admits that the critic may be right and that the fellow may be "just as pitiful as he sees him to be" (Ms. Fol. 2356; 2/20/1959).[32]

Summary Evaluation

The critical reception of *Meeting at the Milestone* was very favorable. Of the criticisms that have been made of the book, none is fatal. The plot may seem a bit contrived and melodramatic, but what to one seems contrived, to another will appear ingenious. Some of the women characters have been criticized as sketchy or unreal: thus, Kari has been called anything from a "phantom" to the product of a "boy's fantasy." However, a Swedish reviewer praised the portrayal of women as well as the book's "erotic atmosphere."[33] Yet, the erotic passages—Hoel's attempt to express the inexpressible—are unashamedly sentimental and laced with purple prose. The essayistic conclusion seems portentously inappropriate: the novel's contents are too private and personal for these comprehensive reflections about humankind. The essay may not be totally unrelated to a shortcoming of Hoel's first-person novels, namely, garrulity. At certain moments the mask of the fictive narrator drops and the voice of Hoel is unmistakably heard. But in *Meeting* such lapses are relatively infrequent.

The novel has received high praise both in Norway and abroad. Audun Tvinnereim points out the lavish wealth of its contents in terms of its synthesis of novelistic forms: it is at the same time development novel and love story, cultural-historical fiction and novel with a purpose.[34] But primarily it is a psychological novel. The chief device responsible for its wide scope is that of projecting what happens on a small scale and in private upon history and the public scene: sex and love become transposed to politics and war. The book demonstrates the intricate interrelationships among different spheres of life. About the treatment of one of these spheres, C.P. Snow in a highly favorable review writes that the portrayal of young manhood alone "would make the book distinguished, for the picture is unsparing: the harsh facts of a young man's first love affairs are set down with truth and an astringent nostalgia."[35] One may mention the book's lyricism, its psychological penetration, intricate narrative structure, and profound moral thought as other merits that help make *Meeting at the Milestone* a great novelistic achievement.

7
Postwar Period Novels

Between 1951 and 1956 Sigurd Hoel published three novels that, whatever their individual merits, lack artistic distinction. With its rapid sociocultural change, the postwar scene more than ever brought out Hoel's satiric bent. The satirist's ethos is clearly evident in the naively utilitarian esthetic advocated in his preface to the *Collected Novels and Stories* (1950): "The question every writer puts (or ought to put) to himself is: Do you have a message?" The esthetic concern is secondary, nothing but a means of conveying that message in the "most effective manner" (I, xvi). Though this statement does not truly describe Hoel's overall esthetic practice, it contains a clue to the decline of his fiction in the early and mid-fifties.

COMMON FEATURES AND PROBLEMS

The three novels in question, *I'm in Love with Someone Else* (*Jeg er blitt glad i en annen*, 1951), *Rendezvous with Forgotten Years* (*Stevnemøte med glemte år*, 1954), and *At the Foot of The Tower of Babel* (1956), have, besides their satirical tendency, several other features in common. All contain a variety of literary modes—tragedy and farce, melodrama and the absurd, heroism and the quotidian. These multifarious contents produce mixed genre qualities. *I'm in Love* combines sociopolitical satire with a story of marriage framed by a generation novel; *Rendezvous* mixes social and moral satire with sentimental romance, psychological novel, and epic; and *Babel* combines anti-utopian satire with artist novel and symbolic romance. As in *Meeting at the Milestone,* the detective story, along with psychoanalysis, provides the model for dealing with the theme of self-examination and quest; psychoanalysis is also an important thematic element.

The presence of disparate materials, modes, and forms does not, of course, explain the artistic weakness of these novels; the problem—since Hoel did not profess an esthetic of dissonance—is due to his failure to integrate these elements. A more serious flaw, however, is the absence of a convincing narrative situation. First-person narrative as here used—even where, as in *Babel,* authorial omniscience determines the overall narrative method—is conducive to intellectual self-indulgence, garrulity, and formal looseness. This problem will be briefly examined.

Already in writing *Meeting at the Milestone* Hoel was concerned with developing a persona he could use as narrator in future works (Ms. Fol. 2324:1). But since *I'm in Love* picks up the thread from *Sinners in Summertime* after some twenty years and uses the same characters and their grown children, its narrator is once more Fredrik, now head (*rektor*) of a junior college (*gymnasium*) in Oslo.[1] The manuscript notes for *Rendezvous* show that Hoel this time originally intended to use the Blameless One as narrator but was advised against doing so (Ms. Fol. 2326:1); the text is produced by another Oslo lawyer, Knut Valstad. Though in both cases Hoel struggled to make the persona plausible, Fredrik and Knut are little more than a flimsy camouflage for Sigurd Hoel—social critic, psychologist, moralist, and general gadfly to the powers that be.

The transparency of these narrative personae is evident in several ways. Though both are shown writing notes, even longer sections of manuscript, there is no accounting for the composition of the novels as such, contrary to the careful motivation of the narrative stance in *Meeting,* where the "I's" dated notes not only constitute the story but provide the editorial framework as well. Secondly, Fredrik's and Knut's esthetic personae as "authors" conflict with their civic roles as educator and lawyer, respectively: they are not credible as both at the same time. However, the most problematic aspect of these personae is their failure to present the necessary challenge to Hoel's imagination. A narrator who was sufficiently distinct from the author himself might have enabled Hoel to maintain a certain distance from the sociopolitical scene that provoked his wrath, to dramatize the problems he saw instead of attacking them head on, and to achieve a more concentrated form. Without such a narrator, with a mere "professional" mask, Hoel had free play for the entire range of his personal opinions, including prejudices, obsessions, and pet ideas, while his artistic personality was largely in abeyance.

Though *Babel* is written in the third person, its narrative situation is not very different. The novel contains chapter-long monologues and extensive speeches by several characters that, as far as language is concerned, are nearly indistinguishable from one another. With rare exceptions, Hoel's handling of free indirect discourse is also rather disappointing in this book and unsatisfactory as a means of character portrayal.

SINNERS ISLAND REVISITED

The following discussion will only touch on a few salient points of these three novels, which, however entertaining and readable—Hoel is always readable—do not merit extensive treatment. In *I'm in Love* the themes of aging, life as play, tragedy and triviality are treated within the context of a radical generation's postfestum disillusionment.[2] The approach of age, the loss of creative zest, and the banality of everyday life are much harder to endure for those who were once idealists, who believed that their generation, that of the 1920s, was going to transform the world. However, for their problems to become real and their harsh fates to move us, they must themselves arouse our interest. This they fail to do. Instead of our becoming engrossed in the marital crises of the former "sinners," their lack of contact with youth as represented by their own children, and their self-deceiving maneuvers to live with their imperfections, regrets, and guilts—instead of this, as one reviewer put it, we keep reading the book because of our interest in the author rather than in the characters.[3]

Though a charming performance, the book is neither well composed nor convincing. The marital crisis of Sigrid and Fredrik seems contrived, founded on a tenuous piece of psychoanalytic reasoning: Sigrid's substitution of an old moral debt to her husband by a newer and much larger debt, with accompanying guilt, to the "hero"—now in a wheelchair—who was wounded while escorting them to Sweden during the Occupation. And their crisis is ultimately resolved not through its own inner psychological momentum but through the melodramatic complications—including the suicide of an escaped Nazi convict—perpetrated by the younger generation, now acting out their own follies on the identical spot of Sigrid's and Fredrik's despair and rapture twenty-three years ago. With Hoel's seeming readiness to sacrifice character and a meaningful plot to journalistic topicality and incidental satire, neither the marital conflict nor the generation theme is satisfactorily handled.

HEROISM AND EROS: EXCURSION INTO HISTORY

Like *I'm in Love, Rendezvous with Forgotten Years* is also focused on the relationship between past and present, but whereas the war and the German Occupation play a relatively minor role in *I'm in Love,* in *Rendezvous* they provide the basis of the book's plot.

The novel begins with an Eastertide dinner·commemorating a war hero, Sven Arneberg, killed in 1940 as the leader of a guerilla troop that continued fighting after its regiment had surrendered to the Germans. The dinner party is given by Vera Bang, a famous actress who, after Sven had lost his wife and child in a bombing accident in the early days of the war, spent one night of love with him in his mountain hideout; since then she has reputedly been living for his memory. At the party their son, Kåre, now thirteen, reacts with outrage at some words allegedly spoken by Sven during the romantic encounter—a string of sentimental-utopian clichés that seem out of place coming from an army officer.[4] Kåre's rage initiates the book's dialectic of real and false heroism, truth and the life-lie, the tragic and the trivial—here as in *I'm in Love* a central theme—and sets the stage for the book's plot. Both guests, Sander Paulsen, who participated in Sven's campaign, and Knut Valstad, at one time Sven's legal associate, hesitate to accept the quoted words as Sven's. But they have been sufficiently shaken to start asking questions—Sander about the

nature of the war he participated in, Knut, who is living apart
from his wife, about Sven, with whose "widow," Vera, we later
discover he is having a not-very-satisfactory affair. This situation
has revived an old problem of his, a sense of inferiority toward
Sven largely caused by his inability to participate in action in
1940 because of his mother's illness and death. At Sander's invitation he decides to join him on an Easter excursion where they
will retrace the campaign trail of fourteen years ago. Consequently, Part II of the novel (X, 175-326) is a kind of temporal
picaresque, a quest for a "fourteen-year-old rainbow" (175).

From this point on, the narrative consists of crosscutting between their excursion experiences and the campaign of 1940 as
related mainly by Sander. In some cases the two intersect, as in
the story of Erik Oppi, who has recently committed suicide, apparently because of unremitting persecution over the years by the
big farmer whose employ he left, without notice, on joining the
troop in April, 1940. Here as in *Meeting at the Milestone*, but
with a different emphasis, Hoel is exploring national attitudes:
now the question largely concerns what happened to those who,
when official government broke down, had the courage to continue the struggle. The answer, though anything but conclusive,
points up the complacency and deficient national spirit of the
mass of Norwegians after 126 years of uninterrupted peace.

By contrast with such attitudes, the guerillas come to seem a
band of adventurers, crusaders, or quixotic knights errant who
renounce the security of civilian life for an absurd ideal at the risk
of their lives. The analogy of Christ and his disciples is the most
sublime expression of their total devotion: it is manifest in the
presence of a Judas figure, in the Emmaus-like apparition of
Sven to Knut toward the end of the novel (X, 396), and in the
commemorative nature of the Eastertide dinner. The troop's high
spirit, self-sacrifice, and potential tragedy also sharply contrast
with, and are heightened by, the moral decadence and emotional
placidity of life in the welfare state as depicted by Hoel. As increasing numbers flock to Sven's banner, attracted by the sense of
adventure that surrounds the campaign, the novel's mid-section
acquires the character of a folk epic. This quality is enhanced by
the plurality of narrative voices, as well as by the perceived analogies with well-known epic quests of the past and, in particular,

with Norwegian fairy tales. Though the novel's ending is one of anticlimax, *Rendezvous* lacks neither external nor internal suspense.

The book's component parts, however, pull in different directions. Thus, its frame is romantic and individualist, its main substance moral-political and collective. This discrepancy can be attributed to implausible character portrayal as well as to weak composition. In terms of character, the psychological complex of the narrator, exacerbated by his affair with Vera, seems a feeble pretext for an exploration of the national past. Similarly, the novel's ending accentuates the narrator's egomania: to Knut, the chief interest of the 1940 campaign seems to be his own attainment of inner peace. From a compositional perspective, the resolution of Knut's problem, with his announced return to a waiting wife after an apocalyptic erotic experience with Vera, ends a work of quasi-epic scope on a trivial note. Furthermore, the detective story follow-up to Vera's affair with Sven, due to her obstetrician's Buchmanite conversion, seems both contrived and inappropriate. While it is a subject of obvious interest to the narrator, who is both Vera's lover and her lawyer, it excessively skews the final portion of the book toward sensationalism, even prurience. The confessing doctor asserts that Kåre's birth certificate was falsified in order to allow Vera to claim Sven's paternity for a child that was not fathered by him. Thus, the dénouements to Sven's and Knut's stories show, first, how heroism is cheapened and trivialized as an exhibit in a shoddy private drama; second, how epic adventure fizzles out in aborted romance and domestic idyll.

Thematically, the novel is almost equally shot through with contradictions. On the one hand, the action is carried forward by the search for truth—the truth about the war, about Sven, about Vera—and by a veritable moral passion that opposes real values to false romanticism. But the narrator's attitude is not consistent, and his final position seems not only ambiguous but vacillating.

Sven and Vera enact, in different form, the same conflict that tore apart Dr. Ravn and his wife, except that eros and scientific research have been replaced by eros and the work of war. However, while *One Day in October* is quite evenhanded in its treatment of the sexes, in *Rendezvous* Sven, the patriotic leader, becomes a shining ideal—a "monumental banality," in one critic's words[5]—whereas Vera is painted in dark, demonic colors suggestive of vampirism. The doctor's story clinches this contrast by casting a curious new light on Sven's predicament immediately before his death. Sven's lonely decision to stay behind with the machine gun when the troop withdrew could be traced to erotic disenchantment: he may have seen through Vera's promiscuity. In a later comment Hoel states that Sven was "fooled both by events in general and by Vera in particular" (Ms. Fol. 2356; 6/10/1960). A similar blackening of Vera comes about through the effect of the doctor's confession on Knut, in that it enables the fugitive husband to free himself from the adventuresome actress's erotic toils. Such implausible attitudes cannot be sustained with consistency, and in the end the narrator, Knut Valstad, places himself in an untenable position.

Having confirmed his old, admiring view of Sven, Knut, as lawyer to Vera, gradually sees through the layers of pretense, fantasy, and myth with which she has embellished her existence. His revulsion is shown by the fact that, after returning from her embrace for the last time, he takes a ritual shower, then calls his wife to tell her he will be moving back home (X, 398). Yet, in defending Vera against the doctor's charge, he has himself had recourse to legal fictions that, to a lay mind, appear to be barefaced lies. The use of Pilate's question, "What is Truth," as a chapter title (354) indicates that the attitude of quest for truth with which the book opens has, wittingly or unwittingly, been subverted.[6]

But there is another side to the narrator's view of Vera and Sven, one that is not unrelated to this ticklish question of truth. Just before his ritual shower, Sven and Vera are juxtaposed in Knut's thoughts as belonging to the same order of being: "Men like Sven, I thought—and women like Vera, why not—must they always . . . be victims of the lying and swindle which overflow the world we live in from east and west, north and south . . . ?" (X, 397-98). Though dismissed as a "sleepwalker's dream," these thoughts acquire a meaningful context from the contemptuous attitude to bourgeois morality expressed by Vera a few hours earlier: to her, the only valid morality is that of art and erotic fulfillment. Vera hates lies, she tells Knut, but she is forced to lie because men cannot bear to know the truth (380, 390). Here Sven and Vera appear as a hero and an avatar of eros, respectively—the necessary sources of courage, vitality, and creativity to ordinary mortals, the latter equally incapable of exemplary heroism as of avowed immoralism. Viewed in this perspective, Knut's acquiescence in being second to Sven—or to the memory of Sven—in Vera's affections and his renunciation of the chance to ascend with her to the "highest peak of existence" as she had done with Sven (389), may express Hoel's recognition that these are largely symbolic figures who, however inspiring or awesome, must eventually be abandoned to the realm of myth.

The difficulty of finding a consistent meaning in the relationship of Sven and Vera and of explaining their treatment in a satisfactory manner is only one of the problems facing the reader of *Rendezvous*. It may point to a serious flaw in the novel's conception: the book's intent is by no means clear. Like Hoel's other novels during the same period, it deals with too many themes and is deficient in unity as well as in concentration. For example, the characters belong to disparate orders of reality. The difference that sets off Sven—lofty, vague, and ideal despite being based on a friend of Hoel's[7]—from everybody else may largely be due to literary reminiscence. Sven's unflinching courage, fidelity, and desire to test himself recall Conrad's Lord Jim, who is referred to in Hoel's notes (Ms. Fol. 2326:1); and both his erotic adventure with Vera in the chalet and his solitary death behind the machine gun to protect his comrades may have been suggested by Hemingway's *For Whom the Bell Tolls*, which deals with a similar kind of warfare. By contrast, Knut Valstad and Sander Paulsen, chief questers and narrators, are supposedly realistic, but their language is so pale and polished as to make them nearly indistinguishable from one another; both have an air of abstraction about them. Most lifelike are some of the rural figures, whose language is individualized through dialectal idiom.

AN ATTEMPT AT ARTISTIC RENEWAL

At the Foot of the Tower of Babel was started, judging by Hoel's manuscript notes, before *Rendezvous* but was put aside because he had not found the right characters to embody his central idea. If he were to write it then, it would turn into more of a "journalistic novel" than he would care to write (Ms. Fol. 2327:1; 5/25/1953). The idea, namely, that we live in a "spiritual interregnum," is mentioned already in his notes for *I'm in Love* (Ms. Fol. 2325:1). Derived, most likely, from Arthur Koestler's *The Yogi and the Commissar* (1945) and mentioned in his 1946 preface to his own translation of the same author's *Arrival and Departure* (*De siste 51 gule*, 41), this notion underlies much of Hoel's thinking in the 1950s. Yet, an early chapter can be traced to 1934, as part of a planned "lightweight" novel that was never written. Several elements stem from that time: the psychoanalytic catchphrase *"Verwirrung der Gefühle"* (confusion of feelings) that lurks behind the book's working title, "Time of Confusion"; the impingement of dreams on reality; the conflict between two kinds of love and a related quest for identity; and the motif of a taxi chase for a lost love (Ms. Fol. 2327:2; 1934). These themes and motifs are obviously connected with the psychoanalysis that Hoel was undergoing at the time.

The book's premise is that the old forms of belief— Christianity, Marxism, psychoanalysis—no longer hold. It is expressed in the following leitmotif: "The gods are dead . . . and people run around confused, like stray dogs." However, the confusion of values is only intermittently conveyed, through characters who often seem like puppets in an authorial performance. More bitterly than ever, Hoel in *Babel* uses his characters as vehicles of social criticism. Moreover, though it deals with important problems and is quite suspenseful, the novel largely fails on account of its weak composition.

Babel deals with four men, friends from the Occupation period whose lives have, for some reason, gone awry in the postwar welfare state. One of the four, Jørgen Bremer, a brilliant economist and philosophical skeptic, commits suicide when he realizes the human costs of the government plan he has devised for rationalizing Norway's shoe industry; he has come to see it as a step on the path to the "soulless" paradise to which modern technology seems to doom the world (XI, 151). The other three, while surviving, are discontented with their lots: Anders Dyring has cynically prostituted his artistic talent as a popular portrait painter; Jens Tofte gave up painting for economics and jour-

nalism in order to support a family; and Klaus Tangen, who left
his engineering position to devote himself to writing, is eking
out a living as a translator. Through these men Hoel seems to say
that, in the welfare society, art and literature—culture, in short—
are anything but matters of first priority, a theme we recognize
from *Open Sesame*. The subject is a topical one, lending itself to
journalistic treatment, a temptation that Hoel has not been able
to resist. The novel's loose, lopsided composition is evident from
the fact that the bulk of the space is devoted to one of the four
characters, Anders Dyring. The fates of Tofte and Tangen are
treated so superficially as to remain indifferent to the reader,
despite the new note of optimism struck by the successful resolution of their problems.

The book's deeper themes are embodied in Bremer and Dyring.
Bremer soon finds his philosophical relativism to be wanting,
and Dyring struggles throughout to move beyond his moral ni-
hilism. More than any of his novels, *Babel* shows Hoel trying to
break through to a new Weltanschauung, one that transcends
scientific rationalism and psychological determinism. The most
extreme example of this is the chilling use of Dyring's parapsy-
chological experience in the first chapter for the purpose of fore-
shadowing (XI, 8). Other experiences of Dyring, while less
dramatic, are more persuasive. To him, so-called reality has been
only a "mocking and distorted dream, or the fragments of such a
dream" (213). Only in certain special states of actual dreaming
and in "rare, sacred moments" of heightened perception of nature do we receive glimpses of a "deeper and more authentic
reality," glimpses that intimate "coherent meaning" as well as
"bliss."[8] It is around such experiences that Dyring has formed
what he calls his religion (249, 215, 248).

Interestingly, in an interview in 1954, Hoel hints at the possibility of religion without god: he speaks of crusaders without a
cross, and states that the human psyche is broad enough to contain both god and devil within it.[9] This is a view of the psyche
that would have met with approval from Carl Jung: if the gods
are dead, the time may have come for new gods to be born from
within. It may be more than a coincidence that the shadowy
mystery woman chased desperately by Anders Dyring throughout
Babel, as in a dream—a woman he needs for his new psychic

integration—seems like an embodiment of the Jungian anima.
Though she eludes him, Anders' constant yearning for her constitutes the chief motive force of the novel's action; only through
fidelity and love will he be able to escape his metaphysical
emptiness.

The new concept of guilt that is embodied in the novel is
equally important. In the same interview of 1954, Hoel sees the
sense of guilt as a sign of "spiritual health and human worth";
without it, for example, no human being would take the trouble
to develop the "life of the intellect."[10] This concept is conveyed
through Jørgen Bremer. In an interesting chapter in modernistic
style, Bremer's psychic fragmentation is expressed by means of a
counterpoint of inner voices; it is one of these voices, a sort of
ethical superego whose moral stringency knows no compromise,
that drives him to render and carry out the death sentence on
himself. Though Bremer's is a pathological case, the inner voice,
like the anima figure, raises the possibility of reconstituting religion and morality, and the values they sanction, on a new basis.

It is evident here that Sigurd Hoel was undergoing significant
intellectual change in the 1950s. The change is quite apparent in
Babel. Yet, the novel does not manifest a corresponding formal
change. Though, as Kjølv Egeland has shown, it draws upon an
unusually varied assortment of devices—omens, dreams, symbols, voices, and powers—that transcend the intellectual universe
of vulgar rationalism, these devices fail to produce the "internal
pattern" that Egeland says is intended.[11] The novel lacks the
radically new esthetic conception that alone would have produced a satisfying novelistic structure. As if to compensate for
this lack, it entertains with diverting digressions and topical satire, turning into what Hoel called a "superficial causerie about
indifferent matters."[12] That is, it gets bogged down in the trivial
"distorted dream" of a reality that, according to the novel's logic,
ought to be transcended or transfigured. Disappointingly, arch-
conventional means are used to convey the new quest: a series of
long psychoanalytic monologues that, however therapeutic, are
nevertheless plodding and dull; a concluding sermon by the
anima figure, now prepared to sign her name; and an exhortatory
poem by Nordahl Grieg (1902-43), quoted by her for everybody's
edification. Hoel does not seem to have been ready to re-educate

himself esthetically as well as to grow spiritually, but it is highly regrettable that he failed to do so.

8
Erotic Romance and Fate Tragedy

The Family Dagger (1941) and *The Troll Circle* (1958) are two historical novels that form a fictional unity, though each can be read and enjoyed independently of the other. Referred to originally under one title, "The Novel from Odalen" (Hoel's birthplace), both novels capture, as Hoel hoped they would, "the fragrance . . . of an old time," "the atmosphere . . . of a remote hamlet in time past" (Ms. Fol. 2323:5). But all the important characters are fictitious. The central figure in both books is Håvard Viland, a young man from Telemark who suffers an exceptionally harsh fate: he is executed at thirty-eight for the alleged murder of his wife. *The Family Dagger* has a time span of about a year (1817-18) and brings the action up to Håvard's marriage. *The Troll Circle,* which relates the turns and twists of circumstance that lead to Håvard's doom, extends over some ten and a half years but with a lightly sketched temporal hiatus of almost nine years. Since *The Troll Circle* is twice the length of *The Family Dagger,* the density of treatment is fairly uniform throughout: both novels have a basically scenic composition.

The differences between the two works pertain to mood, theme, and style. Despite some ominous features, especially toward the end, *The Family Dagger* emits an aura of light and of shimmering lyricism; by contrast, *The Troll Circle* is dark in mood and sardonically ironic in tone. In the former the action is largely shaped by Håvard's erotic escapades, while the latter focuses on a social theme, namely, Håvard's endeavor to modernize the backward community in the East Country where he has settled. Finally, *The Family Dagger* is written in a prefigurative romantic style, whereas *The Troll Circle* is basically realistic. In the light of these differences, *The Family Dagger* could be called erotic romance, *The Troll Circle* fate tragedy. Seen as a continuously unfolding action, however, the story of Håvard Viland fulfills the requirements of tragedy from beginning to end.

GENESIS

The impetus for these two books came from a specific childhood experience. As a boy Hoel heard from his family's head servant—the model of Embret in *The Road*—about an execution for murder that had taken place in his native village in 1833.[1] The spot where the grisly beheading occurred lay behind the place where the Hoels' servants' quarters were later situated. Around age twelve or thirteen, Hoel claims to have found the executioner's block in a rail fence below the meadow; he saw the "crescent-shaped incision" for the head and could make out "five distinct marks" made by the bungling, half-blind executioner's ax. The boy kept his discovery as a "precious, slightly sinister secret." However, his novel was not intended to be the story of that murderer, a "brute" who had killed his pregnant sweetheart. What interested Hoel was the "cycle of myths" that had formed around the murder, myths containing "glimpses from an old time" in which the Nordic Middle Ages were still "vividly alive."[2]

The exceptionally long period of gestation had a profound effect upon the nature of the book's genesis and, in turn, upon its esthetic properties. As his copious manuscript notes show, Hoel usually began a novel with an idea or a set of ideas. Apart from defining these ideas more precisely, the creative process consisted mainly in inventing the necessary characters and shaping an appropriate action. But in this case the process seems to have been reversed. Writing about *The Troll Circle* in 1942, Hoel says that the action is clear "in all essentials," probably because the book has "come into being over a very long time" and "has developed 'by itself' through changing phases of my own life. In those phases I myself have changed and my outlook has changed."

What he hopes for, he notes, is that "the action itself," along with the characters, "will create its own idea, . . . independently of a plan laid in advance." In this way the reader "escapes the hazard which a too conscious idea entails," namely, to have his mood spoiled from seeing through the author's purpose (Ms. Fol. 2323:5). The extraordinary vitality of the characters and the elemental power of the action, especially in *The Troll Circle*, probably stem to a large degree from these circumstances.

The overall plan for the "novel from Odalen" was put together in the early 1940s when Hoel lived in his native village. After *The Family Dagger* appeared in 1941, he went on to its sequel and, before his flight to Sweden in the fall of 1943, wrote several early chapters as well as parts of subsequent ones. But the bulk of *The Troll Circle* was written during seven months of continuous work, "from morning till night," in 1958. When the manuscript was finished on August 14, he wrote his Swedish friend, the publisher Kaj Bonnier: "I ought to be relieved, but I am a little too tired." In other letters he speaks of "insane pressure" and of never before having gone through "such a long continuous period of work *at top capacity*."[3] In an interview in 1959, where he calls *The Troll Circle* his "best work," he said: "In the final section, where Håvard is beheaded, it was terrible. It felt as though I was laying my own head upon the block." When the work was over he thought he would "never again write novels. But at the same time I thought that now I could die in peace."[4] Compared to imaginative labor of this order, the numerous stylistic revisions of his manuscript—changes that testify to a concern with tone and with the mot juste worthy of Flaubert—must have been a relief. Generally, these revisions are aimed toward a more concise, graphic manner of expression, one nearer to vernacular or folk idiom, even in narrative passages (Ms. Fol. 2326:6).

THE UNDERLYING CONCEPTION

It has been stated that the novel's main action was clear to Hoel at an early stage and that he realized the esthetic advantage of its idea emerging from the action and the characters. Yet his manuscript notes bear witness to a protracted struggle to clarify the underlying conception. Seemingly, he started with an analytical definition of what is usually called "fate" in human life—the "inexorable, . . . inescapable quality which marks the lives of all people . . . but occasionally is heightened to something terrifying, monumental." His composite, nonmetaphysical concept of fate is based on the interaction of character and circumstance; it denotes "everything that springs from the conflict between one's own primitive will to life . . . and all that resists it, outside and within oneself." The special form of fate that he will explore is represented by what is called *nemesis*—"that old transgressions, or what is perceived as transgressions, avenge themselves" (Ms. Fol. 2323:3; 11/20/1940). Following this definition, the action would portray a man "who seeks to escape his fate but is thereby precisely overtaken by it" (Ms. Fol. 2323:2; 2/1/1941, 1/31/1941).

However, another theme soon emerges to compete for supremacy in Hoel's thought. Phrased in the poet Henrik Wergeland's words, it formulates a central concern of the Enlightenment: "Why does humankind progress so slowly?" (1831). In an extended note from March, 1941, Hoel says that the book will succeed only if it can present this idea and the original one as a "unity." As a bridge between the two themes he proposes the "fear of happiness," a notion that is familiar from previous novels. Such fear, in Hoel's view, is the fundamental cause of collective inertia and stagnation as well as of the individual's attitude of willing "surrender" to his fate, an attitude that produces that very "fate" (Ms. Fol. 2323:3).

Though Hoel's refinements of these thoughts after the publication of *The Family Dagger* produced nothing radically new, they show that *The Troll Circle*, where the theme of "progress" takes the form of the community's *"reaction to the new"* represented by Håvard, posed further difficulties to thematic unity. Still dubious whether he has brought his two major themes under a "common denominator," he reflects at length on the social and individual ramifications of the "fear of happiness"; the latter, he notes, "ought to be the principal theme" that subsumes all the others. This deepest root of the failure of human self-determination could also, he says, be called "fear of nemesis." He continues: "And the strange thing is that nemesis, the retribution for happiness, strikes precisely *because one was afraid of happiness.* Retribution for happiness strikes the one who, despite everything, seeks happiness but does not dare to seize it for fear of punishment." Here, he says, is a "real vicious circle," what the book's title designates as a "troll circle." Seen in this light, human beings appear as "blind, or at least half-blind, creatures who reel forward and backward, in a circle or a spiral, controlled by irrational impulses—by the past within them and about them—even when they believe they are led by lucid reason." Wergeland's question, "Why does humankind progress so slowly?" is answered thus: "The Middle Ages within us. The past within us. The fear within us. Original sin . . ." (Ms. Fol. 2323:5; 3/14/1942).

These thematic ideas, united by a psychoanalytically based view of man, imply that Hoel's excursion into history was anything but an evasive move away from the reality of his own time. While he admits that the fate of his protagonist would have been less "inexorable" today, the action must, he notes, show "the general features in men and society that are the same at all times." For there to be a tragedy with "real fate" in it, one he will be interested in writing, it must be true to the period but remain of continual interest. With his lifelong struggle against religious obfuscation, intellectual mediocrity, and reactionary politics, Hoel shows particular awareness of the work's relevance to the ideological conflicts of his own time (Ms. Fol. 2323:2). Apart from such substantive considerations, he notes the chief esthetic reason for setting his story in a remote time, namely, to allow its "motive forces" to stand out clearly and in depth. The simple milieu and the temporal distance, at variance with the very nature of a "modern novel," will help to bring out the "interplay" between the forces that shape human destiny, powerful forces from the past such as "heredity, tradition, conscience, guilt"—which we call "irrational when they do not suit us"—as well as from the present, in turn largely "determined by the past" (Ms. Fol. 2323:3).

THE FAMILY DAGGER

With its erotic theme, *The Family Dagger* embodies only part of this tragic conception. The conflict between light and dark, progress and fate, finds adequate expression neither in Hoel's description of the milieu nor in the character portrayal. The East Country backwater where this conflict is enacted is only lightly sketched, and Håvard is not yet a champion of progress and enlightenment. That role belongs to his employer, Peder Thurmann, while Håvard is mainly a figure of erotic romance. The two parts of Hoel's conception have yet to come together in a tragic synthesis.

The Story

The external action is quite simple. In the winter of 1817 Reverend Thurmann, a typical Enlightenment clergyman, leaves Upper Telemark for a larger and richer parish in the East Country. When Håvard, who has been Thurmann's head servant since returning from the war in the fall of 1814, is invited to go along to the new place, he hesitates. Through an itinerant female beggar from Håvard's native hamlet, we discover some of the reasons for his indecision; they are amplified by his own thoughts in a chapter entitled "Håvard Sings and Thinks" (VII, 183-98). Håvard, who cannot resist women's tears, has a tendency to run away from the consequences of having promised too much to too many women. But now the crisis concerns his secret betrothed, Tone, whose faithful love has been a lodestar in his amorous divagations. Tone is the sole heir to a wealthy farmer, who, when Håvard asked for his daughter's hand after she had flatly rejected her father's candidate, refused him with contempt as a fortune hunter. As the second son in a farm family, Håvard is propertyless; and though he has had many different jobs and made a good deal of money since his adventuresome life began at the age of fifteen, he has put little aside. Reluctant to ask his father's help, he decides to accept the clergyman's offer, thinking that, as manager of the new parsonage for a couple of years, he might save enough money to buy his own farm. The alternative—to marry Tone immediately with a special license and settle down as a cotter somewhere, possibly for life—he finds too humiliating even to consider.

Though people say that this time he would be trying to escape

his "fate," not just women, if he left home (VII, 179), Håvard
himself comes to think the contrary: if he left—"ran away as they
called it—he did not run away; but if he did not run away, for fear
of village gossip, then he did run away" (197). Yet, within less
than a year of his departure, his erotic proclivities have involved
him, first, with Anne Margrethe, the parson's daughter; second,
with Rønnau, a bewitching, well-to-do widow; and he barely
escapes being inveigled into an affair with a pretty dairy maid.
Anne Margrethe seduces him with her tears at a posting station
on the way to joining her future husband in Christiania.
Rønnau, who has become interested in him at a country wedding, invites him to visit her on the pretext of wishing to improve
her farming. Before he knows what has happened, he has succumbed to her heady allure. A few months later, after entertaining him and the parson as guests once in between, she tells
Håvard she is pregnant. Håvard decides to do the "honorable"
thing. But in this case doing right by Rønnau involves him in
dishonor at home; for Tone, when she hears the news of his
imminent wedding, throws herself into the waterfall. Thus, the
novel's conventional ending, Håvard and Rønnau's wedding, has
a tragic undertow.

Themes and Structure

The central theme of *The Family Dagger* is articulated by
Reverend Thurmann. Speaking to Håvard of his endeavors to
"deliver" the gifted Norwegian people from its "thousand-year-
long sleep," he compares it to a "bewitched prince" who, during
his inert sleep, dreams of "devils and witches, paralyzing magic,
evil eyes that cause misfortunes, omens and prophecies that have
the power of sorcery." The bewitchment, he says, "consists precisely in this dream from a nocturnal world, which in reality
belongs to a remote past, which *is* this past, namely, the ruins of
it in the minds of men" (VII, 202). The novel's basic conflict pits
these chthonic forces against human reason and freedom. The
benighted local population and Reverend Thurmann—the "potato priest" to whom genuine enlightenment is a synthesis of
"true science and true Christianity" (251)—represent opposing
forces in this conflict; but while the parson complains about the

farmers' unteachableness, no dramatic conflict arises. And though Håvard is Thurmann's disciple, so to speak, having been apprenticed—at the parson's cost—to the greatest agricultural expert in Norway, he is not yet at odds with the community, since he has had no opportunity to try out his ideas. It is chiefly on the psychological level, within Håvard himself, that reason and the irrational, light and darkness, freedom and fate meet in classic conflict.

The dark world emerges in a cluster of folklore motifs, introduced by the itinerant beggar ("The Female Beggar Relates," VII, 169-81) and by Håvard himself. Appearing in legends, ballads, and other bits of folk verse (*stev*), these motifs help to characterize the milieu as well as Håvard; moreover, they have a prefigurative function. Repeated at decisive stages of the action, they shape our view of Håvard's character and foreshadow future plot developments.

Most of these folklore motifs are found in a legend about Håvard's progenitor. This legend exists in two versions, both of which present him as an outlawed knight who suffered a tragic fate. According to the community's version, he ran off with a witch—or the King's daughter—and sought refuge in Håvard's remote valley. When the King tracked him down, the woman jumped into the waterfall and the knight was executed. The family legend that Håvard recalls represents him as a preacher of the "new faith" who was bewitched by a pagan woman, so that he forgot his mission. But one day, after being married to her for many years and living like a heathen, he hears the church bells and returns to the faith (VII, 193). The ballad about Vilemann and Signe that Håvard likes so much is supposedly about this knight, though it differs considerably from both versions of the legend. In the ballad, Vilemann rides to the mountain to release his sister, goes "astray," and falls under the spell of a troll or giantess (*gyger*). She gives him "three magic potions," causing him to forget who he is and why he has come. One day, after living with the mountain troll for many years, he is liberated from the magic spell through his rediscovered sword, whereupon he kills her. With her last glance she imprints a mark on his flesh, right below the heart, the exact spot where Håvard has a birthmark. Due to her dying curse, Vilemann fails even now to recognize his sister, who has been the troll's maid throughout all these years, and marries her. When one day the sound of the church bells causes them to recognize one another, they commit suicide (195).

These ominous legends are extended by family traditions and predictions. Havard's dagger, the family's finest heirloom, was supposedly once a sword owned by a giant who had killed a dragon with it. Afterwards it got into the hand of the outlawed knight. Though diminished, it is still sharp as a razor. Håvard received it from his grandfather, because he had "the birthmark in the right place" (VII, 178). At his sister's wedding, a witchlike cousin of this grandfather scrutinizes Håvard and addresses a couple of sibylline quatrains (*stev*) to him. One is about the family dagger: "If you draw it in your own yard, / it will be your death." Though he dismisses her words as "stuff and nonsense," next day, in a fight provoked by his drunken rival, Håvard is within an inch of murder. The woman's oracular saying is part of an old prophecy that once in every third generation a man of the Viland family will commit murder because of women; the most recent man to whom it happened was Håvard's great-grandfather. The second prediction says that women will be his "fate" and warns him to watch out for widows and orphans (177).

In the actual narrative these motifs are introduced quite naturally, through the beggar's story and Håvard's thoughts, without any impression of romantic excess. The same applies to the subsequent recurrence of selected motifs, especially from the ballad.[5] The dominant ones are those of going "astray" and being put under a spell (*bergtaking;* lit. "being taken into the mountain"), which, along with dreams and visions, turn up whenever Håvard is in a situation of crisis.[6] In *The Family Dagger* three major moments stand out: (1) when, in charge of the parson's move, Håvard must decide whether to recommit himself to his service; (2) when he brings Anne Margrethe to Christiania for her wedding; and (3) when he rides north to appraise Rønnau's farming. Every one of these situations involves an actual or future relationship with a woman.

On the first occasion, while Tone is constantly in Håvard's thoughts, physically he is already moving away from her. Partly to keep awake, partly for sheer pleasure, Håvard sings the ballad of Vilemann and Signe and other snatches of folk lyrics. The first song that occurs to him is about a "dwarf maiden" casting a spell on a rider who has lost his way; a supporting quatrain contains a variant on the same theme. The refrain in both songs expresses the thought of going astray and not finding the "way out" or the "way home." The chthonic nature of the forces at work is suggested by the echo (*dvergemålet*) that comes back to him from the mountain, sounding as though it rises from "under the ice" (VII, 188-89). The part that he sings of Vilemann and Signe—introduced already through Anne Margrethe's humming during the beggar's story (172)—deals characteristically with going astray, being received into the mountain, and being wined by the "lady" (194-95). These songs create a countercurrent to the general direction of Håvard's conscious thoughts, which confirm his love of and loyalty to Tone.

The two remaining situations involve Håvard's seduction by Anne Margrethe and Rønnau, respectively. After hearing the story of Håvard from the beggar, Anne Margrethe views him as a figure of high romance, a mood evoked by the "greenish starlight" that streams "dreamily" through her window (VII, 182). During the seduction, this moonlight motif, suitably varied, appears twice; indeed, their moments together are measured by the changing shape of the illuminated square on the floor (267, 270). But chiefly it is a few lines from the ballad that express the mood and the theme of their encounter. The stanzas cited, again by way of singing, are suited perfectly to their action and conversation. The ceremonial quaffing of wine in the ballad is reflected, in somewhat oblique fashion, by Anne Margrethe's rather heavy drinking, apparently to summon up courage for the seduction (262-64). Moreover, the reference to the sister in the ballad assumes unexpected relevance to the situation when Anne Margrethe tells Håvard that, ever since he saved her from drowning—a faked accident—the day he first arrived, she has looked upon him as a brother. Though these allusions to incest are for the benefit of the reader rather than Håvard, another ballad stanza that he laughingly hums after the episode expresses a strange sense of identification with the incestuous Vilemann, his putative ancestor. The crucial line concerns the magic spell, with all its connotations of lost purpose and identity: "It was as though it had happened to someone else, to a relative of his, as it were. Or as though it had happened far back in time, the kind of thing they made ballads about in the old days" (273).

The climax of *The Family Dagger* is Håvard's seduction by Rønnau, a handsome widow in her early thirties and thus somewhat older than he. In this incident Håvard, the potential lightbringer, is vanquished by the powers of darkness. The titles of the relevant chapters, "Up North in the Woods," and "Now I Lock and Close . . .," allude to the ballad theme. The ride north through the forest to Rønnau's farm is like a passage to a dark realm, unpleasant and frightening, that Håvard equates with the "mountain," with being bewitched. Though the journey reinforces his decision of soon rejoining Tone and leaving these parts—whose inhabitants remind him of gnomes or goblins (*underjordiske*, VII, 314)—ironically it brings him within the troll circle.

At this point the allusions to the ballad are all implicit; even the one line Håvard recalls—about having come under a spell ("found the blue mountain," VII, 339)—is part of a dream during his stay. Whether in the form of dream, thought, or physical movement, Håvard now *enacts* the prefigurations contained in the book's motif structure. There being no proper road, he loses his way and must retrace his steps; the same phrase (*pa villstrå*—"astray") is used in the ballad (194, 317). Once he comes within viewing distance of the "long black" farmhouse, it looks as though it has "grown out of the earth" (318). Rønnau herself, while pretending to be interested in his explanations and advice, is clearly an unregenerate traditionalist who, whatever she may have seen of novelty, has "closed and locked behind her." Through Håvard's occasional sensation that he is up against a "wall" in talking to her (328), one discerns the mountain troll. Håvard does not know what is concealed behind this wall, nor can he understand the meaning of her "hidden smile," a frequent motif that, to the reader, betrays Rønnau's erotic design. The double appearance of the house as a "royal mansion" from afar and a "troll's place" from close up plays with the contrasting fairy-tale themes of fortune's favorite and the bewitched prince (332).

All these hints are preparations for the last evening when,

contrary to his intention of departing before nightfall, Håvard is wined and dined until, as if in a dream, Rønnau "locks and closes" behind him. The seduction, and its anticipation through dream, comes to us by way of Håvard's retrospection during his return. He recalls having dreamed on his first night at Rønnau's that he was out "looking for his own girl, went astray, and got into the mountain of the troll, who was no troll [gyger] but a handsome woman—Rønnau herself" (VII, 338). The text at this point suggests that Håvard's thoughts and physical movements move around and around, without end: he is within the troll circle. A reminder of his light dismissal of the old woman's prediction and warning, "stuff and nonsense" (177, 339), shows the chasm between his superficial rationalism and the dark fate that has overtaken him. All it takes to seal this fate is the parson's illness and the untimely coming of winter, which prevents Håvard's intended trip home. Soon he is heard humming his ballad once more (344), as though enthralled by his tragic ancestor.

Håvard's Character

Though the romantic prefiguration used in *The Family Dagger* seems to spell determinism, even predestination, Håvard comes across as a young man of exceptional intelligence, courage, and humanity; he is determined to lead his life the way he wants to, regardless of family legends and prophecies. To his fellow compatriots in Telemark he has many of the qualities they prize: cheerful and affable, he is a good skier, fiddler, and dancer, an excellent storyteller and singer of ballads. Not surprisingly, these qualities, together with his striking appearance, make him especially attractive to women. His chief faults seem forgivable— a quick temper, suggested by his "impetuous, even violent" appearance, together with a hint of softness as shown in his weak mouth (VII, 159). But these faults are fateful in their outcome: his impetuousness brings him to the brink of murder, and his sensitivity—not only about butchering but anything that might cause pain to people, animals, or even trees or flowers— engenders a compassion so excessive as to cause him to act against his better judgment. Generally, his overall good intentions are not firm enough to carry him through if external cir-

cumstances, such as bad weather, frustrate his immediate plans.
One discerns an underlying internal conflict whose roots are
subconscious. The most tragic aspect of this conflict is seen in the
power exerted upon his behavior, despite his enlightened mind,
by the very omens and predictions that he dismisses. This becomes apparent from the process whereby he decides to go with
the parson's family to the East Country. Recalling that his noble
ancestor committed incest with his own sister, he is reminded
that Tone looks like a sister to himself. Then, as twilight falls
and his relative's lines about the family dagger come to mind, the
face of the "old witch" materializes in front of him: "All at once
what she said had become so menacing." Though he still dismisses the "village gossip" about his "running away from his
fate" (VII, 196), these reflections clearly show his fear of what
might happen if he returned home to Tone. For the dagger was
supposedly a threat to his life only in his "own yard." His
quibble about running away really being the opposite of what it
seemed allows him to follow the drift of his subconscious fear
and move away from Tone, his "fate as it were" (193), while
consciously believing he is doing the opposite. Håvard cannot
read the signs aright: like Oedipus he is the man who, trying to
evade his fate, runs straight into it.

Håvard's weak will, especially in his relations with women,
gradually produces self-division. Only Tone, a symbolic anima
figure as well as his betrothed, holds his self together and makes
it whole after dissipation (VII, 183). His escapades produce symptoms of increasing self-alienation. After the night with Anne
Margrethe, inner division is manifest in his impression that the
entire affair happened to someone else, as well as in a projected
dreamlike stare and "nasty sneer." His very self seems threatened,
as shown by dreams of drowning (273-75). At the subsequent
feasting with Bruflaten, a horse dealer Håvard worked for at one
time, the former's bifurcated shadow plays comic changes on
Håvard's internal schism (291). Similar images are associated
with his seduction by Rønnau, except that now the impression of
drowning and the sneer precede the seduction (338, 317). The
process of seduction itself is an alienated experience: "he was not
there, . . . he had dreamed it all before" (338).

Håvard's self-alienation climaxes during the wedding, where

his brother tells him about Tone's suicide. The news makes him
literally "beside" himself: his body performs the duties of host,
but he himself is "everywhere and nowhere" (VII, 349). Here a
common Hoel theme assumes a very extreme form. Thus, during
a thunderstorm Håvard's brother—who, following superstition,
fears it is the "ride of the dead" (*oskereii*)—sees a "black shadow"
trailing Håvard. In the next moment Håvard sits with a deathlike
face, calm as a stone, "as if he weren't there but had only left his
body behind, while he himself went roaming across land and
sea." Throughout his wedding he experiences the same sensation
of being "two people"; the one they called Håvard was "only an
empty body" (357-58). In view of this persistent experience of
self-alienation, his thought that he would become "one again"
with Rønnau (364) seems the delusion of a man under an erotic
spell. His real endeavor to become "one again" is recounted in
The Troll Circle.

THE TROLL CIRCLE

In the words of one critic, Magli Elster, *The Troll Circle* combines an entire gamut of fictional types: historical novel, regional
tale, criminal drama, novel of marriage, and social novel.[7] One
might add that it is also psychological fiction of a high order.
Finally, Sigurd Evensmo, a fellow writer, has called it Hoel's
pessimistic allegory about the fate of the radical in his own time.[8]
By contrast to Hoel's earlier novels of the 1950s, these multifarious themes are contained within an integral representation of
life and a tragic action without precedent in his production.

Story and Themes

Significantly, the book begins with an overture in which the
local community (*bygda*) presents itself, so to speak: the anonymous narrative voice, using free indirect discourse with a faint
dialectal coloring, shares the outlook of Nordbygda. The ensuing
four chapters, all connected by unity of time, constitute the
novel's exposition. In "Hans Nordby and His Friends" (XII, 15-
39), the account of a drunken spree following Håvard and Rønnau's wedding, the host, Nordby, epitomizes the local ethos as he

finagles a dirt-cheap purchase of timberland from an ineffectual, rather artistic neighbor. Meanwhile Nordby's wife is on her deathbed in a back room. This incident anticipates the unequal future battle between Håvard and the community, an antagonist ruled, in pagan fashion, by the right of the stronger under a veneer of Christianity and respect for the law. The third chapter, where, on riding home after seeing his brother off, Håvard has a "vision" that affirms his role as a pioneering reformer, draws the lines of the coming conflict between him and the remote backward district. Invited next (ch. 4) by Nordby to join the party, Håvard mentions the possibility of raising the cotters' pay if farming were more efficient. This is his first mistake, greeted by jeering words like "missionary" and "stranger." Simultaneously tears and lamentations are heard as Nordby's wife breathes her last. Hoel accentuates the smugly self-enclosed, stagnant, brutally harsh character of the milieu. After Håvard has reached home, the community's hostility to change is mockingly expressed by the sights and sounds of the farmhouse, ringing spectral Aeschylean changes on the insubstantiality of the present in a world where past and future are seamlessly one: the motif "was, will be" (71) leaves little room for the realization of Håvard's visionary plan.

The two parts that comprise the book, of which Part I is by far the longer (XII, 5-272), complicate and eventually resolve this confrontation; but in the meantime it has absorbed other elements of conflict of an interpersonal, marital, and psychological nature. Through Mari, a former dairy maid who now occupies a stall in the cow barn, Håvard learns about the family of his neighbor, Kerstafer Berg, whose hatred and envy of Håvard are evident from their very first meeting in *The Family Dagger* (VII, 333). Kerstafer is only one of five men, farmers and cotters, who either proposed to Rønnau and were refused, or nurtured hopes of winning her favor. The mixture of lust and greed generates emotions that must find periodic outlets in explosive aggression. Håvard is warned by Mari to beware of Kerstafer, whose family history, behavior, and cognomen (*puken*) cast him in the role of a devil figure. He has a local asylum in his basement, where nonconformists are chained to the wall side by side with the insane. This underground chamber, a veritable inferno, grows into a symbol of the entire community. In the chapter "To the Summer Dairy for Hay" (103-26), Jon—who is Håvard's cotter but a free spirit whose favorite occupation is hunting—repeats Mari's warning. With his tales of haunted houses, suicides, and murders—four of the seven neighbors he tells Håvard about are reputed murderers—Jon holds up a terrifying mirror to the hidden evil forces in Nordbygda.

The conflict between Håvard's mission and the benighted village takes on an increasingly menacing character. It is brought to a preliminary climax by two episodes: the draining of the sour meadow and the mutilation of Håvard's horse. After the meadow has been drained, some of the cotters clog up the new covered ditches with clay. The ringleader, Martin, had foolishly hoped to win Rønnau for himself. This episode, which brings Håvard perilously near to killing Martin with the family dagger, is followed by another ("Evening in August," XII, 203-10), in which Håvard on a dark night catches two vandals in the now thriving potato field—Kerstafer and Martin, as it turns out. Kerstafer, who is badly hurt by a blow from Håvard's stick, is also thought to be behind the drainage sabotage. The ghastly climax to this series of skirmishes between Håvard and the local community, namely, the mutilation of his horse, is due to a conspiracy among several of his cotters. But according to Mari, who overheard their debate, Kerstafer was again involved, having guaranteed to pay the eventual penalty. When Martin, after gashing the horse, is crushed to death by its hooves, the other cotters march off to the sheriff to charge Håvard with murder.[9] The charge is dropped only through the intervention of a man of religion, H.A. Tomter, who makes the cotters see their evil ways. This is the "long day" of Part I. Besides forming a dramatic climax to all the intrigues of Håvard's neighbors and cotters, it foreshadows the novel's tragic dénouement.

From the start Håvard's struggle involves his own household. It begins in a semiburlesque spirit with his losing battle about cleanliness in the cow barn with a troll-like dairy maid. However, when Rønnau refuses him the money required for new farm implements and seeds (XII, 145), forcing Håvard to dip into his own savings, she herself proves no better than a troll—an image in keeping with the ballad theme of bewitchment. With her habitual faint smile, Rønnau unconsciously undermines the cotters' respect for Håvard's reforms, putting them down as the vagaries of an overeager boy (159). Since Håvard seems to be the weaker partner sexually—she "plays" on him as on a musical instrument (188)—he is unable to break down Rønnau's resistance to his mission. The repeated disagreements between them come to a head when Håvard's desire to reduce the stock of cattle to avoid the usual spring underfeeding causes Rønnau to taunt him with having acquired the farm by sleeping with her. From this moment on their relationship is irremediably altered. Ironically, by the time Rønnau changes her attitude because of the obvious success of his agricultural reforms, Håvard has lost his zeal. The paralyzing news that her pregnancy—the reason that made him give up Tone and marry Rønnau in the first place—has come to nothing (154) contributes in the long run to Håvard's increasing indifference to his great purpose.

These events are not without a basis in Håvard's psychology. Chiefly, his residual guilt unhinges his senses and perverts his judgment. A hallucinatory scene in the barn after his father's death ("Greetings from Tone," XII, 219-20) is particularly revealing: here, after drinking, he imagines he hears Tone's voice. The sick conscience thus betrayed affects his good judgment, with fateful consequences, in his treatment of Anton, a conniving scoundrel whom Håvard repeatedly protects only to have good repaid with evil. Anton, who worships Rønnau, hates Håvard without the latter's knowledge. Though Håvard's excessive leniency toward him is ultimately a mystery, it can be traced to his permanently guilty conscience: Anton's moral squalor causes Håvard to identify with him, to trust him, and therefore to retain his services, against Rønnau's advice and his own better judgment. Anton's slanderous testimony will have a disastrous effect upon the outcome of the trial in Part II.

At the end of Part I Håvard, like his ancestor in the ballad, has lost his "dream" or his "faith"; his vision of changing the backward community to something "more joyful and better" and turn the cotters into "free people" is gone. Though only a dream, tenuous like a veil, its disappearance has changed everything (XII, 268-69).

Part II of *The Troll Circle,* which begins almost nine years later, brings liberation to Håvard, but its action is under the sign of nemesis. In the first chapter, Håvard kills an encroaching bear at the summer dairy, thus saving the life of his twenty-one-year-old stepdaughter, Kjersti. By a stroke of luck that could happen only once in a thousand, Håvard pierces the huge beast's heart with his scythe—in reality with the family dagger, which since the episode in the sour meadow has been part of the scythe's blade. This stroke of luck and its aftermath, Kjersti's embrace, liberate Håvard from Rønnau's erotic spell to the imagined sounds of church bells. Repeated thrice in his mind, the ringing is previously associated with Vilemann's liberation from enchantment and with Håvard's adolescent awakening to his love of Tone. But the bear episode also seals Håvard's doom, thus fulfilling the ominous prediction of the old crone in *The Family Dagger*. For Håvard's defeat of the bear—in folklore often viewed as the cow of the *hulder*, the alluring troll woman, here Rønnau[10]—leads to the return of his love for Tone in the new relationship to Kjersti. Though he behaves correctly toward Kjersti, Rønnau's behavior changes drastically, at times verging on the abnormal. Her passion assumes a desperate quality which turns Håvard off, and her attitude to Kjersti becomes increasingly hostile. When one evening she swings a knife at her in the kitchen, Kjersti grabs another, whereupon Håvard interposes the ax handle he is working on to stop the fight. Rønnau, evidently suspecting he intends to attack her, abruptly steps back, causing her spine to be pierced by the spike of the extended kitchen crane. Paralyzed, she falls and hits the back of her head against the edge of a flagstone. In less than a day she is dead.

These drastic events are presented from a dual (or triple) perspective, unified by their tragic import. While the titles of certain chapters—"It Is Brewing," "It Strikes," "Omens"—maintain a romantic concept of unleashed natural force fulfilling the mandate of fate, the events themselves are quite understandable on the human level. This level in turn has a double meaning, since almost everything important that happens to Håvard is simultaneously unique and recurrent—part of the seemingly fortuitous web of present circumstance while being a reenactment of the past. Repeatedly Kjersti's words stir vague memories of Tone (XII, 332, 342): Kjersti is Tone resurrected. This aspect of Håvard's experience, reenactment, connects with the theme of fate in the chapter headings. Similarly, Håvard and Kjersti's subsequent discussion of incest, followed by Kjersti's embrace when Håvard admits—in response to her question—that he is "fond of" her (347), picks up the incest theme of the ballad and sets the scene for further tragic developments.

The remainder of the action will be summarized briefly. Rumors start circulating that Rønnau was murdered by Håvard and Kjersti, who reputedly have an incestuous relationship. Soon they are arrested and tried. Though the incest charge is dropped, it lingers in the courtroom to the end. Kjersti is acquitted, but Håvard is sentenced to death for murder. The ghastly execution by beheading takes place on the very meadow where Håvard's mission to Nordbygda was first seriously tested. Before this occurs, Kjersti has been chased across the precipice to her death by a group of self-appointed women witch hunters.

The Nature of Håvard's Tragedy

In *The Troll Circle* Håvard shows none of the erratic behavior he does in *The Family Dagger*. A devoted husband and a potential leader, he is also a kind, compassionate, and trusting human being. His character is marked by pride, nobility, and generosity as well as by the gayety, congeniality, and erotic charm that distinguish him in *The Family Dagger*. How could tragedy, in which character usually interacts with circumstance to produce its inexorable result, overtake such a man?

The outline of Hoel's underlying conception as cited here and as provided in his manuscript notes combines the classical idea of tragedy with a psychoanalytically derived view of man, both individually and collectively; the fear of happiness, or of nemesis, is the cause of man's downfall. Though *The Troll Circle* does embody this conception, the tragedy of Håvard Viland is complex and can be studied from a number of perspectives. Each will elucidate one particular aspect of Hoel's multifaceted creation.

Ritual Drama

In one sense Håvard, admired by all, *must* die, like Christ, a victim of unleashed passions—fear, envy, and hatred (XII, 433).

The Christ allusion is implicit both in Håvard's thought that the
farmers will one day come to ask his advice, just as Nicodemus
came to Jesus at night (51), and in the inveterate enmity of the
diabolic neighbor, Kerstafer Berg. Moreover, the novel's action
contains unmistakable ritual elements: Håvard, the outsider, is
the scapegoat upon whom are projected two of the community's
most notorious transgressions, incest and murder. Incestuous relations must have been commonplace in isolated Nordbygda,
with its endogamous practices (13); and direct or indirect killing
of wives, cotters, and others, for reasons of greed or otherwise, is
referred to more than once. The novel's character of ritual drama
is enhanced by the nature of the trial, in which the two co-judges,
H.O. Tomter and Ola Nordset, are motivated by repressed fears
characteristic of the community. Tomter, a religious pietist, in
whose eyes Kjersti's face "radiates" sin, projects suppressed lust
upon the accused; indeed, the court's "imagination [is] possessed
by the thought of incest" (397). Nordset, whose grandfather was a
stranger to Nordbygda, projects his latent fear of inferiority and
consequent hatred of outsiders. The same effect of a collective
purgation is produced by the ultimate miscarriage of justice, in
which countless private grudges, not only against Håvard but
against those who support him as well, dictate the verdict—to the
almost total neglect of factual evidence and reasoned judgment.
Finally, Hoel's treatment of the execution as an evil epiphany
comes through in references to the "holyday" aspect of the event,
to its being the "usual time for church service," and to the
"witches" (signekjerringer) who try to collect the victim's blood
in their bowls (447). The ritual quality of Kjersti's persecution
and death is equally unmistakable.

The Tragic Rhythm: Purpose

Before analyzing the particular phases of the novel's tragic
rhythm, phases defined by Francis Fergusson with regard to
drama as Purpose, Passion, and Perception,[11] we must consider
briefly the various types of relationships between character and
destiny in *The Troll Circle*. In Rønnau's case, as the mill owner
explains to Håvard, there is a clear connection between the one
and the other: nemesis (XII, 356). Not only does she deal dishon-
estly with Håvard, but her murderous hostility to Kjersti is based

on the assumption that, like herself, Kjersti will use every possible means, fair or foul, to obtain Håvard's love (355). Despite
the ugliness of Rønnau's death, there is a modicum of justice in
it. On the other hand, Tone and Kjersti are innocent tragic victims, both suffering similar deaths. For as the pursuing women
realized afterward, Kjersti could have escaped destruction (429).

Håvard senses an affinity with Rønnau; this becomes evident
when he excuses her lying about the pregnancy on the ground
that, after all, it was done out of love for him. One recalls his
previous tendency to make promises to women, such as eventually turned into lies. He also has features in common with the
two younger women. Thus, during the "long day," he subconsciously thinks of suicide (XII, 253). Yet, Håvard is neither an
innocent victim nor simply an example of the working of
nemesis. If he were, the retributive suffering that in the end he
seems to accept as his due would not seem so totally out of proportion to his faults. Insofar as it exists, the existential logic of
Håvard's destiny must be sought in the relationship between his
mission—that is, his purpose—and his guilt.

Hoel's description of the genesis of Håvard's mission constitutes a marvel of intuitive artistry, intellectually enriched by expert knowledge of the processes of repression and sublimation.
As he rides home after seeing his brother off, Håvard reflects on
his life and what people call "fate." Having failed to find any
particular "meaning" in what happened to him—that is, in his
"fate"—he reflects that, if it were to have a meaning, one had to
"control" it and "turn it where it really did not want to go" (XII,
41). A moment later, looking into the eyes of a female beggar
beside the road, Håvard is reminded of a dream he had at his
wedding, where his one-time wounding of a reindeer was mixed
up with Tone's death. To bring the wounded deer out of its
misery, he had slit its throat with the family dagger; in the dream
Tone cut her throat with the same dagger, which Håvard had
given her to keep as a pledge during his absence. The actual
manner of her death, drowning, is alluded to in the blood that
"gushed forth" (fosset ut; foss means "waterfall") from the
wound (45). After these thoughts have been "forcibly" pushed
aside, Håvard's "vision" comes to him as he considers the lot of
the poor cotters; indeed, an abundance of "dreams, visions,

plans . . . gushed" forth from somewhere within him (46-47). The energies of his utopian "dream" are directly derived from his guilt, as shown by the appearance of the word "gushed" (*fosset*) in the description of both. But Håvard's guilt-based mission, having absorbed his previous reflection on fate, now becomes a means of "turning" that fate and thereby giving meaning to what had happened to him without his knowing why (46). Furthermore, looked at from the vantage point of this superstructure, his entire previous existence takes on "coherence and meaning." What had seemed "confused and fortuitous . . . fell into place, acquired a meaning." Indeed, now that they are recapitulated along with the rest of his adult past, even periods which had seemed hopelessly wasted fit into his new existential synthesis (48).

Since fate in its popular sense *means* nothing to Håvard and is seen under the aspect of facticity, his decision to "turn" his fate can be compared to the existentialist's project of self-creation. As conceived by Håvard, his project touches not only himself but also involves a decision for mankind, embodied in his new community: his purpose embraces a utopian dream of enlightenment for Nordbygda. Among other things, it includes the idea of raising the cotters to a level of economic prosperity that will enable them to become free men (XII, 168, 269). Håvard's social ideal is profoundly humanistic, since economic progress is seen not as an end in itself but as the necessary basis of freedom, dignity, and happiness.

The Tragic Rhythm: Passion

Håvard is not, of course, aware that his new-found purpose is based on unresolved guilt; nor does he realize to what extent it is interlinked with his relationship to Rønnau. When resistance is being offered, by Rønnau and others, he at first reacts in a high-spirited way, as when he relies on his own economic means and his skill as a blacksmith to counteract Rønnau's refusal of money for the planned improvements. When family problems arise, such as his disappointment over Rønnau's "miscarriage," they cause his purpose, as implicit in his work, to become identified even more closely with the meaning of his life. After the drained meadow becomes his "child" (XII, 181), his purpose serves no longer only to sublimate his guilt but also to make up for his frustrated desire for fatherhood.

Eventually these private failures initiate the second moment of the tragic rhythm, foreshadowed from the outset by Håvard's sensation that his head is being pierced by an awl as he faces Nordbygda, thinking: "You will never make it!" (XII, 53). Around the time of the miscarriage, Jon notices that, for some unknown, private reason, Håvard drives his cotters too hard, antagonizing them even further (163). If it had not been necessary to replace his "child" with the meadow, Håvard probably would not have attacked Martin. Even Håvard's confiding to Jon his hope of raising the cotters' pay—a confidence that Jon passes on to them, with the result that they believe Håvard is holding out a lure to squeeze more work out of them—can be traced to the incomplete nature of his relationship with Rønnau, who does not encourage conversation about his hopes and dreams. These smoldering conflicts provide some of the background to the "long day," when the passion phase comes to a preliminary climax with Håvard's bizarre dream of slitting his throat—a sort of hallucinatory expiation for the "murder" of Tone that anticipates the novel's dénouement. His reflections afterward show that, as the purpose and passion phases overlap, so do the passion and perception phases: after the agony he is wiser but even less joyful. He has come to believe it is "no use" to struggle,[12] feels defeated, and loses hope (269). Though in the subsequent years his farming progresses steadily, Håvard seems doomed to sheer materialism, as shown by his repeated dreams of drowning and sinking in the mire: he has lost his purpose.

After the collapse of his self-created mission, which constituted the meaning of his life, the stage is set for a resurgence of eros, desire, which occurs when, during the bear-killing episode, Kjersti steps into the place of Tone. The return of the repressed is strikingly shown in the way this episode is transformed in a recurrent dream, where Kjersti merges with Tone and the bear with Rønnau, whom he is ready to stab with the dagger (XII, 295). Though Håvard dismisses the dream, he senses its menace, especially since it gets confused with a dream about his killing a Swedish soldier during the war. He is also fully aware of his perilous emotional predicament in having to imagine that

Kjersti is in his arms to whet his desire when in bed with Rønnau.[13] Since Rønnau perceives the profound mutual attraction between Håvard and Kjersti and behaves accordingly, Håvard is beleaguered both internally and externally. A recapitulation of his past in an attempt at self-understanding is unsuccessful. He senses that everything that has happened to him is interconnected in a "single strange web with some pattern or other, which he glimpsed a little of but not all. He felt that if he could see the whole pattern, then perhaps he could turn his fate" (298). This purely intellectual way of "turning" fate seems even more precarious than the existentialist "project." In any case, Håvard never does see the whole pattern—who can!—and before he is able to carry out his plan to send Kjersti away, disaster has struck. Though Håvard tried to prevent it from occurring, and therefore seems innocent, the self-recognition that comes to him in prison places his life in a different perspective.

The Tragic Rhythm: Perception

Håvard's transformation in prison stems from an intense need to recover a meaning for his life in the face of death. Even more than before he acts from a sense of guilt. When, after Kjersti changes her testimony and impetuously reveals what Håvard had suppressed to protect his wife's reputation—namely, that Rønnau had threatened Kjersti with a knife—Håvard, in order to save Kjersti, changes his own testimony. This gesture, whereby Håvard reveals the truth of his intervention, is interpreted as a covert confession by the court. It spells doom for him, a doom traceable to his old guilt: one Tone in the waterfall was enough, he reflects (XII, 382). Hoel's intent to demonstrate the working of nemesis, the return of the past, in this instance is evident from a manuscript note where he stresses the irrational quality of Håvard's act (Ms. Fol. 2323:5; 4/8/1943), an act that, while saving Kjersti in the short run, does not alter the ultimate outcome. Håvard's refusal to run away with Kjersti after Rønnau's death or to escape from prison when offered the opportunity through a wartime friend—that is, the refusal to frame a new purpose for his life—these decisions stem from the same source: a stoic nobility of mind and a spirit of self-sacrifice rooted in guilt. Here

Håvard displays that "fear of happiness" which Hoel intended as a link between individual failure and societal stagnancy. In a manuscript note Hoel writes: through "acquiescence" in and "surrender to their 'fate,'" people ensure "that this 'fate' actually becomes their fate" (Ms. Fol. 2323:3; 3/5/1941).

After the verdict, Håvard's suffering—and along with it the passion moment of the tragic rhythm—becomes subsumed by an irrational philosophy of expiation whereby Håvard accepts the role of scapegoat meted out to him in the ritual drama. According to his new perception, he is guilty not only of Tone's death but, indirectly, of Rønnau's as well and therefore deserves to die.[14] In his renewed examination of the past, the incident from the war of 1814 he used to dream about—the killing of the Swedish soldier on a scouting mission—comes to account for part of the pattern. He believes it was this initial act of murder that started him on his fateful course; now he is also expiating his original crime. This expiatory metaphysic, reminiscent of Schillerean and Dostoyevskian tragedy, lends Håvard a dignity on the day of execution that raises him to the level of sublime heroism. However, there is no rational basis to his new self-conception: he is prepared to die for an illusion of guilt. The pattern that he discerns is a purely subjective one and, as in several previous works by Hoel, is set up to be exploded.

The Pattern Exploded: Contingency and Conspiracy

Quite apart from the theme of guilt and expiation, *The Troll Circle* creates a feeling of fate tragedy. Thus, the imagined sounds of church bells after the bear kill, alluding as they do to the ballad of Vilemann, signify Håvard's doom as well as his liberation from the "mountain" of Rønnau; and the repeated use of the number 3 in this episode and elsewhere reinforces the mystery of inexorable fate. But these effects, of reenactment and prefiguration, are purely esthetic; their chief purpose is to enhance the sense of inevitability of the tragic action. These forces of fate are largely external to Håvard's destiny, which can be analyzed in nontranscendent, realistic terms.

Thus analyzed, this pattern of expiatory tragedy becomes suspect. A crucial perspective is offered in the reflections of Hans Nordby, who has posed as a friendly neighbor. With his pagan views, Nordby attributes Håvard's and Kjersti's tragic fate to bad luck, pure evil chance. There are several details in support of this perspective. Thus, there are repeated references to Håvard's good and bad luck: good when he pierces the bear's heart with a single stroke of the scythe, bad when he is confronted with a court dead set against him. It is mentioned that the chance of such things happening is one in a thousand; but they did happen—as did Rønnau's extremely unlikely death, another event placed in the same category. If we take these hints seriously, Håvard's tragedy becomes one of fortuitous circumstance, with no discernible pattern. This is a perspective worth considering, but not Sigurd Hoel's last word.

For Hans Nordby has a secret up his sleeve. Fearing that Håvard, with his uncommon knowledge and initiative, would cut him out of his lumber commission, he has intrigued against him, spied on Håvard and Kjersti, bribed and suborned witnesses, watching the course of events wrapped in a cloak of innocence. One of the things Nordby does not tell his son—in a scene reminiscent of Polonius's advice to Laertes—is how he hired Anton, Håvard's cotter and secret enemy, to play the spy. Anton's testimony that he saw Håvard and Kjersti embrace in the kitchen one evening after Rønnau's death and then retire to Håvard's room, had an electrifying effect on the court. It was Nordby who turned Kjersti's embrace at that time—a token of love for Håvard before her imminent departure so as to forestall nasty rumors—into the prelude to an incriminating act, by suggesting to Anton that they withdrew to Håvard's room. The incident shows the diabolic interweaving of fortuitousness and evil design in Håvard's tragedy: for, with all due respect to Nordby's evil purpose, why should Anton, the stooge of evil, turn up exactly on that night and at that hour.

Nordby's attempt to explain Håvard's destiny, together with his own malign contribution to that destiny, leads the reader of *The Troll Circle* to seek for other patterns than the one Håvard sees. What emerges is a complex network of relationships, where the vagaries of personal nobility and weakness, fortuitous circumstance, and individual and collective evil work together to produce tragedy. Håvard succumbs in large part because of his noble traits—honesty, compassion, and his vision of a new society. While he suffers from certain weaknesses, including an irrational sense of guilt, this fault would not have doomed him in the absence of support from evil chance and a repressive society venting its frustrations upon the hated and envied outsider. More than anything perhaps, what *The Troll Circle* leaves behind is an indelible impression of the implicit peril of collective repression, here, as in "Love One Another," the root cause of fearsome eruptions that wreck human lives in order to preserve the very order from which they spring.

The Esthetics of Analogue

Hoel's diffractive sensibility is also evident from a series of analogues that enrich and implicitly comment on Håvard's story. Hoel follows the same esthetic of analogue favored by Shakespeare, whose Hamlet is partly portrayed by means of foils, such as Horatio, Laertes, and Fortinbras. A great many characters in *The Troll Circle* are thematically related to Håvard; others experience analogous predicaments but handle them differently.

At the very outset the story of Erik Nordby, whose religiously inspired reforms for the benefit of the cotters caused him to lose his farm to Hans, his younger brother, and to be placed in Kerstafer's basement, foreshadows the potential danger to Håvard, a stranger as well as a pioneer (XII, 19). A humorous-pathetic parody of the individual-collective theme is offered through Høgne Lien, who becomes totally alienated from society after Kerstafer's brutal practical joke—promising to be a go-between with the girl he loved, then dressing up Høgne's horse as a bride on the latter's wedding day, meanwhile taking his pleasure with the girl. Høgne spends his days tracing progressively narrower circles in his own yard: he, like Håvard, is within the troll circle. There are also the cited parallels between Håvard and the three important women in his life, Rønnau, Tone, and Kjersti. But Håvard evinces either greater strength of mind and character or a more balanced and rational posture.

Hoel has not forgotten the Fortinbras figure; in fact, there are two: Jon, the hunter, and Amund Moen. The former, Håvard's cotter and occasional companion, despises the local mores but cares little about social progress. However, he has luck. At the end Jon receives from Håvard the large sum of money he had taken along to prison for ransom. The fortune of Jon, now able to buy from Høgne Lien the same farm previously offered to Håvard, is made through the latter's adversity and death. Amund Moen, like Håvard, was accused of killing his wife but staved off the investigation. The marriage to his beautiful young housekeeper and common-law wife, after seven years in which he feared his deceased wife's alleged ability to haunt him, closely coincides with Håvard's execution. The strength of Amund Moen, one of the few who stand up for Håvard during the trial, is his total freedom from guilt, or sense of guilt; he triumphs over the collective mindlessness, marries the woman he loves, and receives an heir—all by contrast to Håvard's fate.

Two more figures, the mill owner and Hans Nordby, are related to Håvard through their actual and potential relationships with Rønnau, respectively. The mill owner, whose housekeeper and mistress Rønnau was before her first marriage, apparently refused to marry her because she was barren. Håvard fell into the trap he had managed to avoid. The mill owner is prosperous, has a wife and family, and seems to enjoy Håvard's discomfiture in failing to interest Rønnau in his reforms. One cannot help wondering whether he testified in Håvard's behalf, knowing full well that his testimony would hurt Håvard because of his own sour relationship with the presiding judge. The values of the mill owner are those of practical common sense, prudence. The attitude of Hans Nordby—who had hoped his wife's death would come in time for him to marry Rønnau—is more aggressive, approaching Machiavellianism. Fearful of Håvard's challenge to his position, Nordby has summoned up all the envy in his greedy soul and come out a winner. Like M. Homais in *Madame Bovary* he represents the triumph of philistinism, without the rhetoric of progress.

The esthetics of analogue has served Sigurd Hoel well in *The Troll Circle*. Its effects are not easy to summarize. On the one hand, the carefully worked-out parallels and contrasts help to show the honesty, purity, and other excellencies of Håvard; on the other, they emphasize the fateful effects of his sense of guilt. More than anything, perhaps, they place Håvard's tragic nobility in relief against the collective average of greed and envy, com-

monplace vices. Accordingly, the complex esthetic structure of
The Troll Circle becomes part of Hoel's penetrating analysis of
society. That analysis can to some extent be extrapolated from the
preceding summary and discussion.

NARRATIVE TECHNIQUE, STYLE, AND SYMBOL IN *THE FAMILY DAGGER* AND *THE TROLL CIRCLE*

Formally, the two novels about Håvard Viland exhibit significant similarities as well as contrasts. The method of presentation
is broadly the same, third-person narrative, with skillful use of
free indirect discourse, individual and collective, so that the
books seem to relate themselves. While the plot of *The Family
Dagger* is one of romantic prefiguration, it takes place in a realistic setting. And though the treatment contains many elements
of lyricism, it occasionally approaches naturalism and the grotesque. In dealing with characteristic themes of the nineteenth-
century novel, such as marriage, the condition of women, and
rural life, Hoel could adopt a far harsher realism that his prede-
cessors, who were hampered by genteel conventions. A relevant
example is Håvard's seduction by a parson's daughter two weeks
before her wedding. Among the many vignettes of rural life, only
a few are picturesque; most show the peasantry to be filthy, su-
perstitious, brutal, and bigoted. Hoel's excellent genre figures are
capped by the broadly humorous portrayal of Bruflaten, a triumph of grotesque art worthy of a Daumier.

Hoel's language in *The Family Dagger*, beautifully adapted to
time, place, and social condition, ranges from dialect to a slightly
archaic Danish officialese, with the moderately oral style of P.C.
Asbjørnsen (1811-83) and Jørgen Moe (1813-82), the collectors of
the Norwegian fairy tales, as the norm. Though formally the
point of view is omniscient, the narrative style is colored by the
mental outlook of whichever character happens to be at the focus
of interest. Particularly notable is the skill with which Hoel
shapes the free indirect discourse of the itinerant beggar in such a
way as to give simultaneously a vivid description of Håvard's
Telemark milieu and a sharply etched portrait of the teller,
another triumph in the grotesque.

In *The Troll Circle*, basically realistic, one feels like pointing up the residual romantic elements, such as the intermittent reappearance of the ballad motifs. Here, though, the evil fatality supposedly inherent in the family history lies within the characters and the happenings themselves. The superiority of *The Troll Circle* over *The Family Dagger* largely consists in its powerful evocation of immanent evil, manifested in daily life, in the relationships bewen neighbors, in sexual jealousies, and so forth. The language and strategies whereby this effect is produced are close to vernacular speech. A good example is the story of Kerstafer Berg and his family as related by Mari, a folklore pendant to the itinerant beggar in *The Family Dagger*. Despite her "chanting tone" (XII, 93), which calls to mind bardic narrative, Mari's disenchanted wisdom pierces to the core of her subjects. Jon, whose language can be both racy and picturesque, relates the brutal tales of Håvard's neighbors in modified dialect. These two folk figures, with their merciless eye for human foibles, are symptomatic of the kind of sensibility that Hoel exhibits in *The Troll Circle*.

Among the many symbols in Hoel's two novels, the troll circle is the most encompassing one. It is related throughout to the imagery of "going astray" and connotes, among other things, social ostracism, moral paralysis, and the return of the past.[15] A related symbol is the sour meadow, where Håvard begins his pioneering reforms, only to end his life there as a convicted criminal. These symbolic images are blended with great artistry in Håvard's dreams and musings: thus, in an early recurrent dream that foreshadows his and Kjersti's plight vis-à-vis the community after Rønnau's death, Håvard is being sucked into a marshy swamp as he walks around in a circle, while the word "astray" sounds in the air as in a tragedy by Aeschylus. Another terrifying image, a counterpart to the constrictive circle, aptly evokes Håvard's sense of the vulnerability of the human condition: a house with one wall knocked out, confronting him directly with the blackness of the night (XII, 251).[16] The staring eye is variously used in both novels to symbolize the community's hatred of outsiders, an alternative self, God's ironic providence, and leering death. The "eye" of God, by its threefold repetition, acquires a particularly terrifying meaning to Håvard.

All the formal aspects of *The Troll Circle*—plot, structure, narrative technique, symbolic motifs, and so forth—are perfectly adapted to the book's tragic mode. This is an open mode. By encapsulating the tragedy of Håvard Viland within a congeries of burlesque, pathetic, and mundane analogues, Hoel has approached the ironic-tragic mode used by so many twentieth-century writers. At the same time he has repeated his own tendency to unite the character's subjective fate—one whose mythic nature is rooted in "family history, dream, clairvoyance, conscience and desire, held together by pervasive symbols"[17]—with a broad, objective vision of that fate. The juxtaposition is disturbing, but not only that; it is also bracing.

9
The Nature of Hoel's Quest

There is no obvious way to conclude a book about the work of Sigurd Hoel. To the question, What is distinctive about Hoel's artistic achievement?, one might answer: He was not, on the whole, a formal innovator, his style is unremarkable, and his range of characters limited. What makes him unusual is the besetting quality of his themes and images, shown best in the way they recur from novel to novel. These elements have been discussed in the preceding chapters. But the central preoccupation in all of Hoel's writing, his quest for coherence in human experience, for the meaning of life, bears further examination.

Georg Simmel, in a little book of 1910—the year in which Sigurd Hoel turned twenty—defined the "philosophical act" as the "unification of the world"; this is an act in which the spirit seeks to lay hold of the multiplicity of being in "*one* concept, *one* meaning, *one* value."[1] Hoel was not a philosopher, but his fiction embodies a quest for coherence and meaning as well as the fragmentation of twentieth-century experience. He shares this concern with many contemporaries, including Joyce, Huxley, and Virginia Woolf, to mention a few who wrote in English. Hoel's artistic and intellectual development is reflected in the changing patterns of meaning that underlie his stories and novels.

The earliest stories (in *The Road We Walk*) are based on the explosion of established orders of meaning, whether Christian or bourgeois. Subnormal sensibilities (of blind man, idiot) relied on for point of view bring out the randomness and the ironic absurdity of experience; and the effect of subconscious, psychoanalytic principles of explanation is less to establish new meaning than to expose and mock bourgeois inanity ("Spleen"). The story-chapters of *Nothing* are structured in similar fashion, in that traditional modes of meaning—religious, communal, and folkloric—chiefly serve as a background to disenchantment: in "Snow," whose nostalgic evocation of Christmas Eve ends in bleak nothingness; or in "The Dream," where the "position with a future" and its bourgeois value system are reduced to futility through a nightmarish confrontation with death. Only "The Star" (in *The Road We Walk*) marvelously explodes *into* meaning; this transcendence of disorder, at the end of a narrative steeped in randomness, is related to the story's fairy-tale quality.

What, Hoel seems to ask in his first novel, *The Seven-Pointed Star*, is the moral predicament of man in a world deprived of the old sources of value? Here, as well as in *Sinners in Summertime*, he grapples with the specter of determinism, the modern paradigm of a human world without self-determination, freedom, or clearly ascertainable values. The theme is impressively orchestrated through Jason's attempt to break out of the inexorable mechanisms of existence by means of insanity. Like Coleman in *Antic Hay* and Spandrell in *Point Counter Point* by Huxley, but with incomparably greater intensity, Jason seeks liberation by a downward transcendence. This means diabolism, culminating in a black mass that celebrates death and annihilation rather than resurrection and grace. Thus, Jason finds refuge from determinism and meaninglessness only through an inversion of the traditional Christian pattern. Though his problem is real and the unconditional freedom that he seeks is attractive to Dr. Conrad as well, Jason's demonic solution is treated ironically: the freedom he seeks, as absolute as the determinism he tries to escape from, is nonhuman. Central to *Sinners* is the ironic treatment of rationality and of the associated concept of self. In this comic novel, the characters' radical dreams of freedom fail because of reason's falling prey to primitive, archaic impulses within the characters. Thus, the bright utopia of perfect rationality fares no better than Jason's dark utopia of infinite freedom. Whereas in *The Seven-Pointed Star*, the projects of unreason are promoted by reason, in

Sinners reason is undermined by unreason.

With *One Day in October* Hoel's fictional world grows more complex and disharmonious, as manifest in the novel's new, modernistic form. Moreover, now for the first time psychoanalytic procedures determine Hoel's treatment of character and event on a broad scale. The book's underlying intent could be called deconstructionist: to unmask, by way of psychoanalytic types of explanation, the traditional vehicles of meaning and coherence in people's lives, such as order, justice, providence, truth, and mythomania. But though the elaborately designed superstructures are dismantled for the reader, for whom they take on the semblance of tier upon tier of self-delusion, the characters revert to the old debunked sources of meaningfulness. The use of mass psychology, here as in *Open Sesame,* accentuates the collective as well as the individual closed circle. Where literary models are discernible, such as initiation (Amund Moen in *October*), Hoel treats them half ironically. In *Open Sesame,* where most traditional ideas evoked—lofty ideals of freedom, heroism, growth—are of a literary nature, they are chiefly used to precipitate effects of parody. Finally, in *October,* Hoel's psychoanalytically inspired embodiment of total fullness of being in Mrs. Ravn's capacity for ecstatic, guiltless erotic joy, is destroyed as Mrs. Ravn succumbs to the raw atavistic persecution of the collective.

In *The Road to the End of the World,* which also juxtaposes a distinctive individual with a collective, the relationship is somewhat different. Here, and sometimes in *The Princess on the Glass Mountain,* Hoel's large-scale use of genre evokes an entire way of life; and repetition, being ritual or commemorative, signifies an immanent wholeness of being rather than enslavement to racial or societal atavism. Myth, legend, and fairy tale, favorite literary forms used in these books, record archetypal experience in a spirit of acceptance. Yet, especially in *The Princess,* the genre coherence is fragmented; thus, in "Love One Another," Hoel probes the social ethos behind the seemingly harmonious surface. Using psychoanalytic insights, he reveals vicious cycles of repression and violence—a virtual inferno of hatred and fear. As in the story of Mrs. Ravn, the primordial vision, utopian in spirit, is defeated by regressive mass hysteria. The development of Anders in *The*

Road reflects a parallel duality. While he realizes that the life to which he belongs is inherently unified and sufficient unto itself, Anders yearns for a freedom that cannot be had within the closed circuit of community life. Yet, his experience—viewed psychoanalytically—is from an early age marked by compulsive repetition. Only the image of the spiral hints at a happier fate, a possibility that Hoel will return to in his next novel.

In that novel, *A Fortnight Before the Nights of Frost*, the alienating bourgeois attitudes touched on in *Nothing* and developed broadly in *October* are explored in detail and debunked through the portrayal of Dr. Holmen. Moreover, the Reichian vision of erotic utopia is undercut, characteristically through the working of psychoanalytic determinism, as Dr. Holmen subconsciously reenacts his childhood traumas. The Blameless One in *Meeting at the Milestone* is in a similar predicament: behind the persona of the perfect patriot that he is, he discovers a traitor who has shut himself off from the richest source of authentic meaning in his life. Again, as in *A Fortnight*, despite his quasi-psychoanalytic exploration of the past, the alienation remains: he is unable to make a fresh start. And the near-mystical vision that comes to him under torture—a peak experience that supposedly unravels the ultimate riddle of existence—seems to appear only in order to be broken, fragmented. Just as in "The Blind Man" (*The Road We Walk*) the divine logic of total justification associated with the Christian theodicy is undercut by the title character's sudden insight into the cruel absurdities of life, so here the all-encompassing idealistic synthesis is put in question by the confusion, paradoxes, and emotional alienation of the "I's" actual existence.

A new order, founded on genuine human freedom, is present only through the image of the spiral, which in the end seems to replace the circle as the form of Dr. Holmen's mental travels. The spiral image shows, by way of a fictional analogue to therapeutic abreaction, how the determinism implicit in Freudianism can be transcended in an order of freedom—on psychoanalytic ground. While the Blameless One makes no comparable claim, both he and Dr. Holmen transpose their dreams—dreams for liberation and a new humanity they despair of finding for themselves—into a hope that their children (in the case of Dr. Holmen) and future generations (in the case of the Blameless One) will overcome the repetition compulsion. In other words, the utopian vision appears again, but now as a mere vicarious hope. Part of Hoel's problem as a writer in the 1950s is that he keeps using the old forms without the requisite belief. By this time, for example, he had recognized the limits of psychoanalysis, yet the closest formal model for both *I'm in Love with Someone Else* and *Rendezvous with Forgotten Years* is psychoanalytic. Whatever new ideas preoccupied him, he could not generate either a new existential concept or a new novel. Although *At the Foot of the Tower of Babel* reflects a philosophic crisis and documents Hoel's search for a new Weltanschauung, the novel remains unsatisfactory: instead of putting his energies to creative use, Hoel seems chiefly concerned with parodying his former beliefs—in psychoanalysis, socialism, or rationalism.

The two novels about Håvard Viland, in particular *The Troll Circle*, are so rich in substance that they contain most of the patterns discussed so far. Here Hoel has offered his most convincing embodiments both of the natural order as represented in myth, the human order based on the need for meaning and freedom, and the explanatory schemas of science. Already *The Family Dagger*, with its genealogical concept of fate, offers a counterpoise to the inexorable repetition of the past that such a concept implies. But it is only in its sequel that the human project of sense-making is fully portrayed. This occurs through Håvard's struggles, in the name of enlightenment and human will, to "turn fate around"; only thus can he make sense of the sheer facticity of existence, meaningless by itself. Håvard's work as a scientific farmer and practical pioneer is his means of realizing this man-made "fate," both for himself and the community. Actually, this sense-making, signifying an achieved order of rational human purpose, no longer has any resemblance to the ancient notion of fate. Håvard's design for his life constitutes Hoel's most convincing and most human example of such a project, more notable and better motivated than Dr. Ravn's rationale for a life of scientific inquiry.

The tragic failure of Håvard's project, which has the virtue of being human without seeming "utopian" in any obvious sense, is due to the sinister interplay of irrational forces operating within society, his family, and himself. In portraying the genesis of Håvard's plan as well as its execution, Hoel draws upon a psychoanalytic perspective, from which Håvard's ambition to "turn fate round" appears as the sublimation of an old unappeased guilt. This implicit interpretation, however, does not reduce Håvard's search for human meaning to mere rationalization. The marvel of *The Troll Circle* is the copresence within it of multiple orders or levels of reality—mythic, existential, epistemic. The religious order of meaning that emerges through Håvard's expiatory faith is of a different kind. First, it is a late, momentary presence; second, it violates the tenor of Håvard's existence; and finally, it would impose a monistic (or dualistic) order upon a pluralist fictional world. Håvard's expiatory concept of his terrible fate is clearly introduced in order to prepare for Hoel's use of his favorite device of *exploding* a traditional pattern, one that is extrinsic to the novel's norm.

It remains to look briefly at Hoel's chief intellectual-artistic quandary, followed by an attempt to place his Weltanschauung within a wider frame.

Paradoxically, Hoel's chief instrument of liberation from the ancient orders of meaning, namely, scientific determinism, also posed a new and formidable obstacle to the attainment of a new, genuinely human order. As a person trained in the natural sciences, Hoel must have been exceptionally aware of the rigorous sequence of cause and effect in events. Very likely, his exposure to the teachings of Freud and Marx confirmed, in his eyes, the validity of determinism for individual as well as collective behavior. But throughout his career Hoel struggles to break out of the closed circle to which determinism doomed him. Unhappily, the possible solutions that he tries out in his fiction— disregarding the obviously insane demonic transcendence in *The Seven-Pointed Star*—are in turn undermined by the same theoretical paradigm that was used to produce them, that of psychoanalysis. The paradisiacal Reichian vision of total, childlike being based on eros—a vision that seems to antedate Reich's influence on Hoel—suffers defeat through the mechanism of the repetition compulsion. Thus, optimistic Reichian salvationism, whose essence can be defined as integral fullness of being in the lyrical instant, is blighted by the pale cast of Freudian reflection and pessimism. Where the salvationism assumes quasi-religious form, as in the great vision of the Blameless One in the Nazi inferno of Heidenreich or in the Jung-inspired quest for an inspirational anima figure (*Babel*), the vision subsequently disintegrates or appears abstract and unconvincing. It can be maintained only by projection into the future. Hoel cannot escape the fate of the utopian.

Only in one novel does Hoel seem to escape this dilemma. The portrayal of Håvard Viland merges utopianism with existentialist thought in a uniquely human manner. And in this case psychoanalysis, far from being an instrument of debunking, illuminates Håvard's struggle with "fate." Hoel's warm empathy with his hero springs from two sources: an early saturation with the folk ethos and a disenchanted urban radical's sense of the meaning of tragedy in our time. Like Håvard, Hoel felt defeated in his "project": to help create a freer, more fulfilling, joyous existence for himself and his fellow countrymen. But he never stopped working for change, because, as he had declared in a speech in 1936, it is "submission to fate that *creates* fate."[2]

Hoel's practical optimism, shown in his ceaseless activity on many fronts, may throw light on a seeming paradox of his work, namely, the coexistence of such themes as absurdity, nothingness, lack of meaning with, in the main, traditional form and a perfectly classical style. His reader's reports at Gyldendal's testify to a veritable loathing for certain kinds of modernistic writing, such as novels in which themes of fragmentation assumed corresponding forms, resulting in much obscurity. By contrast, Hoel's narrative strategies are fairly straightforward, suggesting that the very progression of time is meaningful. True, there are circular patterns in the narrative, but the circles, apart from signifying "no exit," must also have had a less negative meaning for him. Thus he made the ouroboros—symbolizing the union of opposites, "continuity of life," and "self-fecundation"[3]—the emblem of his collected writings, and he deliberately chose an American novel (William Humphrey's *Home from the Hill*) as the last selection in the Yellow Series in order that, in good old fashion, the series could "bite its own tail" (*De siste 51 gule*, 220). Did, after all, some of the ancient, less unhappy meanings of the circle—heaven, perfection, eternity, the state of oneness, and so forth—linger in Hoel's creative unconscious? As for Hoel's language, its crystalline clarity, sparkle, and wit are legendary. Only the ironic manner reveals the hiatus between the elegant form and the fractured content of his works.

In view of these incongruities, one suspects that, like God as understood by certain theologians, Hoel the writer of fiction deliberately withheld from his creation some of his own excellencies, including some of his more affirmative thoughts.[4] A man who considered existentialism merely a philosophical makeshift must have felt, in his bones, that he possessed something better.[5] Is it possible that he concentrated on failure and tragedy in his fiction partly to evoke a dynamic response, one of protest, from the reader? A comment on a book published in the Yellow Series, Margaret Escott's *Show Down* (Norw. tr. 1937), makes this quite likely (*50 gule*, 120).

These assumptions of an excess of spiritual energy and a reservoir of human values are not without support in fact. Thus, Hoel's friends speak of his "irrepressible optimism," his "indomitable faith in human possibilities," and his special ability to "inspire hope in others."[6] Besides, Hoel's essays not only display a high spirit and a confident, sparkling intellect, but also positive ideas that he would defend with great gusto. Hoel was a formidable polemicist, and it was no joking matter to cross swords with him. Such a vigorous, even contentious spirit must have been solidly rooted in a tradition of values that sustained his work. From this perspective it is interesting to note that the fictional subject matter that he handles best, and seems to enjoy the most, is the oldest and most traditional—scenes of folk life, childhood recollections, and quaint or sinister figures from the old days—and he excels in the corresponding forms of genre, fairy tale, and the burlesque character sketch. Through his love of such folk treasures, and others like myth, legend, and ballad, he lends exceeding charm and reality to the completed round of folk life: here, at least, the circle is also *positively* connotative. Hoel's greatest novel, *The Troll Circle*, approaches another ancient form, classical tragedy. The values inherent in these subjects and genres must have meant a great deal to Sigurd Hoel. Furthermore, he demonstrates a lively empathy with the uniqueness of individual characters.

These are only a few hints of values in Hoel's fiction that have largely eluded the preceding summary: a deep sense of the past and of communal life as well as of the transmitted forms of artistic culture, along with a keen, undying awareness of the infinite value of the individual. In his foreword to the collected prefaces to the first fifty novels in the Yellow Series, Hoel writes that perhaps literature can remind us that "the life of a human being is a sacred thing" (*50 gule*, 8). Hoel may secretly have wished, and hoped, that his own writings would leave behind the same impression.

NOTES

PREFACE

All correspondence and manuscript materials cited are available in the Department of Manuscripts, University Library, Oslo, Norway.

1. See letter to Herbert Tingsten of 2/25/1953, Brevs. 355.
2. Letters to Coward McCann of 5/20/1932 and 1/27/1933.
3. Letter to Secker & Warburg of 10/15/1951.
4. Letters to Carroll Atwater of 2/2/1953, and from her to Hoel of 1/14/1953.
5. Martin Joos, "A Lecture on Sigurd Hoel," in *Festskrift til Sigurd Hoel på 60-årsdagen* (Oslo, 1950), p. 110.
6. "Generasjonsskifte?" *Samtiden* 55 (1946), pp. 67-78; and Willy Dahl, *Norges litteraturhistorie,* ed. Edvard Beyer, VI (Oslo, 1975), p. 16.
7. See letter to Georg Svensson of 11/12/1958.
8. "Psychoanalysis in American Literature," Ms. Fol. 2354:1, p. 4; see also Ms. Fol 2365:1; note of 1/13/1929.
9. For discussion of Hoel's achievement as a critic, see Sverre Lyngstad, "Sigurd Hoel: The Literary Critic," *Scandinavica* 22 (Nov. 1983), pp. 141-58.

CHAPTER ONE

1. See interview with M.N. in *Nationen,* 12/24/1954.
2. H.S., "Sigurd Hoel og Vardehytta," *Kongsvinger Arbeiderblad,* 8/7/1937.
3. In an article of 1951, Hoel mentions that, when he read Conrad's *Heart of Darkness* in 1926, he saw it as a prophetic story of Erling Falk ("Joseph Conrad — Erling Falk: Et fem og tyve års minne," *Verdens Gang,* 8/18/1951). And in a manuscript note, both Falk and Reich are seen as examples of the "overly gifted" person's tragic desire for a "quick triumph," causing him to stop being "authentic" (Ms. Fol 2365:13; 6/24/1940).
4. See Wilhelm Reich, *Psychischer Kontakt und vegetative Strömung* (Cophenhagen, 1935), pp. 21-22, where materials from Hoel's psychoanalysis are cited.
5. In a letter to Aksel Sandemose of Dec. 1931, Hoel says that one reason he has not had himself psychoanalyzed is fear that his "desire to write would disappear." Quoted by Johannes Væth, "Sigurd Hoel og *En flyktning krysser sitt spor,*" in *Sandemoses ansikter,* ed. Niels Birger Wamberg (Oslo, 1969), p. 124.
6. "Sigurd Hoel og Wilhelm Reich: Et kapitel av den norske mellomkrigstidens

litteraturhistorie," in *Ideas and Ideologies in Scandinavian Literature since the First World War:* Proceedings of the Tenth Study Conference of the International Association for Scandinavian Studies, ed. Sveinn S. Höskuldsson (Reykjavik, 1975), pp. 277-278.

7. Sigurd Hoel, *Samlede romaner og fortellinger* (1950-58; Hoel's collected fiction), XI, p. 153. References to this work will subsequently be noted in the text; roman numerals designate the volume number, arabic numerals the page or pages.

8. Ms. Fol 2327:1; 5/25/1953. See a similar statement in an interview in *Dagbladet,* 12/9/1950.

9. Interview with Stephan Tschudi, *Vårt Land,* 12/31/1956.

10. "Personlig om Sigurd Hoel," *Vinduet* 14 (1960), pp. 251-52.

11. Olav Storstein, "Musketerens største bedrift," *Vinduet* 5 (1951), p. 719.

12. Arne Stai, *Sigurd Hoel* (Oslo, 1955), p. 177.

13. From a speech on the Danish radio 3/23/1952; Ms. Fol 2345:1.

14. See, for example, S. Hoel, "Mot Dags litteraturnummer," *Mot Dag,* 1923; repr. in *Norsk litteraturkritikk 1914-1945,* ed. Knut Imerslund (Oslo, 1970), p. 111.

15. Sigurd Hoel, "Helge Krog," in *Essays i utvalg,* ed. Nils Lie (Oslo, 1962), p. 167.

16. Sigurd Hoel, *Tanker om norsk diktning* (Oslo, 1955), p. 39.

17. *Essays i utvalg,* p. 127.

18. Ibid., pp. 125-26.

19. In his essay, Hoel admits that "erotic and religious feelings" are related, though not identical (ibid., p. 126).

20. S. Hoel, "Mot Dags litteraturnummer," in Imerslund, p. 110.

21. See letter to Max Ostertag, his German publisher, of 5/11/1932: "I am lazy, and precisely for that reason I have been fooled to do far too much work."

22. The extent to which this could be exceeded is evident from a letter to Harald Grieg of 12/9/1932, in which Hoel reveals that in 1931 he read over two hundred manuscripts.

23. See letters to Harald Grieg of 1/25/1951 and 5/24/1952.

24. In a letter to Gerd Brændstrup of 1/27/1958, Hoel writes that since his sinus infection in the fall of 1945 he has not been really well for a single day.

25. As Helge Krog bears witness, he would spend weeks just correcting "talented but chaotic beginners' manuscripts." "Personlig om Sigurd Hoel," p. 251.

26. For criticism, see especially Eugenia Kielland, "Sigurd Hoel," *Samtiden* 45 (1934), pp. 442-60, and C.J. Hambro *Morgenbladet,* 10/3/1931.

27. "Roman 1960." Ms. Fol 2328; 8/31/1960.

28. "Møte med et medmenneske: Refleksjoner omkring Sigurd Hoels forfatterskap," *Kirke og kultur* 57 (1952), pp. 419, 421.

29. Letter to Sæverud of 11/6/1952.

30. "Tale ved Sigurd Hoels båre," *Aftenposten,* 10/24/1960.

31. Ernst Sørensen, "Ved Sigurd Hoels død," *Ordet* 11 (1960), no. 8, p. 312. For an amusing portrait of Hoel, see Rolf Stenersen, *Aksjer, kunst, kunstnere* (Oslo, 1969), pp. 44-60.
32. Fr. Lange-Nielsen, "Stud. real. Sigurd Hoel, in *Festskrift*, p. 129.

CHAPTER TWO

1. *Norges gymnasiaster*, No. 32, 12/8/1922.
2. Hoel relates he wrote the story in one sitting between 3:30 p.m. on April 30 and 3:30 a.m. May 1, the deadline for submission (I, vii).
3. Hoel expressed similar views shortly before he died: "We stagger blindly toward a goal we do not know. Technological development more and more assumes the form of an avalanche." *Studentene fra 1909* (Oslo, 1959).
4. The leitmotif of the smile, which becomes associated with all the major figures — husband, wife, and baby (I, 56-58) — is reminiscent of the same motif as used in "Jewels" by Guy de Maupassant, one of Hoel's teachers in the art of narrative.
5. In 1920 Hoel had published a brief study of the former, titled *Knut Hamsun*, and Söderberg's name appears in his manuscript notes for *Nothing* (Ms. Fol 2315:1).
6. Gunnar Larsen, a fellow writer, defines the similarity to Söderberg as a "mild and modest malaise that is good for the soul." *"Ingenting,"* in *Festskrift*, p. 45.
7. Published in the Christmas issue of *Mot Dag*, pp. 29-35.
8. This story was written during a two-day interlude in Hoel's work on *Sinners* in 1927, in response to a literary contest arranged by a New York magazine. Hoel, who won the first prize of $500, proudly notes that "seven hundred authors [writing] in . . . fourteen languages had participated" (I, xii). Published as "Christmas Eve" in *The Archer* II (Jan. 1928), pp. 27-36.
9. An autobiographical sidelight on this theme appears in a letter from Sissi Licht, a Swedish painter, who writes Hoel (6/27/1925): "You mustn't feel oppressed and bound by me. I love you and am therefore bound, but you are a free person." The chapter "The Return" contains the most affirmative variant on this theme: "He who has love . . . does not need to be chasing. He has found. He can stop, he dares let himself be bound. Everything binds him, every rock, every blade of grass. And bound he becomes free" (II, 319).
10. Cf. a quotation from Hjalmar Söderberg in the manuscript notes for *Nothing* (Ms. Fol 2315:1): "I can't bear to think that someone sits waiting for me."
11. Johan de Mylius interprets repetition in Hoel's work as a *"category of consciousness* which marks a distance to what is experienced. Repetition is a flight, a state of being bound that gives an illusion of freedom. Its content is

— nothing." *Sigurd Hoel — befrieren i fugleham* (Odense, 1972), p. 161.

12. Hoel was very much interested in dream as a literary technique. His papers contain outlines for no fewer than eight separate dream plays (Ms. Fol 2330).

13. The "hunted" aspect of this particular hunter-hunted image has its counterpart in Hoel's correspondence. In a letter of 9/11/1924, Sissi Licht mentions how thoroughly unhappy one is "when one feels hunted that way." She clearly refers to an expression used by Hoel about his own experience. The expression ("hunted and persecuted") already appears in the story "In the Land of Shadows" in *The Road We Walk* (I, 76), one of several similarities between that story and "The Dream."

14. Some of the previously cited images occur in an actual dream of *"terror and grief"* that Hoel had during the same fall the book was completed (Ms. Fol. 2365:1; 9/2/29).

15. In an essay on Helge Krog of 1949, Hoel wishes Krog could be less of a moralist and try to look "amorally at what happens, that is, simply content himself with being *the eyes that see.*" *Essays i utvalg,* pp. 175-76.

CHAPTER THREE

1. Nils Lie, *"Syvstjernen,"* in *Festskrift,* p. 35. See also Eric Eydoux, "Sigurd Hoel, le groupe et la revue *Mot Dag,*" in *Le Groupe et la revue "Mot Dag"* (Caen, 1973), p. 189.

2. Lie, p. 36.

3. Ibid., pp. 36-37.

4. Ibid., p. 38.

5. Notes for a conversation with Philip Houm on the Danish radio, 1953, Ms. . Fol. 2325:5; and Stai, p. 81.

6. For generally negative reactions, see the reviews by C.J. Hambro (*Morgenbladet,* 12/22/1927), Hans Aanrud (*Aftenposten,* 12/21/1927), and Kristen Gundelach (*Middagsavisen,* 1/16/1928); those by O.R. Müller (*Arbeiderbladet,* 12/13/1927) and C.A. Bolander (*Dagens Nyheter* [Stockholm], 2/11/1928) are more favorable.

7. *Books,* 7/20/1930, p. 5.

8. Arne Røed, "Sommernatt og sommersol," *Edda* 65 (1965), pp. 65-92.

9. Olav Storstein, "Sigurd Hoel og den hellige holmen," *Festskrift,* p. 6.

10. Hoel has given a reason why writers like Wilde and Anatole France were cultivated by "us": they were "just as elegant as we ourselves, peasant clods that we were, dreamed of becoming." "Joseph Conrad — Erling Falk: Et fem og tyve års minne," *VG,* 8/18/1951.

11. Preface to Trygve Braatøy, *Livets cirkel: Bidrag til en analyse av Knut Hamsuns diktning.* 2nd ed. (Oslo, 1954), p. 4.

12. Johannes I. Strømme, *Aftenposten,* 2/16/1928.
13. Trygve Braatøy, "Kjærlighet og hat: Nogen litteratur-psykologiske fragmenter. II. Sigurd Hoel og Aksel Sandemose," *Edda* 33 (1933), pp. 167-73.
14. Arne Lauritz Holden, "Sigurd Hoels *Syndere i sommersol.* En analyse av idéinnholdet og bokens plass i forfatterskapet." Thesis, Oslo, 1960, p. 44.

CHAPTER FOUR

1. See letter to Helge Krog of 3/12/1931.
2. *New York Times Book Review,* 10/23/1932, p. 6.
3. "Psykoanalyse og diktning," *Samtiden* 43 (1932), p. 307.
4. Hoel's assertion that "not a single person in the book is conceived or portrayed psychoanalytically, not a single problem, not a single conflict is traced back to a psychoanalytic basis" (ibid., p. 308), seems disingenuous.
5. According to his own statement, Hoel first heard of Reich in January, 1932. Though Audun Tvinnereim believes Hoel is mistaken and infers that Reich had come to his attention already in the fall of 1931, this would be several months after the completion of *October (Risens hjerte,* p. 59). The thesis of Tvinnereim's book, namely, that the value of Hoel's major works is sustained by their Reichian ideas and, further, that Hoel's alleged artistic decline in the 1950s is due to his dissociation from those ideas, seems not only exaggerated but wrongheaded.
6. Kjell Arild Madssen, "Sigurd Hoel's *En dag i oktober:* Tradisjon og fornyelse." Thesis, Oslo, 1970, pp. 164, 169.
7. *The New York Times Book Review,* 10/23/1932, p. 6.
8. Hoel refers to Adler's psychology in a manuscript note of 12/14/1931 as an analysis of the personality's "defence works" (Ms. Fol 2365:5).
9. *Plays,* with a foreword by Eric Bentley (New York: Signet, 1960), p. 248.
10. Nietzsche's Apollonian-Dionysian dialectic, as well as his ideas in regard to marriage and the philosopher; Freud's hint in *Civilization and Its Discontents* (New York, 1962, p. 50) that woman's desire makes her an enemy of culture; and Hjalmar Söderberg's treatment of the work-eros conflict, especially in *Doktor Glas* (1905), in a spirit akin to Freud's — these are some additional parallels that may have offered intellectual stimulus to Hoel in writing Dr. Ravn's apologia. See Madssen, pp. 172, 175.
11. Ernest Jones, *The Life and Work of Sigmund Freud,* III (New York, 1957), p. 272.
12. Mylius sees the novel's basic theme as the "warmth of feeling" that is defeated by the "coldness of reflection." In this perspective the plot, including Mrs. Ravn's death, becomes a symbol of the characters' "internal death" (*Sigurd Hoel,* p. 52). Another critic, Brikt Jensen, traces Dr. Ravn's inability to love — which he finds to be representative of all the characters except Tordis — to

a mother fixation and "hatred of the father," key Freudian terms for the "unfortunate pattern people follow in Hoel's world" ("Gir diktning svar?," *Minervas kvartalsskrift* 4 [1960], no. 4, p. 421). Mylius, too, sees Dr. Ravn's conflict in Freudian terms: he has been "wounded in his attachment to the mother — and takes revenge upon his sore spot," whereby he is drawn into a "pattern of repetition, a vicious circle" (*Sigurd Hoel*, p. 34).

13. Alf Schjelderup, "Psykoanalyse i vår litteratur," *Samtiden* 43 (1932), pp. 47-48.

14. The image of the child is a pervasive one in the book. Mylius writes: "The child, as it is most purely preserved and developed in woman, is the novel's positive contrast to the frozen world" (*Sigurd Hoel*, p. 41).

15. The cinematic quality of this scene is also noted by the Danish critic (*Sigurd Hoel*, p. 52). Hoel was a long-time student of the "techniques and effects" of cinema and collaborated on several film scripts. For evidence of his interest in the film medium, see letters to Gunnar Meyer of 7/18/1936 and to Ellen Siersted of 6/27/1941.

16. Most reviewers felt it had earned the first prize, which was awarded to Sigurd Christiansen for *Two Living and One Dead*.

17. In *Frontlinjer: Fra mellomkrigstidens kulturkamp*, ed. Leif Longum (Oslo, 1966), pp. 127-29.

18. "Kan psykologi drepe?," *Kirke og kultur* 39 (1932), pp. 9-11.

19. "Sigurd Hoel," *Samtiden* 45 (1934), pp. 442, 458, 453.

20. Johannes A. Dale, *Den 17. Mai*, 9/24/1931; Einar Skavlan, *Dagbladet*, 9/16/1931.

21. The idea of founding a journal can be traced as far back as 1930. See letter to N.C. Vogt of 10/7/1930.

22. Olav Storstein, *Arbeiderbladet*, 12/15/1938.

23. Hoel's article "The Second Moscow Trial" (in *Mellom barken og veden*, 1952, pp. 7-55) is referred to in the book as "The Witch Trials in Moscow" (VI, 280).

24. Interestingly, Hoel describes the plight of the hero of a novel by Louis Guilloux published in the Yellow Series in 1938, *Bitter Blood*, in similar terms: Cripure has become "cowardly and weak and abject because he is lonely and isolated." Caught in the "fateful circle" that only a very few can break out of, he suffers an "intellectual's tragedy." *50 gule* (Oslo, 1939), p. 154.

25. Nicolay Stang, *Tidskifte i maleri og skjønnlitteratur* (Oslo, 1946), pp. 194-95.

26. Harald Beyer, *Bergens Tidende*, 12/7/1938.

CHAPTER FIVE

1. Letter to Georg Svensson of 6/10/1958.

2. Tom Kristensen, *Politiken*, 1/27/1934.

3. Letter to Albert Bonniers Publishers, 10/13/1934, and Ms. Fol. 2319:1. See also the preface to *Vlas* (*50 gule*, pp. 217-18), where Hoel elaborates the same ideas. Moreover, his characterization of Dymov's description of childhood emphasizes qualities — ambition, cruelty, revengefulness, loneliness, and so forth — that are also found in Hoel's portrait.

4. For further information about this accident and its consequences, see Nils Lie, introduction to *Møte ved milepelen* (Oslo, 1967), p. ix.

5. A look at Wilhelm Reich's book, *Psychischer Kontakt und vegetative Strömung* (pp. 21f.), where materials from Hoel's analysis are cited, shows how much of Hoel's recollections of the trip to the hospital and of his understanding of what was happening has been incorporated in the novel. See A. Tvinnereim, *Risens hjerte*, pp. 164-65.

6. In an interview with Johan Borgen, Hoel speaks of "fear of the dark," which, in his opinion, can scarcely be overcome (*Dagbladet*, 11/7/1933). See also Ms. Fol. 2343, A 18.

7. Mylius comments that the anxiety-charged snake and eye are now within himself, as the conscience by which he is bound (*Sigurd Hoel*, p. 113).

8. Mylius associates the troll "without a face" with the previously related fairy tale about a boy who blinded the troll with an ax (IV, 44), an act that entails becoming adult. But the eyeless troll also inspires fear: adults too are afraid, namely, of death. In Sigurd Hoel's work, Mylius says, death is to grow up (*Sigurd Hoel*, p. 66).

9. *Dagbladet*, 11/30/1933; repr. in *Meninger* (Oslo, 1947), pp. 65-68.

10. For more thorough discussion of the style of *The Road*, see Tore Haraldsen, "Sigurd Hoels *Veien til verdens ende:* En analyse." Thesis, Oslo, 1963, pp. 151-56.

11. Tutta Laukholm claims that, in presenting the child's early thinking as "mythic," Hoel was influenced by Carl Jung. "Folkelig tradisjonsstoff i Sigurd Hoels forfatterskap." Thesis, Oslo, 1968, pp. 10ff.

12. Mylius sees the fall as a central image in the book: "*The banishment from the garden of childhood occurs through a series of falls from feeling to consciousness.*" Moreover, Anders' consciousness is presented not as "insight proper" but as the "defense mechanism of the fallen" (*Sigurd Hoel*, pp. 88, 91).

13. Interview with M. G——gg (Johan Borgen) in *Dagbladet*, 11/7/1933.

14. In a contemporary review of Aksel Sandemose's *The Sea Monster (Klabautermannen)*, Hoel defines character in these terms, namely, as a function of recurring "favorite situations": it is the "invisible thread" in each person's life. But his interpretation seems positive, in that these features produce a sense of a "lawful world where there exist coherence and internal tension." "Brev från Norge," *BLM* (Stockholm) II (1933), no. 2, p. 18.

15. In a letter Hoel says that what Anders experienced was the "evil interconnectedness and inevitability of things." To J.J. Alnæs, 8/1/1940.

16. One chapter is available in English, "The World," *The Norseman* 8 (May-June, 1950), pp. 198-202.

17. Audun Tvinnereim believes that Hemingway's *In Our Time*, which Hoel had read in 1926, may have helped him achieve this result through a more "conscious use of point of view" than is evident in earlier regional stories he wrote, specifically through the use of the "peripheral observer." *Risens hjerte*, p. 180.

CHAPTER SIX

1. Sigurd Hoel, "Wilhelm Reich," in *Ettertanker*, ed. Leif Longum (Oslo, 1980), p. 104, and Stai, p. 112.
2. Olav Storstein, "Sigurd Hoel og den hellige holmen," p. 13.
3. In his preface to Eyvind Johnson's *Here Is Your Life* (Norw. tr. 1936) in the Yellow Series, Hoel finds a similar "common fate" in Johnson's hero: the "hunt" for self-understanding has "propelled him in a circle." *50 gule*, p. 199.
4. Mylius sees Ramstad as a Mephisto figure: he puts Holmen in the way of regaining his youth with a woman, whom he will betray because he seeks knowledge and life simultaneously. *Sigurd Hoel*, p. 199.
5. This is the kind of existence Wilhelm Reich called "surrogate life"; in an article, he mentioned Hoel's novel as an incomparable portrayal of this kind of life. Quoted by Tvinnereim, *Risens hjerte*, p. 249.
6. For an extensive analysis of the shadow as symbol, see Mylius, pp. 210-13.
7. As quoted by Kjell Aspaas, "Sigurd Hoels *Fjorten dager før frostnettene.* En litterær analyse." Thesis, Oslo, n.d., p. 40.
8. My interpretation here as elsewhere owes nothing to Mylius or Tvinnereim, whose psychoanalytically based studies I read only after my manuscript was virtually completed. Both carry their theses, Freudian and Reichian respectively, much further than I would be prepared to do.
9. Hoel wrote an essay, "Rebel and Slave" (1934), in which he popularized Reich's idea. See "Rebell og trell," in *Ettertanker*, pp. 17-28.
10. Ole Martin Høystad, "Skyld og erkjennelse." Thesis, Oslo, 1976, p. 151.
11. Mylius suggests that Hoel's imagery, particularly rain, undercuts the optimistic conclusion that the circle is broken (p. 217).
12. Interview with Bjørn Gabrielsen, *Arbeiderbladet*, 1/12/1957.
13. Letter to Harald Grieg, 5/24/1952.
14. See Helge Rønning, "Svikeren, helten og virkeligheten. Noen tanker om krigslitteraturen," *Kontrast*, 1971, no. 1, p. 69.
15. Letter to Harald Grieg, 5/24/1952.
16. Letter to Johannes V. Jensen, 7/7/1948.
17. "Sigurd Hoel og nazismen," in *Nazismen og norsk litteratur*, ed. Bjarte Birkeland and Stein Ugelvik Larsen (Bergen, 1975), p. 111.
18. Asmund Lien, "Sin egen historiker — sin samtids historiker: *Det svundne*

er en drøm og *Møte ved milepelen.* En parallelføring,'' in *Sandemoses ansikter,* pp. 147, 173; Tom Kristensen, *Politiken,* 6/11/1948, repr. in *Til Dags Dato* (Cophenhagen, 1953), pp. 258-63.

19. In parentheses Hoel adds, ''a hell of a program for a novel.''
20. See letter to Harald Grieg, 5/24/1952.
21. Letter to Johannes V. Jensen, 7/7/1948; Ms. Fol 2324:3.
22. Ms. Fol. 2324:6. Contrary to the opinion of Audun Tvinnereim that this intention was due to a late displacement of purpose (*Risens hjerte,* p. 213), it is found in a note from 1944 (Ms. Fol. 2324:3; note of 9/19) where Hoel writes: ''Judge not (But we *must* judge.).''
23. Masahiko Inadomi has pointed out that these portraits serve at the same time as projections of the ''I's'' own problems or weaknesses and as defenses against the ''real'' search for his own guilt. *Den plettfrie* (Oslo, 1968), pp. 42, 62, 67-68.
24. In a very amusing article about the novel, Georg Johannesen makes glorious fun of Hoel's dependence on failure to use prophylactics for the construction of his plot: a missing condom may be sufficient cause for the birth of a Nazi, torturer. ''Forskningsfeltet Norge. Sigurd Hoels *Møte ved milepelen,*'' *Vinduet* 27 (1973), no. 4, p. 15.
25. *Friheten,* 11/20/1947; *Times Literary Supplement,* 9/21/1951.
26. In notes for *Open Sesame* (Ms. Fol. 2321:1; 7/26/1937).
27. Kari's appearnce, which is expressive of her ''primordial'' nature, may owe something to Hoel's recollection of a maid he was in love with as a student. Like Kari, she had a ''Mongolian face'' with ''slanted eyes'' (Ms. Fol. 2319:1, dated 4/29/1932; VIII, 188).
28. *Bread and Wine* (New York: Signet Classics, 1963), p. 43.
29. One is struck by the similarity between this phrasing and Hoel's comments on Arthur Koestler's *Arrival and Departure* (Norw. tr. 1946), which he translated. The childhood of Koestler's hero has produced a guilt which he subsequently seeks to ''pay off'' (*De siste 51 gule* [Oslo], 1959, p. 39). Hoel was very much taken up with Koestler in the 1940s.
30. There exists a meaningful similarity between the ''I's'' experience in Heidenreich's basement and the course of a psychoanalysis, during whch anxiety and terror can give way to a state of rapture (Sigurd Hoel, ''Menneskesynet i moderne litteratur,'' *Kristne Læger,* July 1959, p. 89). In a reader's report on John Knight's *Story of My Psychoanalysis,* Hoel mentions the ''strange atmosphere — a mixture of nursery and subterranean torture chamber — which characterizes an effective analysis (Ms. Fol. 2356; 12/29/1950). Perhaps not only ''effective'' analysis.
31. Letter to Johannes V. Jensen, 7/7/1948.
32. M. Inadomi, who has offered the most deep-probing interpretation of the Blameless One, holds a similar view. The main points of resemblance between his view and mine are coincidental, since this chapter was written before I read his book. Inadomi sees the Blameless One as being hopelessly divided: between

rationalism and religious need, search for self-knowledge and repression, confession of guilt and a tendency toward self-justification and blaming others. He explains not only the "I's" psychology and moral attitudes on this basis but, more interestingly, the entire process of his retrospective story-telling, including the portrayal of others. From this viewpoint, *Meeting* as fiction assumes the character of a vast, intricate construction by an irremediably unreliable narrator. However, Inadomi incorrectly attributes a metaphysical concept of fate to the Blameless One. What the latter calls fate (*skjebne*) is simply the way our lives turn out; and he admits openly that "many of us, even the smallest of us, to a great extent determine our own fate" (VIII, 374-75). Moreover, there is a close correlation between what the "I" calls "the pattern of our fate" and what, using the same image, Hoel calls "character" elsewhere ("Brev från Norge," *BLM*, 2 [1933], no. 2, p. 17). Therefore, contrary to Inadomi's statement, there is no "profound irony" in the fact that the "I's" "mind [*sinn*] became his fate" (151).

33. Jørgen E. Tiemroth, "Hoel — og Panduro," in *Panduro og tredivernes drøm* (Cophenhagen, 1977), p. 143; Paal Brekke, "Syv romaner," *Samtiden* 57 (1948), p. 52; *Dagens Nyheter,* 11/12/1947.

34. "Sigurd Hoel og nazismen," p. 111.

35. *The Sunday Times,* 9/23/1951.

CHAPTER SEVEN

1. The planned title of *I'm in Love,* "Twenty Years After," had to be abandoned because of delay in the writing.

2. The last theme is derived from Koestler. See Hoel's own essay "Det trivielle og det tragiske" (1946), in *Essays i utvalg,* pp. 49-57. In this essay fear of tragedy becomes synonymous with the Reichian "fear of happiness" (p. 53).

3. Øistein Parmann, *Morgenbladet,* 11/17/1951.

4. The Sven-Vera plot was virtually complete on New Year's Eve, 1940. See "Novel Without a Title" (Ms. Fol. 2365:14).

5. Tiemroth, p. 169.

6. A novel by William Sansom, *The Face of Innocence* (1951), which Hoel edited for the Yellow Series in 1952, may have provided a certain stimulus to Hoel in shaping the relationships in *Rendezvous.* The beautiful woman in Sansom's novel is, like Vera, a "pathological" liar, and she is married to the narrator's friend. Similarly, the narrator's chief problem is one of truth. *De siste 51 gule,* pp. 45-46.

7. Ms. Fol. 2326:1; see also Ms. Fol. 2327:1, where his name is given: Gunnar Meyer.

8. Similar ideas appear almost two decades earlier in Hoel's preface to Leo Perutz' *The Swedish Horseman* (1938). *50 gule*, pp. 185-86.

9. Erik Rostbøll, "Samtale med Sigurd Hoel," *Det danske Magasin* 3 (1954), pp. 391, 388.

10. Ibid., pp. 387, 392.

11. *Skyld og skjebne* (Oslo, 1960), pp. 156-57.

12. Letter to Cilla Johnson, 9/2/1956.

CHAPTER EIGHT

1. For an extensive report of this "drama of horror," see *Indlandsposten*, 9/2,3,4,/1935; Ms. Fol. 2323:1.

2. "Da Sigurd Hoel fant bøddelens blokk," *Frisprog*, 10/25/1958; Ms. Fol. 2323:5.

3. Letters to G. Jervin, 7/10 and 8/27/1958; to Kaj Bonnier, 8/15/1958; to Harald Grieg, 6/8/1958.

4. Birger Christoffersen, "Møte med Sigurd Hoel," *Stockholms-Tidningen*, 6/9/1959.

5. Both the ballad and the prophecy were written by Hoel, but all the reviewers assumed they were authentic. See letters to Ellen Siersted, 12/16/1941, and to Aslaug Vaa, 12/14/1941. Hoel's love of folk poetry is verified by Olav Hestenes, who says that at intimate parties he would sing "old ballads" (*Ordet* 9 [1958], no. 8, p. 334). Mylius sees both the ballad and Håvard's story as expressing the Tannhäuser theme (*Sigurd Hoel*, pp. 268, 273ff.).

6. Tutta Laukholm (op. cit., pp. 1, 24, 74 and passim) has pointed to the influence of C.G. Jung in this connection. According to Jung, it is in situations of crisis that the archetypes emerge in consciousness. Jung's conception of myth and folklore as expressions of the unconscius psyche may well be the key to Hoel's use of them in *The Family Dagger* and *The Troll Circle*, where obviously private psychic materials, such as dreams and visions, attain public status through collective literary forms, such as fairy tale and legend. See also Audun Tvinnereim, "*Arvestålet* og *Trollringen*. To romaner av Sigurd Hoel," *Edda* 65 (1965), p. 95.

7. *Arbeiderbldet*, 10/30/1958.

8. *Orientering*, 12/13/1958, p. 14.

9. For several of these acts of criminal mischief, Hoel drew upon information received in 1942 from his elder brother, Olav, based on the latter's experience with his own neighbors in the 1920s (Ms. Fol. 2323:1).

10. Laukholm, p. 99.

11. *The Idea of a Theater* (New York, 1949), p. 31; see also Kenneth Burke, *A Grammar of Motives* (New York, 1945), pp. 39-40.

12. From the 1930s on Hoel used this phrase as well as its positive form (*Det nytter!*, suggesting there is a point in struggling) to indicate acquiescence in the status quo and a radical will to oppose war, tyranny, and injustice, respectively. See "Kulturkamp og litteratur" (1936), in *Tanker i mørketid* (Oslo, 1945), pp. 20-21, and the prefaces to *Paths of Glory* (Norw. tr. 1935), in *50 gule*, p. 85, and William Humphrey's *Home from the Hill* (Norw. tr. 1959), in *De siste 51 gule*, p. 219.

13. This casts doubt on Mylius' thesis that the Tone-Kjersti figure is simply a stand-in for the mother, to whom Håvard subconsciously wishes to return. To escape his incurable split between an erotically possessed body and a free-floating consciousness, Mylius says, Håvard longs "home to — or forward to — a condition beyond individuation," a longing that can only be fulfilled through death. *Sigurd Hoel*, p. 278.

14. In presenting Håvard's development, Hoel is reminiscent of both Kafka and Koestler. The basic theme in Kafka, according to Hoel, is that man can never be "right" before God or "fate" (*50 gule*, p. 177); and Rubashov, the main character in *Darkness at Noon* (1940), feels that the "senseless charge against him is justified, like a nemesis" (*De siste 51 gule*, p. 38).

15. For extensive discussion of these and other meanings, see Tvinnereim, *Risens hjerte*, pp. 355-60.

16. This image seems to derive from a dream that Hoel had almost thirty years earlier (Ms. Fol. 2365:1; 9/2/1929). A variant of it turns up in the preface to Osip Dymov's *Vlas* (1931) to express the utter loneliness of childhood as portrayed there (*50 gule*, p. 218).

17. Torben Brostrøm, "Den onde sirkel," *Vindrosen* 6 (1959), no. 2, p. 160.

CHAPTER NINE

1. *Hauptprobleme der Philosophie* (Berlin, 1950), p. 34.

2. "Kulturkamp og litteratur," in *Tanker i mørketid*, p. 21. It is worth noting that, in 1950, Hoel stated in an interview that the question of determinism versus freedom is meaningless: on a "higher plane" there is no opposition (*Morgenbladet*, 2/13/1950).

3. J.E. Cirlot, *A Dictionary of Symbols* (New York, 1962), p. 235.

4. Hoel uses the author-God analogy in a manuscrilpt note but stresses that the author is not "omnipotent"; he must "follow the laws of his own world" (Ms. Fol. 2354:2).

5. Sigurd Hoel, "Menneskesynet i moderne litteratur, II," *Farmand*, 6/20/1959, p. 21.

6. Ernst Sørensen, "Ved Sigurd Hoels død," *Ordet* 11 (1960), no. 8, p. 313; Nils Lie, introduction to *Meeting at the Milestone*, p. xiii.

SELECTED
BIBLIOGRAPHY

Unless otherwise indicated, all Norwegian books are published by Gyldendal Norsk Forlag, Oslo.

For supplementary listings, see Harald and Edvard Beyer, *Norsk litteraturhistorie* (Oslo: Aschehoug, 1970), p. 455; *Norges litteraturhistorie,* ed. by Edvard Beyer, VI (Oslo: Cappelen, 1975), p. 440; Harald Næss, *Norwegian Literary Bibliography 1956-1970* (Oslo: Universitetsforlaget, 1975), pp. 91-92; Audun Tvinnereim, *Risens hjerte* (Oslo, 1977), pp. 391-99; Reidar Øksnevad, *Norsk litteraturhistorisk bibliografi,* vol. I, 1900-1945 (Oslo, 1951), p. 330; vol. II, 1946-1955 (Oslo, 1958), p. 108.

PRIMARY SOURCES

De siste 51 gule. Oslo, 1959. Prefaces to the last fifty-one novels published in the Yellow Series.

Essays i utvalg. Edited by Nils Lie. Oslo, 1962. Selected essays.

Ettertanker. Etterlatte essays og artikler. Edited and with a foreword by Leif Longum. Oslo, 1980. Essays from the 1930s and the 1950s, the latter chiefly autobiographical.

50 gule. Oslo, 1939. Prefaces to the first fifty novels in the Yellow Series.

Meeting at the Milestone. Translated by Evelyn Ramsden. London: Secker & Warburg, 1951. A readable but flawed translation.

Mellom barken og veden. Oslo, 1952. Chiefly political and cultural essays.

"The Murderer," in *Slaves of Love and Other Norwegian Short Stories.* Edited by James McFarlane. Oxford and New York: Oxford University Press, 1982, pp. 136-43. ("Morderen," in *Prinsessen på glassberget.* Translated by Janet Garton.)

One Day in October. Translated by Sølvi and Richard Bateson. New York: Coward-McCann, 1932. A fairly good translation.

Samlede romaner og fortellinger. With a foreword by Sigurd Hoel. Twelve volumes. Oslo, 1950-58. The standard edition of Hoel's collected fiction.

Sinners in Summertime. Translated by Elizabeth Sprigge and Claude Napier. New York: Coward-McCann, 1930. A fair translation.

Tanker fra mange tider. Oslo, 1948. Mainly travel letters and other journalistic pieces.

Tanker i mørketid. Oslo, 1945. Essays on Nazism.

Tanker om norsk litteratur. Oslo, 1955. Chiefly reviews of Norwegian literature.

SECONDARY SOURCES

Aarbakke, Jorunn Hareide. "Sigurd Hoels novelle 'Spleen' og psykoanalysen." *Norsk litterær årbok 1973,* pp. 64-76. Oslo: Det Norske Samlaget, 1973. Examines the various literary functions of dream in this early story.

Beyer, Harald. *A History of Norwegian Literature.* Translated and edited by Einar Haugen, pp. 318-20. New York: New York University Press, 1956. Brief discussion of Hoel's work up to *Meeting at the Milestone.*

Birn, Randi. Review of Johan E. de Mylius, *Sigurd Hoel — befrieren i fugleham. Scandinavian Studies* 47 (Winter, 1975), pp. 106-7.

Bollvåg, Merete Andersen. *Kjærlighetsbegrepet i Sigurd Hoels forfatterskap.* Oslo-Bergen-Tromsø: Universitetsforlaget, 1981. Examines Hoel's concept of passion-love with the help of Denis de Rougemont's theories.

Braatøy, Trygve. "Kjærlighet og hat. II. Sigurd Hoel og Aksel Sandemose." *Edda* 33 (1933), pp. 167-73. Reprinted in *Kjærlighet og åndsliv,* pp. 64-78. Oslo: Fabritius, 1934. Analyzes *Sinners* from a Freudian viewpoint; discerns latent homoerotic themes.

Dahl, Willy. "Dikteren Sigurd Hoel — og skribenten." In *Perspektiver,* pp. 95-119. Bergen: J.W. Eide, 1968. Elucidates Hoel's work by contrasting Hoel the "poet" *(dikter)* and the journalist *(skribent).* His best characters are created by "one of the most sensitive poets Norway has had."

Egeland, Kjølv. "Sigurd Hoel." In *Fremmede digtere i det 20. århundrede.* Edited by Sven Møller Kristensen, vol. II, pp. 411-27. Copenhagen: Gads Forlag, 1968. A balanced evaluation of Hoel's achievement as a novelist and critic.

_____. *Skyld og skjebne.* Oslo, 1960. Sympathetic examination of four of Hoel's novels, *Meeting at the Milestone* and the three period novels of the 1950s. Interprets the "mystical and magic" internal structure of these works as an expression of "guilt and fate." Exaggerates the philosophical significance of the irrational elements in Hoel's fiction.

Eydoux, Eric. "Sigurd Hoel, le groupe et la revue *Mot Dag.*" In *Le Groupe et la revue "Mot Dag," 1921-1925,* pp. 165-97. Caen: Université de Caen, 1973. Emphasizes Hoel's pivotal importance to the success of the journal *Mot Dag.*

Festskrift til Sigurd Hoel på 60-årsdagen. Edited by Nils Lie, Arnulf Ursin-Holm, and Arnulf Øverland. Oslo, 1950. Contains many interesting reminiscences as well as critical articles.

Haaland, Arild. *Hamsun og Hoel. To studier i kontakt.* Bergen: John Griegs forlag, 1957. A negative view of the human values embodied in Hoel's fiction. Stresses the "nightside" of his characters — lack of human contact, aggressiveness, voyeurism, and so forth.

Hannevik, Arne. "Kjærligheten og trollringen — noen grunnmotiver i Sigurd Hoels diktning." *Ord och bild* 70 (1961), pp. 89-95. Informed commentary on the circle and associated images in Hoel's fiction.

_____. "Sigurd Hoel: A Central Figure on the Norwegian Literary Scene." *The Norseman* (Oslo), 1960, no. 6, pp.8-10. Brief survey of Hoel's work; conservative estimate of its significance. Evaluation somewhat unusual, in that *Sinners* is paired with *The Road* as one of Hoel's two novels with staying power. Unfair judgment of *The Troll Circle.*

Haraldsen, Tore. "Sigurd Hoels 'Veien til verdens ende.' En analyse." Thesis, University of Oslo, 1963. Stresses the double resonance in *The Road,* the tension between figural and authorial points of view.

Havrevold, Finn. "Sigurd Hoel." *Samtiden* 59 (1950), pp. 607-12. Impressionistic, elegantly written characterization of Hoel's style and central themes by a professional writer.

Helseth, Jon Anders. "Kulturradikalisme og kulturkamp. En studie i mellomkrigstidens radikale åndsstrømning — med hovedvekt på Sigurd Hoels essays." Thesis, University of Bergen, 1964. Discusses Hoel's role as a cultural radical between the wars. Notes the contrast between Hoel the novelist, skeptical and pessimistic, and the essayist, a radical idealist with faith in man.

Holden, Arne Lauritz. "Sigurd Hoels *Syndere i sommersol.* En analyse av idéinnholdet og bokens plass i forfatterskapet." Thesis, University of Oslo, 1960. Contains a broad discussion, on a psychoanalytic basis, of the relationship between Fredrik and Erik in *Sinners,* along with references to similar situations in other Hoel novels.

Houm, Philip. *Norges litteratur fra 1914 til 1950-årene: Norsk litteraturhistorie,* vol. VI (Oslo: Aschehoug, 1955), pp. 90-114. Discusses Hoel's fiction, drama, and essays up to the early 1950s. Divides the fiction into deep-probing analyses of the individual and satiric group novels.

Inadomi, Masahiko. *Den plettfrie.* Oslo: Universitetsforlaget, 1968. The best critical study of *Meeting.* Assuming an unreliable narrator, Inadomi interprets the entire narrative, along with its superstructure of mystical and religious ideas, in the light of the narrator's simultaneous search for and escape from self-knowledge and moral responsibility.

Jenssen, Tor Eivind. " 'Fremtidsstillingen' og 'tomhetsfølelsen.' " Thesis, University of Oslo, 1975. Good discussion of the conflicting themes of social adjustment and self-recognition in three novels: *Nothing, A Fortnight,* and *Meeting*.

Johannesen, Georg. "Forskningsfeltet Norge. Sigurd Hoels *Møte ved milepelen.*" *Vinduet* 27 (1973), no. 4, pp. 10-20. A rhymed critical-anthropological fantasy, satirizing the frame and the plot of *Meeting* in a most amusing manner.

Johansson, Lars-Erik. "Kompositionen i Sigurd Hoels *Møte ved milepelen.*" *Edda* 69 (1969), pp. 244-68. Detailed analysis of the structure of *Meeting*. Analyzes the treatment of time, traced partly to Joseph Conrad, partly to psychoanalysis. Stresses, with Inadomi, the narrator's need for confession *and* repression as a determining factor in the book's composition.

Laukholm, Tutta. "Folkelig tradisjonsstoff i Sigurd Hoels forfatterskap." Thesis, University of Oslo, 1968. An interesting study, based on Jung's theory of archetypes, of Hoel's fictional use of traditional material. Jung's theory inspired Hoel to use motifs from saga, fairy tale, and ballad to portray his characters' "inwardness."

Lien, Asmund. "Sin egen historiker — sin samtids historiker: *Det svundne er en drøm* og *Møte ved milepelen*. En parallelføring." In *Sandemoses ansikter*. Edited by Niels Birger Wamberg, pp. 145-73. Oslo: Aschehoug, 1969. Traces the influence of Sandemose's *The Past Is a Dream* upon *Meeting at the Milestone*.

Lyngstad, Sverre. "Sigurd Hoel: The Literary Critic." *Scandinavica* 22 (1983), no. 2, pp. 141-58. Examines the underlying principles of Hoel's criticism on the basis of his reviews, prefaces, literary essays, and editorial judgments.

Madssen, Kjell Arild. "Sigurd Hoels *En dag i oktober*. Tradisjon og fornyelse." Thesis, University of Oslo, 1970. Examination of *October* from the perspective of "tradition and renewal." Discusses possible foreign models, modernistic devices and techniques, and Hoel's relationship to psychoanalysis.

Mannsåker, Jørunn. "Kjærleikssviket — litterært sentralmotiv i Sigurd Hoels dikting." Inaugural lecture, 12/17/1971. *Norsk litterær årbok 1972*, pp. 35-50. Oslo: Det Norske Samlaget, 1972. A survey of a pervasive theme, failure or betrayal in love, in Hoel's fiction.

Michaelsen, Aslaug Groven. *Kjetterier om dikting og sannsynlighet*. Oslo: Dreyer, 1969. Censures Hoel's critics (P. Houm, W. Dahl) for stereotyped judgments based on naturalistic esthetic premises.

Michl, Josef B. "Franz Kafka und die moderne skandinavische Literatur." *Schweizer Monatshefte* 48 (1968/69), no. 1, pp. 57-71. Traces the influence of Kafka upon Hoel's first novel, *The Seven-Pointed Star*. Because of Hoel, Kafka acquired a special position in Norway.

Mylius, Johan E. de. *Sigurd Hoel — befrieren i fugleham*. Odense: Universitetsforlaget, 1972. The best critical study of Hoel, focused on selected major novels. Combines neo-critical close reading with psychoanalytic interpretation. Seeks to penetrate beneath progressive radicalism and preoccupation with fate to the underlying conflicts in Hoel's work.

Nag, Martin. "Franz Kafka og Sigurd Hoel." *Morgenbladet,* 9/22/1965. Examines similarities between Hoel and Kafka, especially in their concepts of alienation and their longing for perfection.

Nøstdal, Kjell. "Sigurd Hoels roman *Trollringen.* Ein analyse av nokre aspekt ved verket." Thesis, University of Bergen, 1970. An extensive literary analysis of Hoel's last novel.

Røed, Arne. "Sommernatt og sommersol." *Edda* 65 (1965), pp. 65-92. Discusses *Sinners* as a "rewriting" of *A Midsummer Night's Dream.*

Sæverud, Ole. "Møte med et medmenneske. Refleksjoner omkring Sigurd Hoels forfatterskap."*Kirke og kultur* 57 (1952), pp. 408-21. A sympathetic critique of Hoel's work from a Christian-religious viewpoint.

Schiff, Timothy. Review of Audun Tvinnereim, *Risens hjerte. Scandinavian Studies* 49 (Spring, 1977), pp. 271-72.

Skartveit, Andreas. "Homo hominibus res sacra est. En Sigurd Hoel studie." *Profil* 18 (1960), no. 5, pp. 10-13. The "sacral" role of love, the root of Hoel's "great respect for the human being," unites Hoel the cultural debater and the novelist.

Stai, Arne. *Sigurd Hoel.* Oslo, 1955. This biography, pronounced a "complete failure" by Hoel, provides much information about Hoel's participation in the struggles of the 1930s. But Stai's method of extrapolating from Hoel's books to his life is questionable.

Storstein, Olav. "Sigurd Hoel og den hellige holmen." In *Fra Jæger til Falk,* pp. 149-87. Oslo: Tiden, 1950. Extravagant praise of *Sinners,* with stress on its mythic qualities.

Sølvhøj, Hans. "Sigurd Hoel — også et politisk forfatterskab." *Dansk Udsyn* 36 (Jan. 1956), pp. 95-104. Sane counterpoise to those critics who minimize the political commitment in Hoel's writing.

Tiemroth, Jørgen E. *Panduro og tredivernes drøm.* Copenhagen: Vinten, 1977. Contains two chapters (pp. 135-69) about Hoel's extensive influence, positive and negative, upon the popular Danish novelist Leif Panduro.

Tofte, Asbjørn Tor. "Sigurd Hoels roman *Sesam sesam.* Ein litterær analyse." Thesis, University of Bergen, 1972. Informed critical analysis of *Open Sesame.*

Tvinnereim, Audun. *Risens hjerte — en studie i Sigurd Hoels forfatterskap.* Oslo, 1975. A broadly based scholarly study of selected novels against the background of Wilhelm Reich's influence on Hoel. An impressive achievement, despite the highly speculative assumption that the separation from Reich is the key to Hoel's alleged decline as a writer in the 1950s.

———. "Sigurd Hoel og nazismen." In *Nazismen og norsk litteratur.* Edited by Bjarte Birkeland and Stein Ugelvik Larsen, pp. 99-121. Bergen: Universitetsforlaget, 1975. An informative article about Hoel's efforts to combat Nazism between the wars.

Væth, Johannes. "Omkring *En flyktning krysser sitt spor.*" In *Sandemoses ansikter*, pp. 79-128. Discusses Hoel's part in the genesis of Aksel Sandemose's *A Fugitive Crosses His Tracks* (1933; Eng. tr. 1936).

Ytreberg, Stein. "Om pessimisme og optimisme hos Sigurd Hoel." *Edda* 65 (1965), pp. 315-24. Rejects the usual argument that Hoel was a pessimist by noting his positive message: his novels are a series of warnings. Stresses Hoel's humor, self-irony, lyricism, and whimsy.

Øyslebø, Olaf. *Sigurd Hoels fortellekunst.* Oslo, 1958. An elaborate analysis of Hoel's narrative strategies and style. While informative, the study is marred by a forbiddingly pedantic terminology, awkward organization (with overlapping categories), and somewhat subjective interpretations.

Index

(The works of Hoel are listed under his name.)

About the Author

SVERRE LYNGSTAD is Professor of English at the New Jersey
Institute of Technology. He is the author of *Jonas Lie*, coauthor
with Alexandra H. Lyngstad of *Ivan Goncharov*, and editor of
Norway, a volume of criticism on modern Norwegian literature.
His articles have appeared in a number of scholarly journals in-
cluding *Scandinavian Studies, Alternative Futures,* and *Scandina-
vica.* He is currently preparing translations of two novels by Sigurd
Hoel.

DUE DATE

	201-6503		Printed in USA